The BIG BOOK *of*
VEGAN
RECIPES

The BIG BOOK of
VEGAN
RECIPES

More Than 500 Easy Vegan Recipes for Healthy and Flavorful Meals

Jolinda Hackett

Avon, Massachusetts

Published by
Adams Media, a division of F+W Media, Inc.
57 Littlefield Street, Avon, MA 02322 U.S.A.
www.adamsmedia.com

Contains material adapted and abridged from *The Everything® Vegan Cookbook* by Jolinda Hackett with
Lorena Novak Bull, copyright © 2010 by F+W Media, Inc., ISBN 10: 1-4405-0216-1, ISBN 13: 978-1-4405-
0216-3; and *The Everything® Vegan Slow Cooker Cookbook* by Amy Snyder and Justin Snyder, copyright
© 2012 by F+W Media, Inc., ISBN 10: 1-4405-4407-7, ISBN 13: 978-1-4405-4407-1.

ISBN 10: 1-4405-7248-8
ISBN 13: 978-1-4405-7248-7
eISBN 10: 1-4405-7249-6
eISBN 13: 978-1-4405-7249-4

Printed in the United States of America.

10 9 8 7 6 5 4 3 2 1

Library of Congress Cataloging-in-Publication Data

Hackett, Jolinda.
The big book of vegan recipes : more than 500 easy vegan recipes for
healthy and flavorful meals / Jolinda Hackett.
pages cm
Includes bibliographical references and index.
ISBN-13: 978-1-4405-7248-7 (paperback : alkaline paper)
ISBN-10: 1-4405-7248-8 (paperback : alkaline paper)
ISBN-13: 978-1-4405-7249-4 (epub)
ISBN-10: 1-4405-7249-6 (epub)
1. Vegan cooking. I. Title.
TX837.H175 2014
641.5'636--dc23
2013031106

Always follow safety and commonsense cooking protocol while using kitchen utensils, operating ovens
and stoves, and handling uncooked food. If children are assisting in the preparation of any recipe, they
should always be supervised by an adult.

Cover image © 123rf.com.

This book is available at quantity discounts for bulk purchases.
For information, please call 1-800-289-0963.

CONTENTS

3   Appetizers, Relishes, and Dips 67

8 Rices and Whole Grains ... 267

9 Classic Pastas 327

INTRODUCTION

THE OLD ADAGE, "Tell me what you eat and I'll tell you who you are," has never been more true. Whether you live in a small town or a big city, you have more choices as to what to eat than ever before in the history of humankind.

Even if you choose something simple such as cereal and milk for breakfast, you're still faced with an entire aisle of boxed cereals and nearly a dozen kinds of milk. Whole grain cereal? Soymilk, rice milk, hemp milk, or coconut milk? Plain, vanilla, or unsweetened? Low-fat or fat-free?

By picking up this book, you've already made one choice: to explore nourishing, animal-friendly, and environmentally sound plant-based meals. No matter whether you're a decades-long herbivore or this is your first exploration into vegan cooking, this book is for you. With more than five hundred recipes, you can try something new every single day for a year and still have ideas leftover.

You'll find plenty of vegan twists on comforting and familiar favorites, such as macaroni and cheese and chocolate chip cookies as well as dishes from around the world with exciting new flavors to keep your palate guessing and your meals fresh.

So if you are what you eat, what are you? Thoughtful? Mindless? Sugar-filled? Wholesome and healthy? Are you adventurous and fiery or simple and traditional?

I hope that after exploring a few of the recipes in this book, you'll be filled with both radiant health and the satisfaction of a good meal. But more than that, I hope you're filled with the joy that accompanies exploring new things and the confidence of knowing that you're someone who makes healthy choices for yourself, your family, the animals, and the planet.

CHAPTER 1

THE VEGAN REVOLUTION

COOK SOME SESAME BOK CHOY and your friends will think you're a talented Chinese food chef. Perhaps even a connoisseur. But when you create a vegan meal, you are literally changing the world. Call it gastronomical activism at the tip of your fork. Just by eating vegan, you become an eco-activist and, within a week or two, a healthier person. Veganism is not just a diet, and not just the food on your plate: it is an active stance against environmental inefficiencies, a boycott against animal cruelty, and a method of preventative medicine. Yes, all that comes just from trading in milk and meat for mushrooms and marinara. One small bite for you is one giant leap toward a healthier planet and a healthier body.

What Are Vegan Foods?

If you're used to eating eggs for breakfast and steak for dinner, you may be wondering, what's left? Rest assured that with a little ingenuity, a plant-centered diet will bring more color, spice, and variety to your plate than ever before.

As a matter of habit, most people reach for the same few foods day after day, but all that stops now! A nearly infinite array of grains, herbs, fruits, vegetables, beans, and legumes from around the world is at your fingertips. There are dozens of varieties of beans alone—navy, cannellini, kidney beans, black beans—and many other pulses, such as chickpeas and lentils, each with its own distinct flavors and textures. There's no need to ever ask, "What do vegans eat?" It's simpler to question what vegans don't eat, as the list is much shorter!

Instead of packaged and processed foods, vegans eat mostly whole foods (fruits, vegetables, beans, nuts, grains) and dairy- and egg-free versions of traditional favorites (cheeseless pizza, bean burritos minus the cheese) flavored with herbs and spices from around the world. Vegans today can savor hundreds of vegan substitute products, including nondairy cream cheese, "beef" jerky, and vegan white chocolate.

Whatever comfort food you crave has a vegan version. There are dozens of brands of the more common substitutes, such as soymilk and vegan meats and cheeses, each with their own texture and taste. Some will fool even the most ardent wrangler, and others, well, won't. You'll also find ways to duplicate many of your favorite comfort foods in this book, without eggs and dairy.

Why Eat Vegan?

Ask one hundred vegans why they pass on animal foods and you may get one hundred different answers. Animal suffering, environmental waste, and personal health usually top the list. But global poverty, food safety and sanitation, or food allergies are valid reasons to reduce reliance on animal foods. People of Western faiths may cite the biblical order for "stewardship" over creation, while others commit to the Eastern spiritual principle of ahimsa—that is, nonviolence and harmlessness. Call it the vegan Hippocratic oath.

So then, what's the harm with eating eggs and dairy?

For the Animals

Concerns over animal suffering understandably lead to a vegetarian diet, but the suffering and killing of animals in dairy and egg production inspires many well-intentioned vegetarians who learn of such practices to quickly go vegan.

Gone are the days of Old MacDonald's happily mooing dairy cows and clucking chickens. Today's cows are relentlessly milked by machines, not cheery, freckle-faced men in overalls. Females must be kept constantly pregnant in order to lactate, but the dairy industry has little use for their male offspring. Sent to slaughter at a few months old for veal, male calves are just leftovers, the collateral damage of dairy production. When her ability to produce milk naturally slows at five or six years of age (think of it as a sort of cow menopause), a dairy cow's final destination is the slaughterhouse.

Egg-laying hens are tightly packed into filthy cages, stacked floor to ceiling in huge warehouses, called CAFOs, or Concentrated Animal Feeding Operations, within the industry. The Occupational Safety and Health Administration (OSHA) recommends that workers only enter when suited up with goggles and respirators, as the air is hazardously putrid with feces.

Here, chickens struggle for space to move and air to breathe. Imagine sharing a porta-potty all summer long with three of your closest friends for a spatial approximation. Under these circumstances, deaths from dehydration and suffocation are common. To avoid pecking conflicts, baby chicks have their beaks sliced off at birth, and the industry has discovered that although a hen's egg-laying ability eventually slows, it can be kick-started through "forced molting," which involves weeks of starvation.

Vegan Advantage

Despite marketing ploys, eggs labeled "free-range" or "cage-free" are no better for your health or the environment than regular eggs, and they're not much better for the chickens. With little regulation, "free-range" hens may still never once see sunlight and still suffer debeaking, and when productivity wanes, they end up in the same place as conventional hens. There's simply no such thing as a "free-range" slaughterhouse.

Such are the lives of animals used for industrialized food production. Not a pleasant life. It's no wonder that more and more people are refusing to support these practices, voting with their stomachs and pocketbooks in favor of tofu scramble over eggs from tortured hens.

For many vegans, inspired by philosophers Jeremy Bentham and Peter Singer, the atrocities of food production are a concern, but dominance, use, and exploitation of some creatures (animals) by another (humans) is the real underlying issue. Agree or disagree, the words of novelist, feminist, and vegan Alice Walker summarize this sentiment: "The animals of the world exist for their own reasons. They were not made for humans any more than black people were made for white, or women created for men." This is the idea of animal rights; that animals may lead their own lives, completely unencumbered by humans.

Many social justice activists, including notable heroes Coretta Scott King and Cesar Chavez, reject animal exploitation as a logical extension of their belief in equality. In the words of Albert Einstein, they have "widened the circle of compassion" to include all victims of oppression and injustice—animals and humans alike.

Some concerned human rights and civil rights activists eat vegan to boycott the sweatshop treatment of slaughterhouse workers, many of whom are illegal immigrants exploited by big businesses to do the dirtiest work. Without basic protections, illegal workers don't object when USDA and OSHA safety violations inevitably occur, and, without health insurance, they are a cheap source of labor that can be ignored when injured performing their dangerous duties.

For the Earth

Modern food production is no friend to local environments, as anyone who has lived near a large death factory can tell you. Neighbors of industrialized farms are constantly complaining of the air and water pollution caused by the concentrated waste of these poor animals. And the larger global environment suffers as well. Everyone from environmental groups to the United Nations agrees that animal agriculture is one of the single largest contributors to global warming and environmental devastation. Because exponentially more water, energy, land, and resources are needed to raise and feed animals than to support a plant-based diet, individuals simply can't call themselves environmentalists while still consuming animal products.

The problem of disposing of the waste produced by the approximately ten billion animals raised for food in the United States is minor in comparison to the very real threat of global climate change. The UN estimates that 20 percent of all greenhouse gases come from the food animal industry; much more than is caused by private jets, SUVs, and all forms of transport worldwide combined. Red meat and dairy are the biggest culprits, closely followed by pigs, chickens, and egg production.

Vegan Advantage
Just one individual switching from a meat-based to a plant-based diet reduces carbon emissions by about one and a half tons a year. That's more than eating locally grown food and trading in your SUV for a hybrid.

With an increasing global population, land and water availability is a concern. More than three-fourths of all agricultural land in the United States is used not to grow food for humans, but rather feed for farm animals or as grazing land. This is a shameful waste of resources that could be redistributed to alleviate hunger worldwide. Yet it's still not enough to feed the selfish American desire for meat. Clear-cutting for grazing land has claimed hundreds of millions of forest acres in the United States, and South American rain forests are now losing timber to provide wealthier nations with imported beef.

A single half-ton cow consumes thousands of pounds of grain, soy, or corn over its short lifetime, yet produces only a few hundred hamburgers. Water used to grow that grain (about half of all water used in the United States goes toward raising animals) and the chemicals and herbicides used to quicken its growth are just more environmental casualties of an animal-based diet. Raising animals for food is a tragically inefficient squandering of water, food, land, chemical fertilizers, and energy.

For Personal and Global Health
Along with humane and environmental concerns, personal health is a strong motivator to eat vegan. From significantly reduced rates of hypertension, arterial hardening, stroke, type 2 diabetes, obesity, heart disease, and several types of cancer (prostate and breast cancer being the most well documented), a plant-based diet helps prevent the vast majority of life-threatening diseases that plague modernity.

Medical research and the Academy of Nutrition and Dietetics affirm that a plant-based diet prevents many ailments, helps reverse some, and eases the symptoms of others. Veganism isn't a bulletproof vest in protecting against these killers, but it just may be the best bet.

Hormone use is a major concern in much of the world, though the American public and lawmakers are less aware of the dangers. In quest of the almighty dollar, U.S. dairy cows are fed a tasty-sounding drug called "recombinant bovine growth hormone" (rBGH), which increases milk production up to 20 percent. Because this powerful hormone ends up in consumers' stomachs, Japan, Australia, Canada, and the European Union have banned the use of rBGH, and the EU bans the import of American beef because of it. Medical studies implicate these hormones in the connection between diet and cancer, particularly breast, prostate, and testicular cancers. The unnatural and unsanitary conditions of production are increasingly convincing the health-conscious to reduce their animal-based food consumption, not only to avoid these hormones, but also to avoid exposure to *E. coli* and the other common pathogens originating in animal feces and contaminating animal products.

The number of children afflicted with one or more food sensitivities has inexplicably grown in recent years, though some people theorize this may be related to the increasing number of unnatural hormones and additives in commonly consumed foods. Trigger foods are more easily avoided on a whole foods diet, and eating vegan or mostly vegan makes this easier. Some food allergy sufferers have even reported the reversal of their sensitivities on a healthy, plant-based diet.

Whatever your reasons for exploring the vegan lifestyle, keep them in mind when confronted with the inevitable naysayers, and remember that your reasons are yours alone. Others may have different motivating factors. Committing yourself 100 percent to your goals will help you in the face of adversity when your deer-hunting uncle cackles at your Thanksgiving tofu turkey.

Vegan Nutrition

Despite a national obsession with protein, most Americans eat much more than recommended, and deficiency in vegans is rare. Professional bodybuilders and pregnant women aside, most vegans easily meet their daily requirement of protein (and most omnivores exceed it exponentially), but beware of your zinc, vitamin D, iron, and calcium intake, and foremost, vitamin B12.

If you are pregnant, you'll need to plan adequately to obtain all the nutrients you need—not just protein—and have likely already consulted with your doctor about this. If not, please do. And, as most bodybuilders already know, the timing of protein consumption coupled with the stress of lifts is more important than whether that protein is plant- or animal-based.

Though not readily supplied by a vegan diet, vitamin D is easily obtained from sunlight. Step outside for a few minutes a day and you're set for vitamin D. Make sure your vegan kids do the same. If you happen to be a vegan living in Antarctica or above the arctic circle, best to rely on a supplement or fortified foods, such as fortified orange juice or soymilk.

Similarly, many soy foods are fortified with calcium, another important nutrient for dairy-free folks, and broccoli, tofu, tahini, almonds, and dark leafy greens provide a good natural source. But to build strong bones, you need exercise as well as calcium, so—vegan or not—diet is only half the equation.

Vegan Advantage

Before you pour that glass of orange juice or soymilk, shake it up! The calcium in these drinks tends to settle at the bottom of the carton, so to get the best bone-boosting effect, shake before you drink. If you're a heavy smoker or coffee drinker, consider taking a supplement, as these inhibit absorption of several nutrients.

When it comes to iron, most vegans and vegetarians actually get more than omnivores, but to be on the safe side, lentils, chickpeas, tahini, and once again, those dark leafy greens like spinach and kale, are good vegan sources.

Noticing a pattern? Dark leafy green vegetables are one of the most nutrient-rich foods on the planet. Find ways to include kale, spinach, or other greens in your diet by snipping them into pasta sauces and casseroles, or include a few spinach leaves along with your other salad greens.

Fish oils and fish such as salmon are often touted as a source of healthy omega-3 fatty acids, but vegetarians and vegans can obtain these from flaxseeds and flax oil, as well as walnuts or hempseeds.

Vegan Advantage

Flaxseed oil is rich in omega-3s, and has a sweet and nutty flavor. Never use flax as a cooking oil, however, as the heat destroys the healthy fats and creates unhealthy free radicals. Instead, add a teaspoonful of flax oil to your favorite salad dressing, or drizzle over already-cooked dishes for your daily omega-3s. Look for a brand that is cold-pressed and stored chilled to keep it fresh.

Vitamin B12 cannot reliably be obtained from vegan foods. Deficiencies of this important nutrient are admittedly rare, and if you're eating vegan meals only occasionally, you don't need to worry. Vegetarians will absorb B12 from food sources, but long-term vegans, and pregnant and breast-feeding women in particular, need a reliable source. Take a supplement and eat fortified foods, such as nutritional yeast. Because the body needs very little B12, and it can be stored for years, some people claim a supplement is not needed, or suggest that omnivores are more likely to be deficient in a variety of nutrients, and thus the B12 issue for vegans is grossly overblown. While this last argument may be true, the bottom line, according to most experts, is to take a supplement. Better safe than sorry.

The Truth about Protein

In 1971 Frances Moore Lappé wrote a book that revolutionized the relationship thousands of Americans had with their plates, effectively launching vegetarianism into the public consciousness. *Diet for a Small Planet* continues to be a widely read and cited book today. Much to the chagrin of generations of vegetarians, however, it was the beginning of a myth still oft retold, including by some nutritionists who ought to know better. This is the myth of "protein combining," or the idea that plant sources provide "incomplete" proteins while meats provide "complete" proteins.

Lappé theorized that in order to digest all nine of the essential amino acids that the human body needs to build protein, vegetarians needed to combine foods so as to consume each essential amino acid in one sitting. Whole grains needed to be consumed at the same time as nuts, for example.

The truth is, by eating a variety of foods, you'll have nothing to worry about. Although you do need a full range of amino acids, and some plant-based foods contain more or less of the essentials, Lappé's error was to assume these nine essentials needed to be consumed at the same meal. Nutritionists, including the Academy of Nutrition and Dietetics and the USDA, have since refuted this claim, and even Lappé herself revised her stance in later editions of the book. Your body will store and combine proteins on its own. Just so this point is not missed: protein combining is a complete myth.

Vegan Advantage

Quinoa, soy, and hempseeds are vegan powerhouses when it comes to protein, as they contain the highest amount of all nine essential amino acids. Hempseeds are also high in essential omega-3 and omega-6 fatty acids.

If however, you tend to go weeks eating nothing but bananas and soda, you'll quickly find yourself deficient in more than just protein. But eat a relatively healthy diet and you'll be just fine. From the Academy of Nutrition and Dietetics: "Plant sources of protein alone can provide adequate amounts of the essential and nonessential amino acids, assuming that dietary protein sources from plants are reasonably varied."

Vegan Health Advantages

While B12 is a genuine concern, the health advantages of a plant-based diet are endless. The average vegan gets twice as much fiber as most omnivores. A vegan diet is naturally cholesterol-free, and is almost guaranteed to lead to marked decreases in cholesterol levels in just two weeks. If lowering your cholesterol naturally is one of your goals, test your levels before and again a few weeks into a vegan diet, and gamble with your skeptical friends, just for fun.

But this is just the tip of the iceberg.

Blood pressure, too, is shown to decrease drastically in a short period of time on a plant-based diet. High blood pressure is rarely a concern for vegans, and making the switch can decrease your blood pressure in less than two months. No need to give up salt as conventional wisdom dictates—just get rid of the meat and dairy!

As an added bonus for men (and for women too, really), it's possible that vegans really do make better lovers. High blood pressure, high cholesterol, and particularly the decreased blood flow associated with blocked arteries are common causes leading to erectile dysfunction, and vegans certainly have fewer instances of these symptoms. Sure, a little pill can help out for the night, but a vegan diet can help forever!

The fountain of youth may not flow with water after all—it may be full of fruits and veggies.

You do need to eat a balanced diet in order to reap these benefits. After all, french fries and potato chips are animal-free, but that doesn't make them healthy. When it comes to vegan nutrition, variety is key. Make sure your protein sources are varied, rather than from just one food group. Eat a rainbow of fruits and veggies, and include green leafy vegetables as often as possible.

But the health benefits of reduced animal consumption go beyond your blood pressure and your bedroom; it's a global concern.

The powerful cocktail of hormones and antibiotics pumped into cows and chickens by today's food industry ends up right back in local water supplies and affects everyone, even vegans. All these antibiotics, combined with the cramped conditions of modern farms, lead to dangerous new drug-resistant pathogens and bacterial strains. Swine flu, bird flu, SARS, and mad cow disease are all traced back to intense animal agriculture practices. Because of our rapidly shrinking planet, the "butterfly effect" is a very real phenomenon: A pig in Mexico sneezed, and a child in Bangkok died.

Getting Started

There's no need to toss out all your old cookbooks and family recipes, as many of them can provide inspiration for fabulous vegan meals—after a few minor tweaks, of course. Most recipes for cookies, muffins, and cakes can be made with nondairy milk, vegan margarine, and a commercial egg replacer. For recipes calling for honey, try an equivalent amount of agave nectar, which is equally lovely in tea and drizzled over vegan pancakes. Store-bought mock ground beef is surprisingly tasty, and TVP (textured vegetable protein) granules provide a meaty texture in dishes like tacos or chili.

Take a look at some of your favorite meals. Like spaghetti with meatballs? Try a vegetable marinara instead, grab some ready-made vegetarian meatballs from your grocery store, or try the Spaghetti with Italian "Meatballs" recipe in Chapter 9. Try your favorite chicken noodle soup recipe without the chicken, and omit the beef from your Chinese beef and broccoli, or use seitan as a beef substitute instead. Often, it's the spices, flavors, and textures that make a meal satisfying and nostalgic, not the actual meat.

For the novice chef, restaurants can offer a tasty introduction to new foods. Check your phonebook or the Internet for vegetarian and vegan restaurants in your area. Thai and Chinese restaurants serve up vegan curries and stir-fries, many with an array of mock meats. As a general rule, ethnic restaurants including Mexican (just hold the cheese), Indian, and Middle Eastern places offer more options for vegetarians and vegans than American chains and diners, which may offer little more than a veggie burger as an afterthought.

Creating Amazing Meals

When eating at restaurants, the flavors often come from an overdose of salt, fat, and sometimes MSG. But when cooking at home, you're better off enhancing your foods with flavors that come from nature.

One flavor enhancer unique to vegan cuisine is the almighty nutritional yeast. It's a yellowish powder universally loved by vegans for its nutty and cheesy taste and ability to add that *je ne sais quoi* to just about any savory dish.

Most chefs agree that sea salt has a superior taste to table salt. Once you've tried sea salt, you'll never go back to regular refined salt, and the trace minerals in sea salt are an added bonus. Similarly, freshly cracked black pepper is always best. Use vegetable broth instead of water whenever possible, stock up on vegetarian bouillon or powdered vegetable broth, and don't be afraid to use it with a heavy hand in stir-fries, soups, gravies, and casseroles—just about anything savory or spicy.

Fresh herbs and spices are an obvious choice for adding flavor, but their true power comes in their variety and combination. No matter how many spices are on your spice rack, there's always room for one or two more! Most of the spices called for in this book are commonly found, but don't let that limit you. Add garam masala to Indian dishes and smoked Spanish paprika to paellas. Same with fresh herbs. If you can find them, add lemongrass and Kaffir lime leaves to your Thai curries!

One or two gourmet or unusual ingredients can add pizzazz to an otherwise standard dish. A salad drizzled with champagne vinegar and avocado oil trumps regular vinaigrette any day, and a meatless pasta salad enhanced with sun-dried tomatoes, dried blueberries, or artichoke hearts, for example, is more exciting than a pasta salad with ordinary grilled chicken. The difference between a simple meal and a culinary affair to remember may be just a handful of wasabi-coated macadamia nuts.

Vegan Machines and Coddled Cooks

The equipment and utensils needed in a vegan kitchen vary little from what any other home cook might need. A blender and food processor are essential. Rather than working up a sweat grating carrots, a food processor will do the trick in ten seconds. Quality chopping knives and a cutting board are standard for any cook, as are a large skillet or sauté pan, a stockpot for soups, and some oven basics, such as a casserole dish and a baking pan. With these few items, you'll be prepared to create almost all of the recipes in this book.

A few convenient luxuries can enliven your whole foods vegan kitchen. Though not an essential, a rice steamer means one less pot on the stove to worry about. After adding liquid and just about any grain (not just rice), you can walk away without worry.

The difference between one stockpot and another is minimal (both the $10 one and the $50 one boil water equally), but splurge for a quality piece when purchasing a nonstick pan. It's essential for making vegan crepes and comes in handy for pancakes and French toast. But the real value of a nonstick pan is in reducing the oil needed to sauté veggies or scramble tofu. If lowering dietary fat is a concern, shop for a quality nonstick pan.

For feeding a large family or baking in quantity, a soymilk maker is a cost-cutter in the long run. Unless the label says "unsweetened," store-bought soymilk is packed with sugar, so homemade is better for you as well. Making soymilk is a bit of an effort by hand, but with a machine, it's a snap. If you're feeding a large family, it's a convenient investment.

Shopping Tips

Health foods stores and gourmet grocers stock vegan specialty goods, but these days, even most regular chain supermarkets carry mock meats and dairy substitutes. Some stores have a separate "natural foods" aisle, while others stock the veggie burgers with the other frozen foods. Most health food stores and co-ops are happy to place special orders, so don't be afraid to ask.

Browse farmers' markets and farm stands for good deals and environmental karma and seek out ethnic and import grocers for hidden treasures. Kosher stores stock enough dairy substitutes to fill a vegan's dreams, Asian grocery stores are a paradise of exotic meatless "meats," sauces, and spices, and Middle Eastern and Mexican grocers supply unusual ingredients and flavors.

Vegan Advantage

Some of you may be wondering if you need to read labels to make sure you're buying animal-free foods. By avoiding foods that contain trace amounts of animal by-products, you're sending a message to companies to use nonanimal sources. Then again, standing in supermarket aisles meticulously reading labels may seem wacky and obsessive rather than healthy and compassionate, the latter being the more exemplary image for vegans to cultivate. Your choice.

Insiders know that the Seventh-day Adventist religion has a long history of vegetarianism and even its own brand of veggie "meats." Check out Adventist book supply stores for a bounty of veggie hams, fish, and sausages if you're lucky enough to have one in your area!

If you live in Manhattan, you'll find vegan foods on literally every corner, but even if you reside in the middle of Mayberry, you can still enjoy a tasty and nutritious vegan diet based on the bounty of grains, beans, fruits, and vegetables that are available anywhere on the planet.

But seriously. Find some nutritional yeast. That stuff is good.

CHAPTER 2

BREAKFAST

APPLE CINNAMON WAFFLES

For perfect vegan waffles, make sure your waffle iron is hot and very well greased, as vegan waffles tend to be stickier than regular waffles.

INGREDIENTS

Serves 4

1¼ cups flour

2 teaspoons baking powder

½ teaspoon cinnamon

2 teaspoons sugar

1 cup soymilk

½ cup applesauce

1 teaspoon vanilla

1 tablespoon vegetable oil

1. In a large bowl, combine the flour, baking powder, cinnamon, and sugar. Set aside.

2. In a separate bowl, combine soymilk, applesauce, vanilla, and oil.

3. Add the soymilk mixture to the dry ingredients, stirring just until combined; do not overmix.

4. Carefully drop about ¼ cup batter onto preheated waffle iron for each waffle, and cook until done.

BAKED "SAUSAGE" AND MUSHROOM FRITTATA

Baked tofu frittatas are an easy brunch or weekend breakfast. Once you've got the technique down, it's easy to adjust the ingredients to your liking. With tofu and mock meat, this one packs a super protein punch!

INGREDIENTS

Serves 4

½ yellow onion, diced

3 cloves garlic, minced

½ cup sliced mushrooms

1 (12-ounce) package vegetarian sausage substitute or vegetarian "beef" crumbles

2 tablespoons olive oil

¾ teaspoon salt

¼ teaspoon black pepper

1 block firm or extra-firm tofu

1 block silken tofu

1 tablespoon soy sauce

2 tablespoons nutritional yeast

¼ teaspoon turmeric (optional)

1 tomato, sliced thin (optional)

1. Preheat oven to 325°F and lightly grease a glass pie pan.

2. Heat onion, garlic, mushrooms, and vegetarian sausage in olive oil in a large skillet for 3–4 minutes until sausage is browned and mushrooms are soft. Season with salt and pepper and set aside.

3. Combine firm/extra-firm tofu, silken tofu, soy sauce, nutritional yeast, and turmeric (if using) in a blender, and process until mixed. Combine tofu with sausage mixture and spread into pan. Layer slices of tomato on top (optional).

4. Bake in oven for about 45 minutes, or until firm. Allow to cool for 5–10 minutes before serving, as frittata will set as it cools.

TOFU FRITTATA

Frittatas are traditionally made with eggs, but you can use tofu instead for a cholesterol-free breakfast dish.

INGREDIENTS
Serves 4

2 tablespoons olive oil

1 cup red potatoes, peeled and diced

½ onion, diced

½ cup red pepper, diced

½ cup green pepper, diced

1 teaspoon jalapeño, minced

1 clove garlic, minced

¼ cup parsley

16 ounces firm tofu

½ cup unsweetened soymilk

4 teaspoons cornstarch

2 tablespoons nutritional yeast

1 teaspoon mustard

½ teaspoon turmeric

1 teaspoon salt

¼ teaspoon black pepper

1. Add the oil to a large pan and sauté the potatoes, onion, peppers, jalapeño, and garlic on medium heat for about 15–20 minutes.

2. Meanwhile, in a blender or food processor, combine the rest of the ingredients until smooth, then pour the mixture into the slow cooker with the potatoes.

3. Cover, and cook on high heat for 4 hours, or until the frittata has firmed.

Make It a Scramble

To shorten the preparation time for this meal while keeping all of the flavors, try making this dish into a scramble by preparing the entire recipe in the slow cooker. Skip the step of blending the tofu and omit the cornstarch. Add remaining ingredients, breaking apart tofu as you stir, and sauté until cooked through.

BREAKFAST TOFU AND VEGGIES

Nutritional yeast has a cheesy flavor, and should not be replaced with other types of yeast.

INGREDIENTS

Serves 4

¼ cup olive oil

1 (16-ounce) package extra-firm tofu, drained and cubed

½ onion, diced

1 cup broccoli, chopped

½ green bell pepper, chopped

½ zucchini, chopped

½ cup yellow squash, chopped

3 tablespoons soy sauce

¼ cup nutritional yeast

1. Add the oil, tofu, vegetables, and soy sauce to a 4-quart slow cooker and stir until well combined. Cover, and cook on low heat for 4 hours.

2. About 1 minute before the tofu and veggies are finished, stir in the nutritional yeast and serve.

BRUNCH SPINACH

While reminiscent of creamed spinach, this vegan version isn't an exact match, so be prepared for something a little different.

INGREDIENTS

Serves 6

4 cups frozen spinach, thawed

1 cup silken tofu

1 cup unsweetened soymilk

1 teaspoon Dijon mustard

¼ cup nutritional flakes

1 teaspoon turmeric

1 teaspoon cup soy sauce

1 teaspoon salt

¼ teaspoon black pepper

Place all ingredients in a 4-quart slow cooker, cover, and cook on low heat for 3 hours.

CAROB PEANUT BUTTER BANANA SMOOTHIE

Yummy enough for a dessert, but healthy enough for breakfast, this smoothie is also a great protein boost after a sweaty workout at the gym. Use cocoa powder if you don't have any carob.

INGREDIENTS

Serves 2

7–8 ice cubes

2 bananas

2 tablespoons peanut butter

2 tablespoons carob powder

1 cup soymilk

Blend together all ingredients until smooth.

CHILI MASALA TOFU SCRAMBLE

Tofu scramble is an easy and versatile vegan breakfast. This version adds chili and curry for subcontinental flavor. Toss in whatever veggies you have on hand—tomatoes, spinach, or diced broccoli would work well.

INGREDIENTS
Serves 2

1 block firm or extra-firm tofu, pressed

1 small onion, diced

2 cloves garlic, minced

2 tablespoons olive oil

1 small red chili pepper, minced

1 green bell pepper, chopped

¾ cup sliced mushrooms

1 tablespoon soy sauce

1 teaspoon curry powder

½ teaspoon cumin

¼ teaspoon turmeric

1 teaspoon nutritional yeast (optional)

1. Cut or crumble pressed tofu into 1" cubes.

2. Sauté onion and garlic in olive oil for 1–2 minutes until onion is soft.

3. Add tofu, chili pepper, bell pepper, and mushrooms, stirring well to combine.

4. Add remaining ingredients, except nutritional yeast, and combine well. Allow to cook until tofu is lightly browned, about 6–8 minutes.

5. Remove from heat and stir in nutritional yeast if desired.

The Next Day
Leftover tofu scramble makes an excellent lunch, or wrap leftovers (or planned-overs!) in a warmed flour tortilla to make breakfast-style burritos, perhaps with some salsa or beans. Why isn't it called "scrambled tofu" instead of "tofu scramble" if it's a substitute for scrambled eggs? This is one of the great conundrums of veganism.

SUNRISE TOFU SCRAMBLE

Go gourmet with this tofu scramble by substituting shiitake mushrooms and Japanese eggplant instead of the broccoli and button mushrooms.

INGREDIENTS

Serves 4

16 ounces firm tofu, drained and crumbled

½ cup broccoli florets, chopped

½ cup button mushrooms, sliced

2 tablespoons olive oil

2 teaspoons turmeric

1 teaspoon cumin

¼ teaspoon garlic powder

⅛ teaspoon red pepper flakes

2 cloves garlic, minced

1 teaspoon salt

¼ teaspoon black pepper

½ cup tomato, diced

1 lemon, juiced

2 tablespoons fresh parsley, chopped

1. Add the tofu, broccoli, mushrooms, oil, turmeric, cumin, garlic powder, red pepper flakes, garlic, salt, and black pepper to a 4-quart slow cooker. Cover, and cook on low heat for 4 hours.

2. Add the tomato, lemon juice, and parsley to the scramble and serve.

TEMPEH SAUSAGE SCRAMBLE

This nutritious alternative to pork sausage and eggs will help you start your day off right.

INGREDIENTS

Serves 4

1 (13-ounce) package tempeh, crumbled

1 (14-ounce) package extra-firm tofu, drained and crumbled

1 teaspoon dried sage

2 teaspoons brown sugar

1/8 teaspoon red pepper flakes

1/8 teaspoon dried marjoram

1/2 cup vegetarian "chicken" broth

1 teaspoon salt

1/4 teaspoon black pepper

Add all ingredients to a 4-quart slow cooker. Cover, and cook on low heat for 4 hours.

CINNAMON APPLE OATMEAL

Allspice may sound like a combination of spices, but it's actually just one, made from the Pimenta dioica *plant.*

INGREDIENTS
Serves 4

2¼ cups water

1½ cups old-fashioned rolled oats

1 tablespoon brown sugar

1 teaspoon sugar

½ teaspoon cinnamon

¼ teaspoon allspice

2 apples, peeled and diced

Place all ingredients in a 4-quart slow cooker, cover, and cook on high 1–2 hours, or until the water is absorbed.

CRANBERRY AND FIGS OATMEAL

Oatmeal is a great source of fiber but be careful not to add too many spoonfuls of sugar!

INGREDIENTS
Serves 4

2¼ cups water

1½ cups old-fashioned rolled oats

1 tablespoon brown sugar

1 teaspoon sugar

½ teaspoon cinnamon

¼ cup frozen cranberries, chopped

¼ cup figs, chopped

¼ teaspoon salt

Place all ingredients in a 4-quart slow cooker, cover, and cook on high 1–2 hours, or until the water is absorbed.

EASY TOFU "EGGS"

Tofu "eggs" are a great form of protein and taste delicious. Build upon this basic recipe to create a variety of tofu scrambles.

INGREDIENTS

Serves 4

2 tablespoons olive oil

1 (16-ounce) package firm tofu, drained and crumbled

¼ cup onion, diced

2 cloves garlic, minced

1 teaspoon turmeric

½ teaspoon salt

¼ teaspoon black pepper

1 lemon, juiced

1. Add all ingredients except the lemon juice to a 4-quart slow cooker. Cover, and cook on low heat for 3–4 hours.

2. About 3 minutes before the "eggs" are finished, stir in the lemon juice.

EASY VEGAN FRENCH TOAST

Kids love golden, fried French toast drowning in powdered sugar and maple syrup, but a fruit compote or some agave nectar would be just as sweet.

INGREDIENTS

Serves 4

2 bananas

½ cup soymilk

1 tablespoon orange juice

1 tablespoon maple syrup

¾ teaspoon vanilla

1 tablespoon flour

1 teaspoon cinnamon

½ teaspoon nutmeg

Oil or vegan margarine for frying

12 thick slices bread

1. Using a blender or mixer, mix together the bananas, soymilk, orange juice, maple syrup, and vanilla until smooth and creamy.

2. Whisk in flour, cinnamon, and nutmeg, and pour into a pie plate or shallow pan.

3. Heat 1–2 tablespoons of vegan margarine or oil in a large skillet.

4. Dip or spoon mixture over bread on both sides, and fry in hot oil until lightly golden brown on both sides, about 2–3 minutes.

The Perfect Vegan French Toast

Creating an eggless French toast is a true art. Is your French toast too soggy or too dry? Thickly sliced bread lightly toasted will be more absorbent. Too mushy, or the mixture doesn't want to stick? Try spooning it onto your bread, rather than dipping.

FAT-FREE BANANA BREAD

You can add ½ cup chopped walnuts to this simple banana bread, but then, of course, it won't be fat-free. If you want a bit of texture and crunch without the fat, try adding chopped dates or raisins instead.

INGREDIENTS
Yields 1 loaf

4 ripe bananas

⅓ cup soymilk

⅔ cup sugar

1 teaspoon vanilla

2 cups all-purpose flour

1 teaspoon baking powder

½ teaspoon baking soda

½ teaspoon salt

¾ teaspoon cinnamon

1. Preheat oven to 350°F. Lightly grease a loaf pan.

2. Mix together the bananas, soymilk, sugar, and vanilla until smooth and creamy.

3. In a separate bowl, combine the flour, baking powder, baking soda, and salt.

4. Combine the flour mixture with the banana mixture just until smooth.

5. Spread batter in loaf pan and sprinkle the top with cinnamon. Bake for 55 minutes, or until a toothpick inserted in the middle comes out clean.

FRENCH TOAST CASSEROLE

This recipe is a wonderful way to use bread that is slightly stale.

INGREDIENTS
Serves 8

12 slices raisin bread

2 teaspoons cornstarch mixed with 2 tablespoons water

1 cup soymilk

1 teaspoon vanilla

2 tablespoons dark brown sugar

1 teaspoon cinnamon

¼ teaspoon nutmeg

1. Spray a 4-quart slow cooker with nonstick spray. Layer the bread in the slow cooker.

2. In a small bowl, whisk the cornstarch mixture, soymilk, vanilla, brown sugar, cinnamon, and nutmeg. Pour over the bread.

3. Cover, and cook on low for 6–8 hours.

4. Remove the lid and cook uncovered for 30 minutes, or until the liquid has evaporated.

GRANDMA'S CORNMEAL MUSH

This recipe cooks into a thick cornmeal porridge and makes for a tasty and inexpensive breakfast food.

INGREDIENTS

Serves 4

2 cups yellow cornmeal

8 cups water

1 teaspoon salt

2 tablespoons vegan margarine

1. Add all ingredients to a 4-quart slow cooker. Cover, and cook on low heat for 4 hours.

2. Allow the mush to cool slightly before serving.

Serving Suggestions

Cornmeal-based dishes are usually served differently depending on what part of the country you live in. In the North and Midwest it's most likely to be served up sweet and topped with syrup or sugar, but in the South it's usually accompanied by heaping scoops of butter and cheese.

GRANOLA BREAKFAST PARFAIT

Sneak some healthy flax meal or wheat germ into your morning meal by adding it to a layered soy yogurt and granola parfait. If you don't have fresh fruit on hand, try adding some dried fruit, such as chopped dried apricots or pineapples. Serve in glass bowls or cups for presentation.

INGREDIENTS

Serves 2

¼ cup flax meal or wheat germ

2 (6-ounce) containers soy yogurt, any flavor

2 tablespoons maple syrup or agave nectar (optional)

½ cup granola

½ cup sliced fruit

1. In a small bowl, mix together the flax meal or wheat germ, yogurt, and maple syrup until combined.

2. In 2 serving bowls, place a few spoonfuls of granola, then a layer of soy yogurt. Top with a layer of fresh fruit, and continue layering until ingredients are used up. Serve immediately.

HOME FRIES

Home fries are traditionally made in a pan or skillet on the stovetop but they can be easily adapted for the slow cooker.

INGREDIENTS
Serves 6

2 pounds red potatoes, peeled and chopped

1 onion, chopped

1 green bell pepper, chopped

⅛ cup olive oil

½ teaspoon cumin

2 teaspoons paprika

1 teaspoon chili powder

1 teaspoon salt

¼ teaspoon black pepper

Place all ingredients in a 4-quart slow cooker, cover, and cook on high 2 hours.

HOMEMADE GRANOLA

Unlike most slow cooker recipes, this one calls for cooking with the lid off in order to dry out the granola. You don't want to be left with oats that are too liquidy.

INGREDIENTS
Serves 8

5 cups old-fashioned rolled oats

1 cup slivered almonds

¼ cup agave nectar

¼ cup canola oil

1 teaspoon vanilla

¼ cup unsweetened flaked coconut

1½ cups cashews

1½ cups raisins

1. Place the oats and almonds into a 4-quart slow cooker. Drizzle with agave nectar, oil, and vanilla. Stir the mixture to distribute the syrup evenly.

2. Cook on high, uncovered, for 1½ hours, stirring every 15–20 minutes.

3. Add the coconut, cashews, and raisins and reduce the heat to low. Cook for 2 hours, stirring every 20 minutes. Allow the granola to cool completely before serving.

Storage Suggestions
To cool granola faster, spread it evenly over wax paper that is placed over a countertop or baking sheet. Once cool and completely dry, place it in an airtight container and store for up to 1 month.

HOMEMADE NUT MILK

Homemade Nut Milk is delicious in breakfast cereal or oatmeal, smoothies, or to use in baking.
If you don't have a sieve or cheesecloth, you can still enjoy this recipe, but it will be a bit grainy.

INGREDIENTS

Yields 4 cups

1 cup raw almonds or cashews

Water for soaking

4 cups water

½ teaspoon salt

½ teaspoon vanilla

1 teaspoon sugar (optional)

1. In a large bowl, cover nuts with plenty of water and allow to soak for at least 1 hour, or overnight. Drain.

2. Blend together soaked nuts with 4 cups water and purée on high until smooth.

3. Strain through a cheesecloth or sieve.

4. Stir in salt, vanilla, and sugar, and adjust to taste.

Does It Taste Different from What You Expected?

If you read the label of most nondairy milks, you'll find them loaded with sugar! The first few times you make a homemade batch, you may need to add extra sugar to replicate the store-bought taste. Or try using a healthier sweetener, such as maple syrup or agave nectar.

HOMEMADE RICE MILK

When blending, add a bit more water to get the consistency you prefer. If you don't have cheesecloth, you can pour the milk into a new container, leaving most of the grainy bits at the bottom of the first container.

INGREDIENTS

Yields 1 quart

½ cup long-grain rice

6½ cups water

½ teaspoon vanilla

2 tablespoons maple syrup

Dash salt, to taste

1. Slowly simmer rice in water, covered, for 1 hour. Remove from heat, add vanilla, stir to combine, then cover and allow rice and water to cool.

2. Transfer to a blender and purée until smooth, working in batches as needed. Chill for at least 30 minutes.

3. Strain through a cheesecloth and add maple syrup and salt, to taste.

How to Use Rice Milk

Though it's not as thick and creamy as dairy milk, rice milk is sweet and delicious in its own right. Use rice milk in your morning cereal and in smoothies or tea.

JALAPEÑO HASH BROWNS

The type of jalapeños you choose for this dish can make the heat vary greatly, so be careful if you don't like it hot.

INGREDIENTS

Serves 6

2 tablespoons olive oil

2 pounds red potatoes, peeled and shredded

1 onion, diced

¼ cup pickled jalapeños, chopped

1 teaspoon salt

¼ teaspoon black pepper

Place all ingredients in a 4-quart slow cooker, cover, and cook on high 2 hours.

MIXED BERRY QUINOA

Quinoa is an excellent source of vegan protein and fiber, and it's tasty too!

INGREDIENTS

Serves 6

2 cups quinoa

4 cups water

2 teaspoons brown sugar

1 teaspoon dried ginger

½ teaspoon cinnamon

⅛ teaspoon nutmeg

1 cup strawberries, sliced

1 cup blueberries

Place all ingredients except the berries into a 4-quart slow cooker. Cover, and cook on low heat for 2–3 hours, or until the quinoa is fully cooked. When the quinoa is finished, mix in the berries and serve.

MORNING CEREAL BARS

Store-bought breakfast bars are often loaded with artificial sugars, and most homemade recipes require corn syrup. This healthier method makes a sweet and filling snack or breakfast to munch on the run.

INGREDIENTS

Yields 12–14 bars

3 cups breakfast cereal, any kind

1 cup peanut butter

⅓ cup tahini

1 cup maple syrup

½ teaspoon vanilla

2 cups muesli

½ cup flax meal or wheat germ

½ cup diced dried fruit or raisins

1. Lightly grease a baking pan or 2 casserole pans.

2. Place cereal in a sealable bag and crush partially with a rolling pin. If you're using a smaller cereal, you can skip this step. Set aside.

3. Combine peanut butter, tahini, and maple syrup in a large saucepan over low heat, stirring well to combine.

4. Remove from heat and stir in the vanilla, and then the cereal, muesli, flax meal or wheat germ, and dried fruit or raisins.

5. Press firmly into greased baking pan and chill until firm, about 45 minutes, then slice into bars.

NO-SUGAR APRICOT APPLESAUCE

You don't really need to peel the apples if you're short on time, but it only takes about 5 minutes and will give you a smoother sauce. Try adding a touch of nutmeg or pumpkin pie spice for extra flavor.

INGREDIENTS

Yields 4 cups

6 apples

⅓ cup water

½ cup dried apricots, chopped

4 dates, chopped

Cinnamon to taste (optional)

1. Peel, core, and chop apples. Add apples and water to a large soup pot or stockpot and bring to a low boil. Simmer, covered for 15 minutes, stirring occasionally.

2. Add chopped apricots and dates and simmer for another 10–15 minutes.

3. Mash with a large fork until desired consistency is reached, or allow to cool slightly and purée in a blender until smooth.

4. Sprinkle with cinnamon to taste.

ONION, PEPPER, AND POTATO HASH

Use a cheese grater to achieve finely grated potatoes for this dish.

INGREDIENTS

Serves 4

2 tablespoons olive oil

4 cups russet potatoes, peeled and grated

½ onion, diced

1 poblano pepper, cored and diced

2 cloves garlic, minced

1 teaspoon chili powder

½ teaspoon paprika

½ teaspoon cumin

1 teaspoon salt

¼ teaspoon pepper

Add all ingredients to a 4-quart slow cooker. Cover, and cook on high heat for 4 hours.

Better Hash Browns

After you have grated the potatoes for the hash browns, make sure to rinse them in a colander to get rid of the extra starch. Then, allow the potatoes to dry so they will get extra crispy in the slow cooker.

PEANUT BUTTER GRANOLA WRAP

Eating on the go? This wrap has all you need for a healthy breakfast, including whole grains, fresh fruit, and protein. It's the perfect breakfast for the busy health nut!

INGREDIENTS

Serves 1

1 whole-wheat flour tortilla

2 tablespoons peanut butter
(or other nut butter)

2 tablespoons granola (or any vegan
breakfast cereal)

½ banana, sliced thin

¼ teaspoon cinnamon

1 tablespoon raisins

1 teaspoon agave nectar (optional)

1. Spread peanut butter down the center of the tortilla and layer granola and banana on top.

2. Sprinkle with cinnamon and raisins, and drizzle with agave nectar if desired.

3. Warm in the microwave for 10–15 seconds to slightly melt peanut butter.

Exploring Nut Butters

Peanut butter is a great source of protein and kids love it, but shop around for other nut butters for variety. Cashew nut butter is a rich and creamy treat, and soy nut butter is similar to peanut butter but with an earthy taste. If you've got a food processor, mix and match your favorites to make your own homemade nut butters (like Tropical Cashew Nut Butter, Chapter 3).

POTATO POBLANO BREAKFAST BURRITOS

With or without the optional ingredients, this is a filling breakfast. Plan on two servings without the ground beef, and stretch it to three servings with the mock meat.

INGREDIENTS

Serves 2–3

2 tablespoons olive oil

2 small potatoes, diced small

2 poblano or Anaheim chilies, diced

1 teaspoon chili powder

Salt and pepper to taste

1 tomato, diced

$2/3$ cup vegetarian ground beef or sausage substitute (optional)

2–3 flour tortillas, warmed

Grated vegan cheese (optional)

Ketchup or hot sauce (optional)

1. Heat olive oil in a pan and add potatoes and chilies, sautéing until potatoes are almost soft, about 6–7 minutes.

2. Add chili powder, salt and pepper, tomato, and meat substitute if desired, and stir well to combine.

3. Continue cooking until potatoes and tomatoes are soft and meat substitute is cooked, another 4–5 minutes.

4. Wrap in warmed flour tortillas with vegan cheese and ketchup or a bit of hot sauce if desired.

SPICY BREAKFAST BURRITO

Tofu is a great alternative to eggs in breakfast dishes and tofu is naturally cholesterol-free!

INGREDIENTS

Serves 4

2 tablespoons olive oil

1 (16-ounce) package firm tofu, drained and crumbled

¼ cup red onion, diced

1 tablespoon jalapeño, minced

¼ cup red bell pepper, diced

¼ cup poblano pepper, diced

1 cup cooked black beans, drained

2 teaspoons turmeric

1 teaspoon cumin

½ teaspoon chili powder

½ teaspoon salt

¼ teaspoon black pepper

4 flour tortillas

1 avocado, peeled and sliced

½ cup tomatoes, diced

¼ cup cilantro, chopped

½ cup chipotle salsa

1. Add olive oil, tofu, onion, jalapeño, red bell pepper, and poblano pepper to a 4-quart slow cooker and sauté on medium-high for 5–8 minutes.

2. Add the black beans, turmeric, cumin, chili powder, salt, and black pepper. Cover, and cook on low heat for 4 hours.

3. Scoop the filling onto the tortillas and add the avocado, tomatoes, cilantro, and salsa. Fold the sides of the tortilla in and roll up the burrito.

Steaming Tortillas

For best results, steam tortillas on the stovetop using a steamer basket. If you're in a hurry, throw the tortillas into the microwave one at a time and heat for about 30 seconds.

QUICK TOFU BREAKFAST BURRITO

Toss in a fresh diced chili if you need something to really wake you up in the morning. There's no reason you can't enjoy these burritos for lunch, either!

INGREDIENTS

Serves 2

1 block firm or extra-firm tofu, well pressed

2 tablespoons olive oil

½ cup salsa

½ teaspoon chili powder

Salt and pepper to taste

2 flour tortillas, warmed

Ketchup or hot sauce, to taste

2 slices vegan cheese

½ avocado, sliced

1. Cube or crumble the tofu into 1" chunks. Sauté in olive oil over medium heat for 2–3 minutes.

2. Add salsa and chili powder, and cook for 2–3 more minutes, stirring frequently. Season generously with salt and pepper.

3. Layer each warmed flour tortilla with half of the tofu and salsa mix and drizzle with ketchup or hot sauce.

4. Add vegan cheese and avocado slices and wrap like a burrito.

QUICK AND EASY VEGAN BISCUITS

Use these vegan biscuits to mop up your Mushroom Gravy (Chapter 3) or top with vegan margarine or jam, pour some Earl Grey tea, and enjoy a British afternoon tea.

INGREDIENTS

Yields 12–14 biscuits

2 cups flour

1 tablespoon baking powder

½ teaspoon onion powder

½ teaspoon garlic powder

½ teaspoon salt

5 tablespoons cold vegan margarine

⅔ cup unsweetened soymilk

1. Preheat oven to 425°F.

2. Combine flour, baking powder, onion powder, garlic powder, and salt in a large bowl. Add margarine.

3. Using a fork, mash the margarine with the dry ingredients until crumbly.

4. Add soymilk a few tablespoons at a time and combine just until dough forms. You may need to add a little more or less than ⅔ cup.

5. Knead a few times on a floured surface, then roll out to ¾" thick. Cut into 3" rounds.

6. Bake for 12–14 minutes, or until done.

SAVORY RED PEPPER GRITS

Grits are a true Southern staple but this recipe has a slight twist and calls for vegetable broth and red pepper flakes.

INGREDIENTS

Serves 6

2 cups stone-ground grits

3 cups water

3 cups Vegetable Broth (Chapter 6)

2 tablespoons vegan margarine

1 teaspoon red pepper flakes

1 teaspoon salt

¼ teaspoon black pepper

Place all ingredients in a 4-quart slow cooker, cover, and cook on high 2 hours.

Choosing Grits

You may be most familiar with instant or fast-cooking grits, but those should be avoided in slow cooker recipes. Choose stone-ground or whole kernel grits instead, which will hold up better during the long cook time.

STRAWBERRY PROTEIN SMOOTHIE

Add silken tofu to a simple fruit smoothie for a creamy protein boost.

INGREDIENTS

Serves 2

½ cup frozen strawberries (or other berries)

½ block silken tofu

1 banana

¾ cup orange juice

3–4 ice cubes

1 tablespoon agave nectar (optional)

Blend together all ingredients until smooth and creamy.

Protein Shakes

If you're tempted by those rows of fancy-looking dairy-and-egg–based protein powders sold at your gym, try a vegan version! Well-stocked natural foods stores sell a variety of naturally vegan protein powders that you can add to a smoothie for all your muscle-building needs. Look for hemp protein powder or flax meal blends and don't be afraid of the green proteins—some of them are quite tasty!

SUPER GREEN QUICHE

Get your greens in before noon with this veggie quiche. To avoid a crumbly mess, you'll have to be patient and let it cool before slicing.

INGREDIENTS
Serves 4

1 (10-ounce) package frozen chopped spinach, thawed and drained

½ cup broccoli, diced small

1 block firm or extra-firm tofu

1 tablespoon soy sauce

¼ cup soymilk

1 teaspoon mustard

2 tablespoons nutritional yeast

½ teaspoon garlic powder

1 teaspoon parsley

½ teaspoon rosemary

¾ teaspoon salt

¼ teaspoon pepper

Prepared vegan crust (see sidebar)

1. Preheat oven to 350°F.

2. Steam the spinach and broccoli until just lightly cooked, then set aside to cool. Press as much moisture as possible out of the spinach.

3. In a blender or food processor, combine the tofu with the remaining ingredients until well mixed. Mix in the spinach and broccoli by hand until combined.

4. Spread mixture evenly in prepared pie crust.

5. Bake for 35–40 minutes, or until firm. Allow to cool for at least 10 minutes before serving. Quiche will firm up a bit more as it cools.

An Easy Whole-Wheat Crust
Combine ¾ cup whole-wheat flour with ¾ cup all-purpose flour, and a teaspoon of salt. Cut in ⅓ cup vegan margarine until it's crumbly, then add ice-cold water, a few tablespoons at a time, until you can form a dough. You'll need about ½ cup. Roll out the dough and press it into your pie pan and you're ready to fill it up!

SWEET POTATO APPLE LATKES

Use your food processor to quickly process the potatoes, apples, and onion to a fine grate and cut the preparation time in half for this recipe. Serve topped with a homemade Easy Applesauce (Chapter 14) or nondairy sour cream.

INGREDIENTS

Yields 1 dozen latkes

3 large sweet potatoes, grated

1 apple, grated

1 small yellow onion, grated

Egg replacer for 2 eggs

3 tablespoons flour

1 teaspoon baking powder

½ teaspoon cinnamon

½ teaspoon nutmeg

½ teaspoon salt

Oil for frying

1. Using a cloth or paper towel, gently squeeze out excess moisture from potatoes and apples, and combine with onion in a large bowl.

2. Mix together remaining ingredients except the oil, and combine with potato mixture.

3. Heat a few tablespoons of oil in a skillet or frying pan. Drop potato mixture in the hot oil a scant ¼ cup at a time and use a spatula to flatten, forming a pancake. Cook for 3–4 minutes on each side until lightly crisped.

TEMPEH BACON BAKE

The combination of soy sauce, liquid smoke, and brown sugar are what help give the tempeh a faux-bacon flavor in this dish.

INGREDIENTS

Serves 6

1 (13-ounce) package tempeh, cut into bite-size pieces

⅛ cup soy sauce

1 teaspoon liquid smoke

⅛ cup apple cider vinegar

1 tablespoon brown sugar

2 pounds red potatoes, peeled and chopped

2 cups tomatoes, diced

1 onion, chopped

1 green bell pepper, chopped

1 teaspoon salt

¼ teaspoon black pepper

Place all ingredients in a 4-quart slow cooker, cover, and cook on high 2 hours.

TOFU FLORENTINE

Satisfy your comfort food cravings with this "eggy" tofu and spinach mixture drowning in a creamy vegan Quick Hollandaise Sauce (Chapter 4) on toast.

INGREDIENTS

Serves 2

1 block firm or extra-firm tofu, well pressed

2 tablespoons flour

1 teaspoon nutritional yeast

1 teaspoon garlic powder

2 tablespoons canola or safflower oil

1 (10-ounce) box frozen spinach, thawed and drained

½ cup vegan Quick Hollandaise Sauce (Chapter 4)

2 slices bread, lightly toasted (or English muffins or bagels)

1. Slice tofu into ½"-thick slabs.

2. In a small bowl, combine the flour, nutritional yeast, and garlic powder. Dredge tofu in this mixture, then fry in oil for 2–3 minutes on each side until lightly browned.

3. Reduce heat and add spinach and 2 tablespoons of Quick Hollandaise Sauce, gently coating tofu. Cook for just 1–2 minutes over low heat until spinach is heated through.

4. Stack spinach and 2 strips of tofu mixture on each piece of toasted bread and cover with remaining sauce.

Benedict Versus Florentine

For a variation on this classic brunch recipe, skip the spinach and add a layer of lightly browned, store-bought vegan bacon for eggs Benedict instead of Florentine.

TOFU RANCHERO

Bring Mexican cuisine to the breakfast table with an easy Tofu Ranchero.

INGREDIENTS

Serves 4

3 tablespoons olive oil

1 (16-ounce) package firm tofu, drained and crumbled

½ onion, diced

2 cloves garlic, minced

1 lemon, juiced

½ teaspoon turmeric

1 teaspoon salt

¼ teaspoon black pepper

1 cup cooked pinto beans

8 corn tortillas

½ cup chipotle salsa

1. Add the olive oil, tofu, onion, garlic, lemon, turmeric, salt, black pepper, and pinto beans to a 4-quart slow cooker. Cover, and cook on low heat for 4 hours.

2. When the ranchero filling is nearly done, brown the tortillas on both sides using a small sauté pan.

3. Serve by scooping a little bit of the tofu mixture onto each tortilla and topping with salsa.

Choosing Salsa

Salsa comes in many delicious and unique varieties. Most are clearly labeled "mild," "medium," and "hot," but one's interpretation of those words can vary greatly. Chipotle salsa has a deep, earthy spice, but you can also use plain tomato salsa or tomatillo salsa in this recipe.

VANILLA DATE BREAKFAST SMOOTHIE

Adding dates to a basic soymilk and fruit smoothie adds a blast of unexpected sweetness. This is a healthy breakfast treat or a cooling summer snack.

INGREDIENTS

Serves 1

4 dates

Water

¾ cup soymilk

2 bananas

6–7 ice cubes

¼ teaspoon vanilla

1. Cover the dates with water and allow to soak for at least 10 minutes. This makes them softer and easier to blend.

2. Discard the soaking water and add the dates and all other ingredients to the blender.

3. Process until smooth; about 1 minute on medium speed.

For a Smoother Smoothie

Soaking your dates first will help them process a little quicker and results in a smoother consistency. Place dates in a small bowl and cover with water. Let them sit for about 10 minutes, then drain.

VANILLA FLAX GRANOLA

Making your own granola allows you to create whatever flavors you desire. Crystallized ginger, chopped dates, a sprinkle of cinnamon, coconut flakes, dried papaya—the possibilities are endless!

INGREDIENTS

Yields 2½ cups

⅔ cup maple syrup

⅓ cup vegan margarine

1½ teaspoons vanilla

2 cups oats

½ cup flax meal or wheat germ

¾ cup dried fruit, small dices

1. Preheat oven to 325°F.

2. Melt and whisk together maple syrup, vegan margarine, and vanilla over low heat until margarine is melted.

3. Toss together oats, flax meal or wheat germ, and dried fruit on a large baking tray in a single layer (you may need to use 2 trays).

4. Drizzle maple syrup mixture over oats, gently tossing to combine as needed.

5. Bake for 25–30 minutes, carefully tossing once during cooking. Granola will harden as it cools.

VEGAN CREPES

Crepes make a lovely brunch or even dessert, depending on what you fill them with!

INGREDIENTS
Serves 4

1 cup flour

¾ cup soymilk

¼ cup water

2 teaspoons sugar

1 teaspoon vanilla

¼ cup vegan margarine, melted

¼ teaspoon salt

1. Whisk together all ingredients. Chill for at least 1 hour. Remove from fridge and remix.

2. Lightly grease a nonstick pan and heat over medium-high heat.

3. Place about ¼ cup batter in pan and swirl to coat. Cook for just 1 minute, until set, then carefully flip, using a spatula or even your hands. Heat for just 1 more minute, then transfer to a plate.

It's All in the Wrist
Don't worry if the first one or two turn out less than perfect; it always seems to happen. As you master the swirl technique, you'll soon be churning out perfect crepes every time. If you've never tried, you may want to make a double batch so you can practice. Be sure to use a nonstick pan!

VEGAN MIGAS

Serve this breakfast dish just as you would many other Tex-Mex dishes: taco-style in a tortilla!

INGREDIENTS

Serves 4

2 cups tortilla chips, slightly crumbled

2 cups silken tofu

1 cup unsweetened soymilk

1 teaspoon Dijon mustard

¼ cup nutritional flakes

1 teaspoon turmeric

⅛ cup soy sauce

1 teaspoon salt

¼ teaspoon black pepper

Place all ingredients in a 4-quart slow cooker, cover, and cook on high 2 hours.

Tex-Mex Migas

Tex-Mex migas, like this recipe, are slightly different than other versions with the same name. Tex-Mex migas are usually made with eggs and crumbled tortilla chips, while other versions are bread-based breakfast dishes.

VEGAN PANCAKES

A touch of sugar and hint of sweet banana flavor more than make up for the lack of eggs and butter in this pancake recipe.

INGREDIENTS

Yields 1 dozen pancakes

1 cup flour

1 tablespoon sugar

1¾ teaspoons baking powder

¼ teaspoon salt

½ banana

1 teaspoon vanilla

1 cup soymilk

1. Mix together flour, sugar, baking powder, and salt in a large bowl.

2. In a separate small bowl, mash banana with a fork. Add vanilla and whisk until smooth and fluffy. Add soymilk and stir to combine well.

3. Add soymilk mixture to the dry ingredients, stirring just until combined.

4. Heat a lightly greased griddle or large frying pan over medium heat. Drop batter about 3 tablespoons at a time and heat until bubbles appear on surface, about 2–3 minutes. Flip and cook other side until lightly golden brown, another 1–2 minutes.

Don't Overmix!

When it comes to mixing pancake batter, less is more! Pancakes should be light and fluffy, but overmixing the batter will make them tough and rubbery. Gently combine the wet ingredients with the dry ones and don't be afraid of a few lumps; they'll sort themselves out when heated. If you let the batter sit for about 5 minutes, you'll need to stir even less.

WHOLE-WHEAT BLUEBERRY MUFFINS

Because these muffins have very little fat, they'll want to stick to the papers or the muffin tin. Letting them cool before removing them will help prevent this, and be sure to grease your muffin tin well.

INGREDIENTS

Yields approximately 1½ dozen muffins

2 cups whole-wheat flour

1 cup all-purpose flour

1¼ cups sugar

1 tablespoon baking powder

1 teaspoon salt

1½ cups soymilk

½ cup applesauce

½ teaspoon vanilla

2 cups blueberries

1. Preheat oven to 400°F.

2. In a large bowl, combine the flours, sugar, baking powder, and salt. Set aside.

3. In a separate small bowl, whisk together the soymilk, applesauce, and vanilla until well mixed.

4. Combine the wet ingredients with the dry ingredients, stirring just until mixed. Gently fold in half of the blueberries.

5. Spoon batter into lined or greased muffin tins, filling each muffin about ⅔ full. Sprinkle remaining blueberries on top of muffins.

6. Bake for 20–25 minutes, or until lightly golden brown on top.

Making Vegan Muffins

Got a favorite muffin recipe? Try making it vegan! Use a commercial egg replacer brand in place of the eggs, and substitute a vegan soy margarine and soymilk for the butter and milk. Voilà!

CHAPTER 3

APPETIZERS, RELISHES, AND DIPS

AVOCADO AND SHIITAKE POT STICKERS

Once you try these California-fusion pot stickers, you'll wish you had made a double batch! These little dumplings don't need to be enhanced with a complex dipping sauce, so serve them plain or with soy sauce.

INGREDIENTS

Yields 12–15 pot stickers.

1 avocado, diced small

½ cup shiitake mushrooms, diced

½ block silken tofu, crumbled

1 clove garlic, minced

2 teaspoons balsamic vinegar

1 teaspoon soy sauce

Vegan dumpling wrappers

Water for steaming or oil for pan-frying

1. In a small bowl, gently mash together all ingredients except wrappers and water or oil, just until mixed and crumbly.

2. Place about 1½ teaspoons of the filling in the middle of each wrapper. Fold in half and pinch closed, forming little pleats. You may want to dip your fingertips in water to help the dumplings stay sealed if needed.

3. To pan-fry: Heat a thin layer of oil in a large skillet. Carefully add dumplings and cook for just 1 minute. Add about ½ cup water, cover, and cook for 3–4 minutes.

4. To steam: Carefully place a layer of dumplings in a steamer, being sure the dumplings don't touch. Place steamer above boiling water and allow to cook, covered, for 3–4 minutes.

Whether Steamed or Fried . . .

In dumpling houses across East Asia, dumplings are served with a little bowl of fresh grated ginger, and diners create a simple dipping sauce from the various condiments on the table. To try it, pour some rice vinegar and a touch of soy sauce over a bit of ginger and add hot chili oil to taste.

BARBECUE "MEATBALLS"

Enjoy these "meatballs" as a two-bite snack or use them as the filling in a hearty sub.

INGREDIENTS

Serves 6

1 pound vegan ground beef, such as Gimme Lean Beef

½ onion, diced

1 clove garlic, minced

½ cup panko bread crumbs

1 (18-ounce) bottle barbecue sauce

1. In a large mixing bowl, combine the vegan ground beef, onion, garlic, and bread crumbs, and mix until well combined. (Using your hands is the easiest method.) Roll the "beef" mixture into 12 meatballs.

2. To a 4-quart slow cooker, add the "meatballs."

3. Cover with barbecue sauce; cover, and cook over high heat for 1 hour.

Panko Bread Crumbs

Panko is a type of bread crumb made from white bread without crusts. It typically creates a crispier texture when used as the coating on food than regular bread crumbs. To make your own, bake crustless white bread crumbs until they are dry, but not browned.

CINNAMON AND SUGAR PEANUTS

This is a festive treat that can be packaged in cellophane bags and given as party favors or gifts.

INGREDIENTS
Serves 6

12 ounces unsalted, roasted peanuts

½ tablespoon ground cinnamon

⅓ cup sugar

1 tablespoon melted vegan margarine

1. In a 4-quart slow cooker, place the peanuts.

2. Add the cinnamon and sugar and drizzle with vegan margarine. Stir.

3. Cook on low, uncovered, for 2–3 hours, stirring occasionally.

4. Spread the peanut mixture onto a cookie sheet or parchment paper and cool until dry.

EGGPLANT BABA GHANOUSH

Whip up a batch of Eggplant Baba Ghanoush, Roasted Red Pepper Hummus, and some Vegan Tzatziki (this chapter) and make a Mediterranean appetizer spread. Don't forget some vegan pita bread to dip into your Baba.

INGREDIENTS
Yields 1½ cups

2 medium eggplants

3 tablespoons olive oil, divided

2 tablespoons lemon juice

¼ cup tahini

3 cloves garlic

½ teaspoon cumin

½ teaspoon chili powder (optional)

¼ teaspoon salt

1 tablespoon chopped fresh parsley

1. Preheat oven to 400°F. Slice eggplants in half and prick several times with a fork.

2. Place on a baking sheet and drizzle with 1 tablespoon olive oil. Bake for 30 minutes, or until soft. Allow to cool slightly.

3. Remove inner flesh and place in a bowl.

4. Using a large fork or potato masher, mash eggplant together with remaining ingredients until almost smooth.

5. Adjust seasonings to taste.

FRESH BASIL BRUSCHETTA WITH BALSAMIC REDUCTION

Your guests will be so delighted by the rich flavors of the balsamic reduction sauce that they won't even notice that the cheese is missing from this vegan bruschetta. Use a fresh artisan bread if you can, for extra flavor.

INGREDIENTS

Serves 4

8–10 slices French bread

¾ cup balsamic vinegar

1 tablespoon sugar

2 large tomatoes, diced small

3 cloves garlic, minced

¼ cup chopped fresh basil

2 tablespoons olive oil

Salt and pepper to taste

1. Toast bread in toaster or for 5 minutes in the oven at 350°F.

2. Whisk together the balsamic vinegar and sugar in a small saucepan. Bring to a boil then reduce to a slow simmer. Allow to cook for 6–8 minutes until almost thickened. Remove from heat.

3. Combine the tomatoes, garlic, basil, olive oil, salt, and pepper in a large bowl. Gently toss with balsamic sauce.

4. Spoon tomato and balsamic mixture over bread slices and serve immediately.

A Tuscan Tradition

A true Italian chef will prepare the bread for bruschetta by toasting homemade bread over hot coals, then quickly rubbing a sliced clove of garlic over both sides of the bread before drizzling with just a touch of the finest olive oil. In lieu of hot coals, a toaster or 5 minutes in the oven at 350°F will work just fine.

FRESH MINT SPRING ROLLS

Wrapping spring rolls is a balance between getting them tight enough to hold together, but not so tight the thin wrappers break! It's like riding a bike: once you've got it, you've got it, and then spring rolls can be very quick and fun to make.

INGREDIENTS

Serves 4

1 (3-ounce) package clear bean thread noodles

1 cup hot water

1 tablespoon soy sauce

½ teaspoon powdered ginger

1 teaspoon sesame oil

¼ cup shiitake mushrooms, diced

1 carrot, grated

10–12 spring roll wrappers

Warm water

½ head green leaf lettuce, chopped

1 cucumber, sliced thin

1 bunch fresh mint

1. Break noodles in half to make smaller pieces, then submerge in 1 cup hot water until soft, about 6–7 minutes. Drain.

2. In a large bowl, toss together the hot noodles with the soy sauce, ginger, sesame oil, mushrooms, and carrot, tossing well to combine.

3. In a large shallow pan, carefully submerge spring roll wrappers, 1 at a time, in warm water until just barely soft. Remove from water and place a bit of lettuce in the center of the wrapper. Add about 2 tablespoons of noodles mixture, a few slices of cucumber and place 2–3 mint leaves on top.

4. Fold the bottom of the wrapper over the filling, fold in each side, then roll.

To Dip, or Not to Dip?

Store-bought sweet chili sauce, spicy sriracha sauce, or a Japanese salad dressing or marinade will work in a pinch, but a simple homemade dip is best. Try a Thai Orange Peanut Dressing (Chapter 5) or an Easy Asian Dipping Sauce (this chapter).

FRIED ZUCCHINI STICKS

You don't have to deep-fry these zucchini sticks, just sauté them in a bit of oil if you prefer.
This is a great appetizer or snack for kids!

INGREDIENTS

Serves 4

¾ cup flour

½ teaspoon garlic powder

¾ teaspoon Italian seasoning

¼ teaspoon salt

4 zucchinis, cut into strips

Oil for frying

Vegan ranch dressing or ketchup
   for dipping

1. In a large bowl or pan, combine the flour, garlic powder, Italian seasoning, and salt.

2. Lightly toss the zucchini strips with the flour mixture, coating well.

3. Heat oil in a large skillet or frying pan. When oil is hot, gently add zucchini strips to pan.

4. Fry until lightly golden brown on all sides. Serve with vegan ranch dressing or ketchup.

MARINATED MUSHROOMS AND GARLIC

Although white button mushrooms are most common, there are a variety of other exotic mushrooms,
such as shiitake and chanterelles, that will work perfectly in this recipe.

INGREDIENTS

Serves 6

2 (8-ounce) packages mushrooms

5 cloves garlic, minced

1 cup red wine

1 cup soy sauce

1 cup water

½ teaspoon tarragon

⅛ teaspoon salt

⅛ teaspoon black pepper

Add all ingredients to a 4-quart slow cooker, cover, and cook on medium heat for 3–4 hours.

MUSHROOM FONDUE

Nutritional yeast lends a rich flavor to this fun party fondue. If you don't have a fondue pot, you can mix the ingredients over low heat and serve hot. Don't forget plenty of dippers—French bread, mushrooms, or lightly cooked baby potatoes would work well. Long live the '70s!

INGREDIENTS

Serves 4

2 tablespoons vegan margarine

2 cups sliced mushrooms

½ cup soymilk or soy cream

1 teaspoon onion powder

½ teaspoon garlic powder

½ teaspoon celery salt

2 tablespoons flour

3 tablespoons nutritional yeast

1. Melt the vegan margarine over low heat and add mushrooms. Allow to cook for 5 minutes, then add soymilk or soy cream, onion powder, garlic powder, and celery salt. Cook over low heat for 8–10 minutes until mushrooms are soft.

2. Allow mixture to cool slightly, then purée in a blender.

3. Place puréed mushrooms in a fondue pot and add soymilk mixture. Over medium heat, whisk in flour and heat until thickened. Stir in nutritional yeast and serve immediately.

Dust Off Your Disco Ball . . .

What could be more fun than a vegan fondue-themed party? The retro trend is in! Melt some vegan chocolate with soy cream, or try a wine reduction with fresh herbs. A Nacho "Cheese" Dip (this chapter) can be warmed in a fondue pot. Get together with friends for some Saturday night fun, and don't double-dip! Fondue sets also make a fun gift for the vegan cook who has everything.

SIMPLE SCALLION PANCAKES

Whether you eat them as an accompaniment to a Chinese feast, or just as a snack or appetizer, these salty fried pancakes are a popular street food snack served up hot in East Asia. Plain soy sauce is the perfect dip.

INGREDIENTS

Yields 6 large pancakes

2 cups flour

½ teaspoon salt

¾ cup hot water

2 teaspoons sesame oil

6 scallions, chopped (green parts only)

Oil for frying

Soy sauce for dipping

1. In a large bowl, combine flour and salt. Slowly add water and sesame oil, mixing, just until a dough forms. You may need a little bit less than ¾ cup water.

2. Knead dough for a few minutes, then let sit for 30 minutes.

3. Divide dough into 6 (2") balls. Roll out each ball on a lightly floured surface. Brush with sesame oil and cover with scallions. Roll up dough and twist to form a ball. Roll out again ¼" thick.

4. Fry each pancake in hot oil 1–2 minutes on each side. Slice into squares or wedges and serve with soy sauce.

SOUTHERN BOILED PEANUTS

On a warm summer day in the South, you can find roadside stands selling boiled peanuts by the bagful.

INGREDIENTS

Serves 8

4 cups raw peanuts, rinsed

8 cups water

¼ cup kosher salt

Add all ingredients to a 4-quart slow cooker, cover, and cook on high heat for 5–6 hours. When the peanuts are tender, drain and serve.

SPICY SEITAN BUFFALO STRIPS

Most bottled buffalo wing sauces contain butter, so be sure to read the label or make your own by following the steps below.

INGREDIENTS
Serves 6

⅓ cup vegan margarine

⅓ cup hot sauce

1 tablespoon vinegar

1 teaspoon garlic powder

2 (7-ounce) packages Gardein Chick'n Strips

1. Place the vegan margarine in a small bowl and microwave for 30 seconds, or until melted.

2. Add the hot sauce, vinegar, and garlic powder and stir well.

3. In a 4-quart slow cooker, add the prepared hot sauce and Chick'n Strips and cook over low heat for 1 hour.

Serving Strips

Faux buffalo chicken strips can be added to sandwiches or salads, but if you'd like to serve them as an appetizer or snack, place in a small basket lined with parchment paper and add sides of celery sticks, carrot sticks, and vegan ranch.

TERIYAKI VEGGIE SKEWERS

If you are using an oval slow cooker or one that is very large, save time by prepping the skewers the night before cooking and storing in the fridge.

INGREDIENTS
Serves 4

1 red bell pepper, cut into 16 (1") chunks

1 eggplant, cut into 16 large chunks

1 pineapple, peeled and cut into 16 large chunks

1 tablespoon vegetable oil

¼ cup soy sauce

1 cup water

⅓ cup brown sugar

1 tablespoon fresh ginger, grated

2 cloves garlic, minced

1 package of 6" skewers

1. In a large bowl, toss the red bell pepper, eggplant, and pineapple with the vegetable oil. Whisk the soy sauce, water, brown sugar, ginger, and garlic together in a small bowl.

2. Add all the ingredients to a 4-quart slow cooker, cover, and cook on medium-high heat for 3–4 hours.

3. Assemble the skewers with the bell pepper first, then eggplant, then pineapple, bell pepper, eggplant, and pineapple.

TOMATO AND DILL–STUFFED GRAPE LEAVES (DOLMAS)

Little Middle Eastern dolmas overflow with flavors and travel well in lunchboxes. Look for canned or jarred grape leaves in the ethnic foods aisle of your grocery store.

INGREDIENTS

Yields approximately 2 dozen dolmas

3 scallions, chopped

1 tomato, diced small

¼ cup olive oil, divided

1 cup uncooked rice

½ cup water

½ teaspoon salt

1 tablespoon chopped fresh dill

1 teaspoon dried parsley

1 tablespoon chopped fresh mint (optional)

Approximately 40 grape leaves

Water for boiling

2 tablespoons lemon juice

1. Heat scallions and tomato in 2 tablespoons of olive oil for 2 minutes, then add rice, water, salt, dill, parsley, and mint if desired. Cover, and cook for 5 minutes. Remove from heat and cool.

2. Place about 2 teaspoons of the rice filling in the center of a grape leaf near the stem. Fold the bottom of the leaf over the filling, then fold in the sides and roll. Continue with each grape leaf.

3. Line the bottom of a pan with extra or torn grape leaves to prevent burning. Add wrapped and filled leaves and add enough water just to cover the dolmas. Add remaining 2 tablespoons of olive oil and bring to a slow simmer.

4. Cook for 20 minutes. Drizzle with lemon juice just before serving.

In a Hurry?
Mix together some leftover rice with vegan pesto for the filling. Wrap, simmer just a few minutes, and eat!

WALNUT ASPARAGUS "EGG" ROLLS

It's not traditional, but it's certainly delicious. Spring roll wrappers or wonton wrappers are just fine if you can't find eggless egg roll wraps.

INGREDIENTS

Yields 15 egg rolls

1 bunch asparagus

2 avocados

½ onion, minced

1 teaspoon lime juice

1 tablespoon soy sauce

1 teaspoon chipotle powder

½ cup walnuts, finely chopped

¼ cup chopped fresh cilantro

15 vegan egg roll wrappers

Oil for frying

1. Steam the asparagus until crisp-tender, then chop into ½" slices.

2. Mash together the asparagus with the avocados, onion, lime juice, soy sauce, chipotle, walnuts, and cilantro.

3. Place 2–3 tablespoons of filling in each wrapper. Fold the bottom up, then fold the sides in and roll, wetting the edges with water to help it stick together.

4. Fry in hot oil for 1–2 minutes on each side.

VEGAN CHEESEBALL

Use this recipe to make one impressive-looking large cheeseball or cheeselog, or make individual bite-size servings for a party or the holidays. Everyone will be asking you for the recipe!

INGREDIENTS

Makes 1 large cheeseball or 12–14 bite-size cheeseballs

1 block vegan nacho or Cheddar cheese, room temperature

1 container vegan cream cheese, room temperature

1 teaspoon garlic powder

½ teaspoon hot sauce

¼ teaspoon salt

1 teaspoon paprika

¼ cup nuts, finely chopped

1. Grate vegan cheese into a large bowl, or process in a food processor until finely minced. Using a large fork, mash the vegan cheese together with the cream cheese, garlic powder, hot sauce, and salt until well mixed. (You may need to use your hands for this.)

2. Chill until firm, at least 1 hour, then shape into ball or log shape, pressing firmly. Sprinkle with paprika and carefully roll in nuts. Serve with crackers.

VEGAN "PIGS" IN A BLANKET

Use store-bought vegetarian hot dogs to make this great little appetizer that kids and adults both love. Serve with ketchup or hot mustard.

INGREDIENTS
Makes 16 "pigs"

1 batch dough from Quick and Easy Vegan Biscuits recipe (Chapter 2)

8 vegan hot dogs, sliced in half

1. Preheat oven to 400°F and lightly grease a baking sheet.

2. Divide dough into sections and roll into ovals.

3. Place each hot dog piece on the edge of each dough circle and wrap. Place on baking sheet.

4. Bake for 10–12 minutes or until lightly golden brown.

Party Pigs

Head to enough vegan parties, and you'll inevitably run into a variation of this recipe sooner or later—it's an old vegan favorite. If you're short on time, roll out some store-bought vegan crescent roll dough, and to try something a bit different, add a thin slice of vegan cheese or a generous sprinkle of red pepper flakes before wrapping.

BLACK BEAN GUACAMOLE

Sneaking some extra fiber and protein into a traditional Mexican guacamole makes this dip a more nutritious appetizer.

INGREDIENTS
Yields 2 cups

1 (15-ounce) can black beans

3 avocados

1 tablespoon lime juice

3 scallions, chopped

1 large tomato, diced

2 cloves garlic, minced

½ teaspoon chili powder

¼ teaspoon salt

1 tablespoon chopped fresh cilantro

1. Using a fork or a potato masher, mash the beans in a medium-size bowl just until they are halfway mashed, leaving some texture.

2. Combine all the remaining ingredients, and mash together until mixed.

3. Adjust seasonings to taste.

4. Allow to sit for at least 10 minutes before serving to allow the flavors to set.

5. Gently mix again just before serving.

CRANBERRY JALAPEÑO RELISH

If you can't take the heat, leave the jalapeños out of this recipe for a more traditional relish.

INGREDIENTS

Serves 6

1 (12-ounce) bag frozen cranberries

2 oranges, juiced

1 lemon, juiced

1 cup sugar

1 jalapeño, minced

⅛ cup water

¼ teaspoon salt

¼ black pepper

Add all ingredients to a 4-quart slow cooker, stir, cover, and cook on medium heat for 2–3 hours.

EASY ASIAN DIPPING SAUCE

Tangy, salty, spicy, and a bit sour—this easy dipping sauce has it all! Use it for dipping vegetarian sushi, Avocado and Shiitake Pot Stickers, and Fresh Mint Spring Rolls (this chapter). It also makes an excellent marinade for a baked tofu dish.

INGREDIENTS

Yields ⅓ cup

¼ cup soy sauce

2 tablespoons rice vinegar

2 teaspoons sesame oil

1 teaspoon sugar

1 teaspoon fresh ginger, minced

2 cloves garlic, minced and crushed

¼ teaspoon crushed red pepper flakes, or to taste

Whisk together all ingredients.

GARLIC CONFIT

Use this garlic in place of fresh garlic in appropriate recipes, or you can enjoy it smashed and spread on toasted bread.

INGREDIENTS
Yields 5 heads of garlic

2–3 cups olive oil

5 heads of garlic, cloves peeled

3 dried red chilies

1. Add all ingredients to a 4-quart slow cooker. Make sure there is enough oil to cover all the garlic cloves. Place the cover on the slow cooker and cook on low heat for 4 hours, or until the garlic is tender.

2. Remove the garlic with a slotted spoon and place in canning jars. Pour the oil over the garlic and seal the top.

Preserving Garlic
Garlic confit is a great and easy way to preserve garlic when it is in season and at its peak. Garlic prepared using this method can be jarred and stored for up to 3 months.

GREEN AND BLACK OLIVE TAPENADE

Mediterranean olive tapenade can be used as a spread or dip for baguettes or crackers. If you don't have a food processor, you can mash the ingredients together with a mortar and pestle or a large fork instead.

INGREDIENTS
Yields 1 cup

½ cup green olives

¾ cup black olives

2 cloves garlic

1 tablespoon capers (optional)

2 tablespoons lemon juice

2 tablespoons olive oil

¼ teaspoon oregano

¼ teaspoon black pepper

Process all ingredients in a food processor until almost smooth.

HOMEMADE TAHINI

If you're serving this as a Middle Eastern dip or spread, use the paprika for extra flavor, but leave it out if your tahini will be the basis for a salad dressing or a noodle dish.

INGREDIENTS
Yields 1 cup

2 cups sesame seeds

½ cup olive oil

½ teaspoon paprika (optional)

1. Heat oven to 350°F.

2. Once oven is hot, spread sesame seeds in a thin layer on a baking sheet and toast for 5 minutes in the oven, shaking the sheet once to mix.

3. Allow sesame seeds to cool, then process with oil in a food processor or blender until thick and creamy. You may need a little more or less than ½ cup oil. Garnish with paprika if desired. Tahini will keep for up to 1 month in the refrigerator in a tightly sealed container, or store your tahini in the freezer and thaw before using.

MANGO CITRUS SALSA

Salsa has a variety of uses, and this recipe adds color and variety to your usual chips and dip or Mexican dishes.

INGREDIENTS
Yields 2 cups

1 mango, chopped

2 tangerines, chopped

½ red bell pepper, chopped

½ red onion, minced

3 cloves garlic, minced

½ jalapeño pepper, minced

2 tablespoons lime juice

½ teaspoon salt

¼ teaspoon black pepper

3 tablespoons chopped fresh cilantro

1. Gently toss together all ingredients.

2. Allow to sit for at least 15 minutes before serving to allow flavors to mingle.

MUSHROOM GRAVY

Stir, stir, stir! Just like regular gravy, the secret to perfect vegan gravy is in the stirring, to prevent those pesky lumps. That and the hefty added flavors!

INGREDIENTS

Yields 1½ cups

¼ cup vegan margarine

¾ cup sliced mushrooms

2½ cups Vegetable Broth (Chapter 6)

1 teaspoon garlic powder

1 teaspoon onion powder

½ teaspoon sage

½ teaspoon thyme

¼ teaspoon marjoram (optional)

3 tablespoons flour

2 tablespoons nutritional yeast (optional)

Salt and pepper to taste

1. Heat the vegan margarine in a large skillet over medium heat and add mushrooms. Sauté for 2–3 minutes.

2. Reduce heat to medium-low and add Vegetable Broth, garlic powder, onion powder, sage, thyme, and marjoram if desired, stirring well to combine.

3. Add flour, 1 tablespoon at a time, whisking constantly to combine well and prevent lumps. Allow to cook for 2–3 minutes before adding the next tablespoon of flour. Continue simmering over low heat until thick.

4. Remove from heat and stir in nutritional yeast, if using. Taste, and add a bit of salt and pepper, as needed. Gravy will thicken as it cools.

ROASTED CASHEW AND SPICY BASIL PESTO

The combination of spicy purple Thai basil or holy basil instead of Italian sweet basil and the bite of the garlic creates an electrifying vegan pesto.

INGREDIENTS
Serves 3

4 cloves garlic

1 cup Thai basil or holy basil, packed

2/3 cup roasted cashews

1/2 cup nutritional yeast

3/4 teaspoon salt

1/2 teaspoon black pepper

1/3–1/2 cup olive oil

1. Process all ingredients except olive oil in a blender or food processor just until coarse and combined.

2. Slowly incorporate olive oil until desired consistency is reached.

Traditional Pesto
For a more traditional Italian pesto, you can, of course, use regular Italian basil. In this case, cut back on the garlic a bit, and use pine nuts or walnuts instead of roasted cashews.

TROPICAL CASHEW NUT BUTTER

You can make a homemade cashew nut butter with any kind of oil, so feel free to substitute, using whatever you have on hand, but you're in for a real treat when you use coconut oil in this recipe!

INGREDIENTS
Yields 3/4 cup

2 cups roasted cashews

1/2 teaspoon sugar (optional)

1/4 teaspoon salt (optional)

3–4 tablespoons coconut oil or other vegetable oil

1. Process the cashews and sugar and salt (if using) in a food processor
on high speed until finely ground. Continue processing until cashews form a thick paste.

2. Slowly add coconut oil until smooth and creamy, scraping down sides and adding a little more oil as needed.

Making Nut Butters
Nut butters can be very expensive to purchase, but are so easy to make at home! Try making almond, walnut, or macadamia nut butter for a delicious alternative to store-bought peanut butter. Roasted nuts work best, so heat them in the oven at 400°F for 6–8 minutes or toast them on the stovetop in a dry skillet for a few minutes.

VEGAN CHOCOLATE HAZELNUT SPREAD

Treat yourself or your family with this rich, sticky chocolate spread. This one will have you dancing around the kitchen and licking your spoons!

INGREDIENTS

Yields 1 cup

2 cups hazelnuts, chopped

½ cup cocoa powder

¾ cup powdered sugar

½ teaspoon vanilla

4–5 tablespoons vegetable oil

1. Process hazelnuts in a food processor until very finely ground, about 3–4 minutes.

2. Add cocoa powder, sugar, and vanilla, and process to combine.

3. Add oil just a little bit at a time until mixture is soft and creamy and desired consistency is reached. You may need to add a bit more or less than 4–5 tablespoons.

Besides Just Licking the Spoons . . .

Europeans spread it on toast, and Asian teenagers spread it on pancakes and stuff it inside waffles, but you can use it however you want, perhaps to top Vegan Crepes (Chapter 2) for dessert, spread over apple slices for the kids, or—go ahead—just eat it plain. No one will know! If you can't find hazelnuts, cashews will lend a similar creamy consistency.

VEGAN MAYONNAISE

The secret to getting a really creamy homemade vegan mayonnaise is to add the oil very, very slowly—literally just a few drops at a time—and use the highest available speed on your food processor.

INGREDIENTS
Yields 1 cup

1 (12-ounce) block silken tofu

1½ tablespoons lemon juice

1 teaspoon prepared mustard

1½ teaspoons vinegar (apple cider or white)

1 teaspoon sugar

¾ teaspoon onion powder

½ teaspoon salt

⅓ cup canola or safflower oil

1. Process all ingredients except oil in a food processor until smooth.

2. On high speed, slowly incorporate the oil just a few drops at a time until smooth and creamy.

3. Chill for at least 1 hour before serving to allow flavors to blend. Mayonnaise will also thicken as it sits.

From Aioli Sauce to Thousand Island Dressing

Mayonnaise is used in so many comfort foods that you'll really want to have a good one on hand most of the time. If you prefer to try a store-bought vegan mayo, shop around or try a couple of different types, as there's a vast range of brands and flavors available.

VEGAN TZATZIKI

Use a vegan soy yogurt to make this classic Greek dip, which is best served very cold. A nondairy sour cream may be used instead of the soy yogurt if you prefer.

INGREDIENTS
Yields 1½ cups

1½ cups soy yogurt, plain or lemon-flavored

1 tablespoon olive oil

1 tablespoon lemon juice

4 cloves garlic, minced

2 cucumbers, grated or chopped fine

1 tablespoon chopped fresh mint or fresh dill

1. Whisk together yogurt with olive oil and lemon juice until well combined.

2. Combine with remaining ingredients.

3. Chill for at least 1 hour before serving to allow flavors to mingle. Serve cold.

KALAMATA OLIVE HUMMUS

This hummus can easily be spiced up with the addition of red pepper flakes.

INGREDIENTS

Serves 6

1 pound dry chickpeas

7 cups water

⅓ cup tahini

2 lemons, juiced

¼ cup kalamata olives, chopped

2 cloves garlic, minced

4 tablespoons olive oil

2 teaspoons cumin

¾ teaspoon salt

¼ teaspoon black pepper

1. Place the dry chickpeas and water in a 4-quart slow cooker, cover, and cook on high heat for 4 hours. Drain the chickpeas.

2. Combine the chickpeas and the rest of the ingredients in a food processor and purée until smooth.

Protein Punch

Hummus is a great source of protein and iron, making it an excellent choice for vegans. Even little ones love the creamy treat!

ROASTED RED PEPPER HUMMUS

You'll rarely meet a vegan who doesn't love hummus in one form or another. As a veggie dip or sandwich spread, hummus is always a favorite. Up the garlic in this recipe if that's your thing, and don't be ashamed to lick the spoons or spatula.

INGREDIENTS

Yields 1½ cups

1 (15-ounce) can chickpeas, drained

⅓ cup tahini

⅔ cup chopped roasted red peppers

3 tablespoons lemon juice

2 tablespoons olive oil

2 cloves garlic

½ teaspoon cumin

⅓ teaspoon salt

¼ teaspoon cayenne pepper (optional)

Process all ingredients together in a blender or food processor until smooth, scraping the sides down as needed.

Do-It-Yourself Roasted Red Peppers

Sure, you can buy them from a jar, but it's easy to roast your own. Here's how: Fire up your oven to 450°F (or use the broiler setting) and drizzle a few whole peppers with olive oil. Bake for 30 minutes, turning over once. Direct heat will also work if you have a gas stove. Hold the peppers with tongs over the flame until lightly charred. Let your peppers cool, then remove the skin before making hummus.

ZESTY LEMON HUMMUS

Serve this zesty Middle Eastern spread with pita, vegetables, or falafel.

INGREDIENTS
Serves 20

1 pound dried chickpeas

Water, as needed

3 tablespoons tahini

4 tablespoons lemon juice

Zest of 1 lemon

3 cloves garlic

¼ teaspoon salt

1. In a 4-quart slow cooker, place the chickpeas and cover with water. Soak overnight, drain, and rinse. The next day, cook on low for 8 hours. Drain, reserving the liquid.

2. In a food processor, place the chickpeas, tahini, lemon juice, lemon zest, garlic, and salt. Pulse until smooth, adding the reserved liquid as needed to achieve the desired texture.

Easy Snacking
Keeping hummus and fresh vegetables around makes healthy snacking easy. Cut carrots, celery, and radishes into snack-friendly sizes. Place them in a bowl with a tightly fitting lid. Fill the bowl ⅔ with water. They will keep crisp in the refrigerator up to 1 week.

HOT ARTICHOKE SPINACH DIP

Serve this creamy dip hot with some baguette slices, crackers, pita bread, or sliced bell peppers and jicama. If you want to get fancy, you can carve out a bread bowl for an edible serving dish.

INGREDIENTS
Serves 8

1 (12-ounce) package frozen spinach, thawed

1 (14-ounce) can artichoke hearts, drained

¼ cup vegan margarine

¼ cup flour

2 cups soymilk

½ cup nutritional yeast

1 teaspoon garlic powder

1½ teaspoons onion powder

¼ teaspoon salt

1. Preheat oven to 350°F.

2. Purée spinach and artichokes together until almost smooth and set aside.

3. In a small saucepan, melt the vegan margarine over low heat. Slowly whisk in flour, 1 tablespoon at a time, stirring constantly to avoid lumps, until thick.

4. Remove from heat and add spinach and artichoke mixture, stirring to combine. Add remaining ingredients.

5. Transfer to an ovenproof casserole dish or bowl and bake for 20 minutes. Serve hot.

CARAMELIZED ONION DIP

Caramelized onions give this dip an amazing depth of flavor.

INGREDIENTS

Serves 32

²/₃ cup Caramelized Onions (Chapter 7)

8 ounces vegan cream cheese

8 ounces vegan sour cream

1 tablespoon vegan Worcestershire Sauce

¼ teaspoon white pepper

⅛ teaspoon flour

1. Place all ingredients into a 1½- to 2-quart slow cooker.

2. Heat on low for 2 hours. Whisk before serving.

Vegan Worcestershire Sauce

While most brands of Worcestershire sauce contain anchovies, vegans need not worry! Many store brands are accidentally vegan and omit fish from the recipe. Just be sure to read the label.

CREAMY CILANTRO DIP

This versatile dip can be served with tortilla chips, pita wedges, vegetables, or as a sandwich condiment.

INGREDIENTS

Serves 6

½ pound dry white beans

3¼ cups water, divided

1 bunch cilantro, washed and stemmed

1 tablespoon olive oil

1 lime, juiced

½ teaspoon salt

⅛ teaspoon black pepper

1. Place the dry white beans and 3 cups of the water in a 4-quart slow cooker, cover, and cook on high heat for 4–5 hours, or until the beans are tender. Drain the white beans.

2. While the beans are cooking, purée the cilantro, olive oil, lime juice, salt, and pepper in a food processor. Set the herb mixture aside in a small bowl.

3. Add the drained white beans and ¼ cup of water to the food processor and purée until it reaches a smooth consistency.

4. In a large bowl, combine the white beans and the herb mixture. Cover, and chill for 2 hours before serving.

Cilantrophobia

You either love it or you hate it, and those who hate cilantro really hate it. Studies suggest that the aversion to the green leafy herb may be genetic but it's still largely unknown why some people can't stomach the herb that is described as tasting like soap.

EDAMAME-MISO DIP

The Asian flavors of this unique dip are both subtle and satisfying.

INGREDIENTS

Serves 4

½ pound frozen shelled edamame

3 cups water

1 tablespoon soy sauce

2½ tablespoons miso paste

2 green onions, thinly sliced

⅛ teaspoon salt

1. Add all ingredients to a 4-quart slow cooker, stir, cover, and cook on low heat for 2 hours, or until the edamame is tender.

2. Using a slotted spoon, remove the edamame and place it in a food processor or blender. Purée the edamame, adding enough of the cooking liquid to create a smooth consistency. Serve cold or at room temperature.

MIXED VEGGIE DIP

Try this vegetable-rich dip with pita chips or baked potato chips.

INGREDIENTS

Serves 20

8 ounces vegan cream cheese, room temperature

½ cup vegan sour cream

½ teaspoon white pepper

½ teaspoon garlic powder

½ teaspoon onion powder

½ teaspoon vegan Worcestershire sauce

1 carrot, minced

1 stalk celery, minced

3 tablespoons fresh spinach, minced

¼ cup broccoli, minced

1. In a 2-quart slow cooker, thoroughly mix all ingredients.

2. Cook on low for 2 hours. Stir before serving.

NACHO "CHEESE" DIP

Peanut butter in cheese sauce? No, that's not a typo! Just a touch of peanut butter creates a creamy and nutty layer of flavor to this sauce, and helps it to thicken nicely. Use this sauce to dress plain steamed veggies or make homemade nachos.

INGREDIENTS

Yields about 1 cup sauce

3 tablespoons vegan margarine

1 cup unsweetened soymilk

¾ teaspoon garlic powder

½ teaspoon onion powder

½ teaspoon salt

1 tablespoon peanut butter

¼ cup flour

¼ cup nutritional yeast

¾ cup salsa

2 tablespoons chopped canned jalapeño peppers (optional)

1. Heat margarine and soymilk together in a pan over low heat. Add garlic powder, onion powder, and salt, stirring to combine. Add peanut butter and stir until melted.

2. Whisk in flour, 1 tablespoon at a time, until smooth. Heat until thickened, about 5–6 minutes.

3. Stir in nutritional yeast, salsa, and jalapeño peppers if desired.

4. Allow to cool slightly before serving, as cheese sauce will thicken as it cools.

Chili Cheese

Add a can of store-bought vegetarian chili for a chili cheese dip, or smother some french fries to make chili cheese fries.

PARSLEY AND ONION DIP

If you like packaged onion dip mixes, try this tofu-based version with fresh parsley and chives. Perfect for carrots or crackers.

INGREDIENTS

Serves 6

1 onion, chopped

3 cloves garlic, minced

1 tablespoon olive oil

1 block firm tofu, well pressed

½ teaspoon onion powder

3 teaspoons lemon juice

¼ cup chopped fresh parsley

2 tablespoons chopped fresh chives

¼ teaspoon salt

1. Sauté onions and garlic in the olive oil for 3–4 minutes until onions are soft. Remove from heat and allow to cool slightly.

2. Process the onion and garlic with the tofu, onion powder, and lemon juice in a food processor or blender until onion is minced and tofu is almost smooth.

3. Mash together with remaining ingredients by hand.

PARSLEY AND THYME WHITE BEAN DIP

Don't substitute dried herbs for fresh in this recipe because fresh herbs are needed to complement the lemon and give the dip a light and refreshing flavor.

INGREDIENTS

Serves 6

2 tablespoons olive oil

½ onion, diced

3 cloves garlic, minced

½ pound dry white beans

3 cups water and additional water for processing

1 lemon, juiced

1 tablespoon fresh parsley, chopped

½ tablespoon fresh thyme

¼ teaspoon salt

⅛ teaspoon black pepper

1. Add the olive oil to the slow cooker and sauté the onion and garlic on medium-high heat for 3–4 minutes. Add the dry white beans and 3 cups of water to the slow cooker, cover, and cook on high heat for 4–5 hours, or until the beans are tender. Drain the white beans.

2. In a food processor, purée the white beans, adding enough water to create a smooth consistency. Add the lemon juice, parsley, thyme, salt, and pepper, and continue to blend until very smooth.

3. Cover, and refrigerate for at least 2 hours before serving.

Storing Bean Dips

Dried beans take a while to cook; to save time in the kitchen you can make a large batch of your favorite bean dip, then freeze the unused portions. Store the desired amount in a freezer-safe bag, label, and store for up to 3 months.

PINTOS, CERVEZA, AND LIME DIP

If you don't have a Mexican beer on hand, a domestic beer will work just fine.

INGREDIENTS

Serves 6

2 tablespoons olive oil

½ onion, diced

3 cloves garlic, minced

½ pound dry pinto beans

3 cups water and additional water for processing

1 (12-ounce) Mexican beer

1 fresh jalapeño, minced

2 limes, juiced

¼ teaspoon, salt

⅛ teaspoon, black pepper

1. Add the olive oil to the slow cooker and sauté the onion and garlic on medium-high heat for 3–4 minutes.

2. Add the dry pinto beans, 3 cups of water, and beer to the slow cooker, cover, and cook on high heat for 4–5 hours, or until the beans are tender. Drain the pinto beans.

3. In a food processor, purée the pinto beans, minced jalapeño, lime juice, salt, and pepper, adding enough water to create a smooth consistency. Serve hot or at room temperature.

SWEET BEET DIP

Beets have another culinary use aside from being eaten. They can be used as red or pink food coloring that is vegan-friendly.

INGREDIENTS

Serves 6

6 large beets, peeled and quartered

½ cup apple juice

½ cup orange juice

1 teaspoon red wine vinegar

¼ teaspoon salt

⅛ teaspoon black pepper

1. Add all ingredients to a 4-quart slow cooker, cover, and cook on medium-high heat for 5–6 hours, or until the beets are tender.

2. Purée the beets in a food processor or blender, adding just enough of the liquid to create a smooth consistency. Serve cold or at room temperature.

Beet Greens

Don't toss the tops! The greens at the top of beets can be cooked and eaten too. Sauté them in some olive oil and season with salt and pepper.

CHAPTER 4

SAUCES

BOLOGNESE SAUCE

If you'd like to add a protein punch to this sauce, toss in one cup of cooked white beans before cooking.

INGREDIENTS

Serves 6

2 tablespoons olive oil

1 onion, diced

½ cup celery, chopped

½ cup carrots, chopped

3 cloves garlic, minced

2 (14-ounce) cans tomatoes, crushed

1 lemon, juiced

1 bunch parsley, chopped

1 teaspoon salt

½ teaspoon black pepper

1. Add the oil to the slow cooker and sauté the onion, celery, and carrots on medium-high heat for 3–5 minutes. Add the garlic and sauté for 1 minute more.

2. Add the rest of the ingredients and cook on low heat for 4 hours.

CAROLINA BARBECUE SAUCE

This tasty sauce has a more acidic taste than the sweeter, mainstream, ketchup-based sauces.

INGREDIENTS

Serves 6

¼ cup vegan margarine

1 cup apple cider vinegar

⅓ cup brown sugar

1 tablespoon molasses

1 tablespoon mustard

2 teaspoons vegan Worcestershire sauce

⅛ teaspoon cayenne pepper

Add all of the ingredients to the slow cooker and cook on medium-high heat for 1 hour, stirring occasionally.

COCONUT CURRY SAUCE

Red curry paste is ideal for this recipe, but any variety will do.

INGREDIENTS
Serves 6

1 (14-ounce) can coconut milk

1 cup Vegetable Broth (Chapter 6)

1 teaspoon soy sauce

1 tablespoon curry paste

1 tablespoon lime juice

2 cloves garlic, minced

½ teaspoon salt

¼ cup chopped cilantro

1. In a 4-quart slow cooker, add all ingredients except cilantro. Cover, and cook on low heat for 2 hours.

2. Add the chopped cilantro and cook for an additional 30 minutes.

EASY PEANUT SAUCE

Choose a peanut butter that is free of added flavors and is as natural as possible, so that it won't distort the flavors in your dish.

INGREDIENTS
Serves 6

1 cup smooth peanut butter

4 tablespoons maple syrup

½ cup sesame oil

1 teaspoon cayenne pepper

1½ teaspoons cumin

1 teaspoon garlic powder

1½ teaspoons salt

2 cups water

1. In a blender, add all ingredients except the water. Blend as you slowly add the water until you reach the desired consistency.

2. Pour the sauce into a 2-quart slow cooker and cook over low heat for 1 hour.

Uses for Peanut Sauce
Peanut sauce can be used to dress Asian noodles such as udon or soba noodles. It may also be used as a dipping sauce for steamed broccoli or spring rolls.

MOLE

Just like barbecue sauce in the United States, mole sauce recipes vary greatly by region, and no two are exactly the same.

INGREDIENTS

Serves 6

2 tablespoons olive oil

½ onion, finely diced

3 garlic cloves, minced

1 teaspoon ground cumin

¼ teaspoon ground cinnamon

¼ teaspoon ground coriander

1 tablespoon chili powder

2 chipotles in adobo, seeded and minced

1 teaspoon salt

4 cups Vegetable Broth (Chapter 6)

1 ounce vegan dark chocolate, chopped

1. In a sauté pan over medium heat, add the oil, onion, and garlic and sauté about 3 minutes. Add the cumin, cinnamon, and coriander and sauté for 1 minute.

2. Transfer the sautéed mixture to a 4-quart slow cooker. Add the chili powder, chipotles, and salt, then whisk in the Vegetable Broth. Finally, add the chocolate.

3. Cover, and cook over medium heat for 2 hours.

QUICK HOLLANDAISE SAUCE

A classic hollandaise sauce is made from raw eggs, but this vegan cheater's version uses prepared vegan mayonnaise with a bit of turmeric for a yellow hue. Pour over steamed asparagus, artichokes, or cauliflower for an easy side dish, or make a vegan Tofu Florentine (Chapter 2) or "eggs" Benedict.

INGREDIENTS

Yields ½ cup sauce

⅓ cup vegan mayonnaise

¼ cup lemon juice

3 tablespoons unsweetened soymilk

1½ tablespoons Dijon mustard

¼ teaspoon turmeric

1 tablespoon nutritional yeast (optional)

½ teaspoon salt

¼ teaspoon black pepper

¼ teaspoon hot sauce, or to taste (optional)

Whisk together all ingredients and heat over low heat before serving. Adjust seasonings to taste.

Soy, Almond, and Rice Milks

Though soymilk is the most common, vegans can also choose from almond and rice milk substitutes. Rice milk is thinner and sweeter than soymilk, and almond milk has a grainier texture. For baking, soy or almond milk is best, and in savory casseroles and sauces such as this one, use soymilk for its neutral flavor. Choose brands fortified with vitamin D, B12, and calcium, particularly if you've got kids.

RED PEPPER COULIS

This versatile sauce can be tossed with ingredients such as cooked pasta or gnocchi, or even enjoyed as a dip or spread.

INGREDIENTS
Serves 6

2 tablespoons olive oil

2 shallots, minced

2 red bell peppers, diced

2 cloves garlic, minced

1 cup Vegetable Broth (Chapter 6)

¼ cup plain unsweetened soymilk

¼ teaspoon salt

⅛ teaspoon black pepper

1. Add the oil to the slow cooker and sauté the shallots and red peppers on medium-high heat for 3–5 minutes. Add the garlic and sauté for 1 minute more.

2. Add the rest of the ingredients and cook on medium-high heat for 2 hours.

What Is a Coulis?

A coulis is a thick sauce made from puréed fruits or vegetables. In this recipe, the slow cooking eliminates the need for puréeing because the peppers cook down until they are very soft.

TOMATILLO SAUCE

Tomatillos look like small green tomatoes, but are actually related to the gooseberry.

INGREDIENTS
Serves 4

12 tomatillos, husked

Water

1 onion, diced

2 cloves garlic, minced

1 jalapeño, seeded and minced

½ tablespoon fresh cilantro, chopped

1 teaspoon salt

1. Place the tomatillos in the slow cooker with enough water to cover them. Set the slow cooker to high and allow the tomatillos to cook for 1–2 hours or until tender. Drain the tomatillos.

2. Place the tomatillos, onion, garlic, jalapeño, cilantro, and salt in a food processor and purée. Place the mixture in a bowl and add water until it has the consistency of a sauce.

CHUNKY TOMATO SAUCE

When tomatoes are in season, try replacing the canned diced tomatoes in this recipe for one cup of fresh Roma tomatoes.

INGREDIENTS
Serves 6

2 tablespoons olive oil

1 onion, diced

4 cloves garlic, minced

1 teaspoon dried oregano

1 teaspoon dried parsley

1 teaspoon dried basil

1 lemon, juiced

½ cup water

1 (14-ounce) can diced tomatoes

1 (14-ounce) can crushed tomatoes

2 teaspoons sugar

1 teaspoon salt

½ teaspoon black pepper

1. Add the oil to a 4-quart slow cooker and sauté the onion on medium-high heat for 3–5 minutes. Add the garlic and sauté for 1 minute more.

2. Add the rest of the ingredients and cook on low heat for 6 hours.

Crushed Tomatoes

Crushed tomatoes vary greatly by brand—some are thick, like a paste, and others are quite watery. When using crushed tomatoes in combination with other tomatoes, choose a thicker blend of crushed tomatoes.

SLOW ROASTED GARLIC AND TOMATO SAUCE

Canned, diced tomatoes are a good substitute for fresh, vine-ripened tomatoes when fresh tomatoes are not in season.

INGREDIENTS

Serves 6

2 tablespoons olive oil

2½ pounds fresh, vine-ripened tomatoes, peeled and diced

1 teaspoon dried parsley

1 teaspoon dried basil

1 tablespoon balsamic vinegar

½ teaspoon granulated cane sugar

Salt, to taste

Freshly ground black pepper, to taste

3 heads roasted garlic, cloves removed from peel

In a 4-quart slow cooker, add all ingredients. Cover, and cook on low for 3–4 hours.

Roasting Garlic

Roast whole heads of garlic by cutting off the top ¼, drizzling with olive oil, and then wrapping in aluminum foil. Cook in an oven preheated to 400°F for about 45 minutes.

RED WINE REDUCTION

Try using bolder wines, such as merlot, for heavier dishes and less bold wines, such as pinot noir, for lighter dishes.

INGREDIENTS

Serves 4

2 tablespoons olive oil

1 shallot, minced

2 cloves garlic, minced

1 cup red wine

1 cup Vegetable Broth (Chapter 6)

¼ cup vegan margarine

1. Add the oil to the slow cooker and sauté the shallot on medium-high heat for 3 minutes. Add the garlic and sauté for 1 minute more.

2. Add the remaining ingredients and cook on medium-high heat until the sauce has reduced by half, approximately 1–2 hours.

SUN-DRIED TOMATO SAUCE

Although sun-dried tomatoes lose over 90 percent of their weight when they are being dried in the sun, they maintain most of their nutritional value.

INGREDIENTS

Serves 6

¼ cup vegan margarine

¼ cup white flour

3½ cups plain unsweetened soymilk

1 cup sun-dried tomatoes, chopped

1 tablespoon vegan Worcestershire sauce

1 teaspoon salt

¼ teaspoon black pepper

1. Set the slow cooker to medium-high and add the vegan margarine. Once melted, slowly stir in the flour to create a roux. Once the roux is created, whisk in the soymilk until smooth.

2. Add the rest of the ingredients and continue cooking on low heat for 2 hours, stirring occasionally.

Sun-Dried at Home

You can make homemade sun-dried tomatoes by, you guessed it, halving tomatoes and leaving them out to dry in the sun for about a week. Other methods are available too, such as using the oven or a dehydrator.

VEGAN ALFREDO SAUCE

Top cooked fettuccine with this updated version of a classic sauce.

INGREDIENTS

Serves 8

1 cup raw cashews

1 cup water

½ cup unsweetened soymilk

3 cups Vegetable Broth (Chapter 6)

Juice of ½ lemon

½ cup nutritional yeast

1 teaspoon mustard

2 cloves garlic, minced

2 teaspoons salt

1 teaspoon pepper

1. In a blender, place the cashews, water, and soymilk. Process until very smooth.

2. In a 4-quart slow cooker, pour the blended cashew sauce and all remaining ingredients and stir well. Cover, and cook over low heat for 1 hour.

Cooking with Cashews

Cashews are an excellent ingredient to use when you want to create a creamy vegan dish, but be sure to use raw cashews, not roasted or cooked in any other way. Also, remember that nuts are high in calories and fat, so they should be consumed in small quantities.

WHITE WINE–DILL SAUCE

Toss this sauce with cooked angel hair pasta and enjoy the rest of the wine with dinner.

INGREDIENTS

Serves 6

¼ cup vegan margarine

¼ cup white flour

3½ cups plain unsweetened soymilk

¼ cup white wine

1 teaspoon dried dill weed

1 tablespoon vegan Worcestershire sauce

1 teaspoon salt

¼ teaspoon black pepper

1. Set the slow cooker to medium-high and add the vegan margarine. Allow the vegan margarine to melt, while slowly stirring in the flour to create a roux. Once the roux is created, whisk in the soymilk until smooth.

2. Add the rest of the ingredients and continue cooking on medium-high heat for 2 hours, stirring occasionally.

CHAPTER 5

SALADS AND SALAD DRESSINGS

SESAME AND SOY COLESLAW SALAD

You don't need mayonnaise to make a coleslaw! Make it a full meal by adding some marinated tofu from the Italian Balsamic Baked Tofu recipe (Chapter 11).

INGREDIENTS

Serves 4

1 head Napa cabbage, shredded

1 carrot, grated

2 green onions, chopped

1 red bell pepper, sliced thin

2 tablespoons olive oil

2 tablespoons apple cider vinegar

2 teaspoons soy sauce

½ teaspoon sesame oil

2 tablespoons maple syrup

2 tablespoons sesame seeds (optional)

1. Toss together the cabbage, carrot, green onions, and bell pepper in a large bowl.

2. In a separate small bowl, whisk together the olive oil, vinegar, soy sauce, sesame oil, and maple syrup until well combined.

3. Drizzle dressing over cabbage and veggies, add sesame seeds if desired, and toss well to combine.

SPICY SOUTHWESTERN TWO-BEAN SALAD

This cold bean salad with Tex-Mex flavors is even better the next day—if it lasts that long!

INGREDIENTS
Serves 6

1 (15-ounce) can black beans, drained and rinsed

1 (15-ounce) can kidney beans, drained and rinsed

1 red or yellow bell pepper, chopped

1 large tomato, diced

⅔ cup corn (fresh, canned, or frozen)

1 red onion, diced

⅓ cup olive oil

¼ cup lime juice

½ teaspoon chili powder

½ teaspoon garlic powder

¼ teaspoon cayenne pepper

½ teaspoon salt

¼ cup chopped fresh cilantro

1 avocado, diced

1. In a large bowl, combine the black beans, kidney beans, bell pepper, tomato, corn, and onion.

2. In a separate small bowl, whisk together the olive oil, lime juice, chili powder, garlic powder, cayenne, and salt.

3. Pour dressing over bean mixture, tossing to coat. Stir in fresh cilantro.

4. Chill for at least 1 hour before serving to allow flavors to mingle.

5. Add avocado and gently toss again just before serving.

Make It a Pasta Salad

Omit the avocado and add some cooked pasta and extra dressing to turn it into a high-protein Tex-Mex pasta salad!

RASPBERRY VINAIGRETTE

Create a colorful and inviting salad with this purplish dressing. Dress up a plain fruit salad, or toss some cranberries, pine nuts, and baby spinach with this vinaigrette for a gourmet touch.

INGREDIENTS

Yields 1¼ cups

¼ cup balsamic or raspberry vinegar

2 tablespoons lime juice

¼ cup raspberry preserves

2 tablespoons Dijon mustard

½ teaspoon sugar

¾ cup olive oil

Salt and pepper to taste

1. Process together vinegar, lime juice, raspberry preserves, mustard, and sugar in a food processor or blender until smooth.

2. Slowly add olive oil, just a few drops at a time on high speed to allow oil to emulsify.

3. Season generously with salt and pepper.

NO-MAYO APPLE COLESLAW

There's nothing wrong with grabbing a store-bought pre-shredded coleslaw mix from the produce section to make this vegan salad; just double the dressing if you find it's not enough.

INGREDIENTS

Serves 4

1 head cabbage, shredded

1 apple, diced small

1 (15-ounce) can pineapple, drained (reserve 2 tablespoons of juice)

1 tablespoon apple cider vinegar

2 tablespoons olive oil

1 tablespoon tahini

2 tablespoons agave nectar or 1 teaspoon sugar

2 tablespoons sunflower seeds (optional)

1. In a large bowl, combine the cabbage, apple, and pineapple.

2. In a separate small bowl, whisk together 2 tablespoons of the pineapple juice with the cider vinegar, olive oil, and tahini. Pour over cabbage and apples, tossing gently to coat.

3. Drizzle with agave nectar, again tossing to coat.

4. Chill for at least 30 minutes before serving, and toss with sunflower seeds if desired.

Make It Vegan!

If you have a favorite family coleslaw recipe, there's no need to give it up when eating vegan. Just use a vegan store-bought or homemade Vegan Mayonnaise (Chapter 3) or dressing. Whatever recipe you use, coleslaw works best if it sits for several hours to soften up the cabbage, so make this recipe in advance if possible. The night before would be best.

DAIRY-FREE RANCH DRESSING

An all-American creamy homemade ranch dressing, without the buttermilk. Get those baby carrots ready to dip!

INGREDIENTS
Yields 1 cup

1 cup Vegan Mayonnaise (Chapter 3)

¼ cup soymilk

1 teaspoon Dijon mustard

1 tablespoon lemon juice

1 teaspoon onion powder

¾ teaspoon garlic powder

1 tablespoon minced fresh chives

1. Whisk or blend together all ingredients except chives, until smooth.

2. Stir in chives until well combined.

CREAMY MISO SESAME DRESSING

A creamy and tangy Japanese-inspired salad dressing. A bit of minced fresh ginger would add another layer of flavor if you happen to have some on hand.

INGREDIENTS
Yields 1 cup

¼ cup miso

2 tablespoons rice wine vinegar

¼ cup soy sauce

2 tablespoons sesame oil

½ cup soymilk

2 tablespoons lime juice

Process all ingredients together in a blender or food processor until smooth.

Miso Trivia

Miso is available in a variety of interchangeable flavors and colors—red, white, and barley miso being the most common. The type you use is really a personal preference. Asian grocers stock miso at about ⅓ the price of natural food stores, so if you're lucky enough to have one in your neighborhood, it's worth a trip.

ASIAN RANCH DRESSING

An Asian combination of flavors fuses with all-American mayonnaise for a twist on the usual ranch dressing.

INGREDIENTS

Yields ⅔ cup

½ cup Vegan Mayonnaise (Chapter 3)

⅓ cup rice vinegar

¼ cup soy sauce

2 tablespoons sesame oil

2 teaspoons sugar

½ teaspoon powdered ginger

¾ teaspoon garlic powder

1 tablespoon chopped fresh chives

Combine all ingredients except chives in a blender or food processor until smooth and creamy. Stir in chives by hand.

THAI ORANGE PEANUT DRESSING

A sweet and spicy take on traditional Thai and Indonesian peanut and satay sauce. Add a bit less liquid to use this salad dressing as a dip for veggies.

INGREDIENTS

Yields ¾ cup

¼ cup peanut butter at room temperature

¼ cup orange juice

2 tablespoons soy sauce

2 tablespoons rice vinegar

2 tablespoons water

½ teaspoon garlic powder

½ teaspoon sugar

¼ teaspoon crushed red chili flakes (optional)

Whisk together all ingredients until smooth and creamy, adding more or less liquid to achieve desired consistency.

DELI-STYLE MACARONI SALAD

A classic creamy pasta salad with vegan mayonnaise. Add a can of kidney beans or chickpeas for a protein boost.

INGREDIENTS

Serves 6

3 cups cooked macaroni

1 carrot, diced small

½ cup green peas

½ cup corn

1 rib celery, diced

½ cup Vegan Mayonnaise (Chapter 3)

1½ tablespoons prepared mustard

2 tablespoons white or apple cider vinegar

2 teaspoons sugar

2 tablespoons pickle relish

1 tablespoon chopped fresh dill (optional)

Salt and pepper to taste

1. Combine the macaroni, carrot, peas, corn, and celery in a large bowl.

2. In a separate small bowl, whisk together the mayonnaise, mustard, vinegar, sugar, and relish. Combine with macaroni.

3. Stir in the fresh dill if desired and season with salt and pepper, to taste.

4. Chill for at least 2 hours before serving, to allow flavors to combine and to soften veggies.

Pasta Salad Secrets

One secret to making flavorful vegan pasta salads is to use heavily salted water when boiling the pasta. So go ahead, dump a full tablespoon (or even two!) of salt into the cooking water.

TEMPEH DILL "CHICKEN" SALAD

Turn it into a sandwich, or slice up some tomatoes and serve on a bed of lettuce.

INGREDIENTS
Serves 3

1 (8-ounce) package tempeh, diced small

Water for boiling

3 tablespoons Vegan Mayonnaise (Chapter 3)

2 teaspoons lemon juice

½ teaspoon garlic powder

1 teaspoon Dijon mustard

2 tablespoons sweet pickle relish

½ cup green peas

2 stalks celery, diced small

1 tablespoon chopped fresh dill (optional)

1. Cover tempeh with water and simmer for 10 minutes, until tempeh is soft. Drain and allow to cool completely.

2. Whisk together mayonnaise, lemon juice, garlic powder, mustard, and relish.

3. Combine tempeh, mayonnaise mixture, peas, celery, and dill if desired, and gently toss to combine.

4. Chill for at least 1 hour before serving to allow flavors to combine.

Curried Chicken Tempeh

For curried chicken salad, omit the dill and add ½ teaspoon curry powder and a dash cayenne and black pepper. If you don't feel up to dicing and simmering tempeh, try combining the dressing with store-bought mock chicken, or even veggie turkey or deli slices.

KIDNEY BEAN AND CHICKPEA SALAD

This marinated two-bean salad is perfect for summer picnics or as a side for outdoor barbecues or potlucks.

INGREDIENTS

Serves 6

¼ cup olive oil

¼ cup red wine vinegar

½ teaspoon paprika

2 tablespoons lemon juice

1 (14-ounce) can chickpeas, drained

1 (14-ounce) can kidney beans, drained

½ cup sliced black olives

1 (8-ounce) can corn, drained

½ red onion, chopped

1 tablespoon chopped fresh parsley

Salt and pepper to taste

1. Whisk together olive oil, vinegar, paprika, and lemon juice.

2. In a large bowl, combine the chickpeas, kidney beans, olives, corn, red onion, and parsley. Pour the olive oil dressing over the bean mixture and toss well to combine.

3. Season generously with salt and pepper, to taste.

4. Chill for at least 1 hour before serving to allow flavors to mingle.

HOT GERMAN DIJON POTATO SALAD

Tangy deli-style German potato salad requires potatoes that are thinly sliced and not overcooked. This vegan version is just as good—if not better—than any other recipe you'll find.

INGREDIENTS

Serves 4

4 large potatoes, precooked and cooled

½ yellow onion, sliced thin

2 tablespoons olive oil

⅓ cup water

⅓ cup white or apple cider vinegar

1 tablespoon Dijon mustard

1 tablespoon flour

1 teaspoon sugar

2 scallions, chopped

3 tablespoons vegetarian bacon bits (optional)

Salt and pepper, to taste

1. Slice potatoes into thin coins and set aside.

2. In a large skillet, heat onion in olive oil over medium heat and cook until just barely soft, about 2–3 minutes.

3. Reduce heat and add water, vinegar, mustard, flour, and sugar, stirring to combine. Bring to a simmer and cook until thickened, just 1–2 minutes.

4. Reduce heat and stir in potatoes, scallions, and bacon bits if desired. Season with salt and pepper to taste.

Perfect Potatoes

To prepare your potatoes for a potato salad, give them a quick scrub. Peeling is an aesthetic preference entirely up to you. Either way, chop them into chunks (or thin coins, for a German-style salad), then simmer just until soft, about 15 minutes or less. Drain and rinse your potatoes immediately under cold water to stop them from cooking further and getting too soft.

CUCUMBER CILANTRO SALAD

Cooling cucumbers and cold creamy yogurt are coupled with a dash of cayenne pepper for a salad that keeps you guessing.

INGREDIENTS
Serves 3

4 cucumbers, diced

2 tomatoes, chopped

½ red onion, diced small

1 cup soy yogurt, plain or lemon flavored

1 tablespoon lemon juice

2 tablespoons chopped fresh cilantro

Salt and pepper to taste

¼ teaspoon cayenne (optional)

1. Toss together all ingredients, stirring well to combine.

2. Chill for at least 2 hours before serving, to allow flavors to marinate. Toss again just before serving.

LEMON CUMIN POTATO SALAD

A mayonnaise-free potato salad with exotic flavors, this one is delicious either hot or cold.

INGREDIENTS
Serves 4

1 small yellow onion, diced

2 tablespoons olive oil

1½ teaspoons cumin

4 large cooked potatoes, chopped

3 tablespoons lemon juice

2 teaspoons Dijon mustard

1 scallion, chopped

¼ teaspoon cayenne pepper

2 tablespoons chopped fresh cilantro (optional)

1. Heat onion in olive oil just until soft. Add cumin and potatoes, and cook for just 1 minute, stirring well to combine. Remove from heat.

2. Whisk together the lemon juice and Dijon mustard and pour over potatoes, tossing gently to coat. Add scallion, cayenne pepper, and cilantro if desired, and combine well.

3. Chill before serving.

The Family Recipe

Traditional American potato salads are easy to veganize, so if you've got a family favorite, take a look at the ingredients. Substitute vegan mayonnaise or sour cream for regular, omit the eggs, and use mock meats in place of the bacon bits or other meats.

BASIC BALSAMIC VINAIGRETTE

No need to purchase expensive and sugar-laden salad dressings at the grocery store! This simple vinaigrette will serve you well for a last-minute salad dressing.

INGREDIENTS

Yields 1 cup

¼ cup balsamic vinegar

¾ cup olive oil

1 tablespoon Dijon mustard

¼ teaspoon salt

⅛ teaspoon black pepper

½ teaspoon dried basil

½ teaspoon dried parsley

Whisk together all ingredients with a fork until well combined.

YOU ARE A GODDESS DRESSING

Turn this zesty salad dressing into a dip for veggies or a sandwich spread by reducing the amount of liquids.

INGREDIENTS

Yields 1½ cups

⅔ cup tahini

¼ cup apple cider vinegar

⅓ cup soy sauce

2 teaspoons lemon juice

1 clove garlic

¾ teaspoon sugar (optional)

⅓ cup olive oil

1. Process all the ingredients except olive oil together in a blender or food processor until blended.

2. With the blender or food processor on high speed, slowly add in the olive oil, blending for another full minute, allowing the oil to emulsify.

3. Chill in the refrigerator for at least 10 minutes before serving; dressing will thicken as it chills.

In Search of Tahini

Tahini is a sesame seed paste native to Middle Eastern cuisine with a thinner consistency and milder flavor than peanut butter. You'll find a jarred or canned version in the ethnic foods aisle of large grocery stores, or a fresh version chilling next to the hummus if you're lucky. Check the bulk bins at co-ops and natural foods stores for powdered tahini, which can be rehydrated with a bit of water, or, try the Homemade Tahini recipe in Chapter 3.

ITALIAN WHITE BEAN AND FRESH HERB SALAD

Don't let the simplicity of this bean salad fool you! The fresh herbs marinate the beans to flavorful perfection, so there's no need to add anything else!

INGREDIENTS

Serves 4

2 cans cannellini or great northern beans, drained and rinsed

2 ribs celery, diced

¼ cup chopped fresh parsley

¼ cup chopped fresh basil

3 tablespoons olive oil

3 large tomatoes, chopped

½ cup sliced black olives

2 tablespoons lemon juice

Salt and pepper to taste

¼ teaspoon crushed red pepper flakes (optional)

1. In a large skillet, combine the beans, celery, parsley, and basil with olive oil. Heat, stirring frequently, over low heat for 3 minutes, until herbs are softened but not cooked.

2. Remove from heat and stir in remaining ingredients, gently tossing to combine. Chill for at least 1 hour before serving.

VEGAN PESTO VINAIGRETTE

Turn vegan pesto into a flavorful salad dressing. Perfect on a green salad with red onions, black olives, and diced avocado. You may need a little more or less liquid, depending on how thick the pesto is.

INGREDIENTS

Yields 1¼ cups

⅔ cup vegan pesto

¼ cup red wine vinegar

1 tablespoon lemon juice

⅓ cup olive oil

1 tablespoon Dijon mustard

Whisk together all ingredients until well combined.

MESSY TACO SALAD

If you're bored by the usual salads but still want something light and green, try this taco salad. The taste and texture is best with iceberg lettuce, but if you want something more nutritious, use a blend of half iceberg and half romaine. Top with a handful of shredded vegan cheese if you'd like.

INGREDIENTS
Serves 4

2 heads iceberg lettuce, chopped

½ cup sliced black olives

½ cup corn

1 jalapeño pepper, deseeded and sliced, or 2 tablespoons canned green chilies (optional)

1 can refried black beans

2 tablespoons taco sauce or 1 teaspoon hot sauce

¼ cup salsa

¼ cup vegan mayonnaise

10–12 tortilla chips, crumbled

1 avocado, diced (optional)

1. Combine the lettuce, olives, corn, and jalapeño peppers if desired in a large bowl.

2. Warm the beans slightly over the stove or in the microwave, just until softened. Combine beans with taco sauce or hot sauce, salsa, and mayonnaise, breaking up the beans and mixing to form a thick sauce.

3. Combine bean mixture with lettuce, stirring to combine as much as possible. Add tortilla chips and avocado if desired, and stir gently to combine. Add a dash or two of extra hot sauce, to taste.

Baked Tortilla Chips

Why not make your own tortilla chips! Slice whole-wheat tortillas into strips or triangles, and arrange in a single layer on a baking sheet. Drizzle with olive oil for a crispier chip, and season with a bit of salt and garlic powder if you want, or just bake them plain. It'll take about 5–6 minutes on each side in a 300°F oven.

SPICY SWEET CUCUMBER SALAD

Japanese cucumber salad is cool and refreshing, but with a bit of spice. Enjoy it as a healthy afternoon snack, or as a fresh accompaniment to takeout.

INGREDIENTS

Serves 2

2 cucumbers, thinly sliced

¾ teaspoon salt

¼ cup rice wine vinegar

1 teaspoon sugar or 1 tablespoon agave nectar

1 teaspoon sesame oil

¼ teaspoon red pepper flakes

½ onion, thinly sliced

1. In a large shallow container or baking sheet, spread the cucumbers in single layer and sprinkle with salt. Allow to sit at least 10 minutes.

2. Drain any excess water from the cucumbers.

3. Whisk together the rice wine vinegar, sugar or agave nectar, oil, and red pepper flakes.

4. Pour dressing over the cucumbers, add onions, and toss gently.

5. Allow to sit at least 10 minutes before serving to allow flavors to mingle.

TANGERINE AND MINT SALAD

Fennel and mint are a wonderful combination, but the sweet tangerines will carry the salad if you can't find fennel. A small drizzle of gourmet oil if you have some would kick up the flavor even more. Try walnut or even truffle oil.

INGREDIENTS

Serves 2

1 head green lettuce, chopped

2 tablespoons chopped fresh mint

2 tangerines, clementine or satsuma oranges, sectioned

⅓ cup chopped walnuts

1 bulb fennel, sliced thin (optional)

2 tablespoons olive oil

Salt and pepper to taste

1. Gently toss together the lettuce, mint, tangerines, walnuts, and sliced fennel.

2. Drizzle with olive oil, salt, and pepper.

Homemade Flavored Oils

A flavored oil will beautify your kitchen and add flavor to your food. Simply combine several of your favorite herbs, whole garlic cloves, peppercorns, dried lemon or orange zest, or dried chilies with a quality olive oil. For safety's sake, avoid fresh herbs and zests, and always use dried. Oils infused with dried herbs will keep for up to one year, while fresh herbs can cause spoilage after less than a week.

CARROT AND DATE SALAD

If you're used to carrot and raisin salads with pineapples and drowning in mayonnaise, this lighter version with tahini, dates, and mandarin oranges will be a welcome change.

INGREDIENTS

Serves 4

⅓ cup tahini

1 tablespoon olive oil

2 tablespoons agave nectar or 2 teaspoons sugar

3 tablespoons lemon juice

¼ teaspoon salt

4 large carrots, grated

½ cup chopped dates

3 satsuma or mandarin oranges, sectioned

⅓ cup coconut flakes (optional)

1. In a small bowl, whisk together the tahini, olive oil, agave nectar or sugar, lemon juice, and salt.

2. Place grated carrots in a large bowl, and toss well with tahini mixture. Add dates, oranges, and coconut flakes if desired, and combine well.

3. Allow to sit for at least 1 hour before serving to soften carrots and dates. Toss again before serving.

EDAMAME SALAD

If you can't find shelled edamame, try this recipe with lima beans instead.

INGREDIENTS

Serves 4

2 cups frozen shelled edamame, thawed and drained

1 red or yellow bell pepper, diced

¾ cup corn kernels

3 tablespoons chopped fresh cilantro (optional)

3 tablespoons olive oil

2 tablespoons red wine vinegar

1 teaspoon soy sauce

1 teaspoon chili powder

2 teaspoons lemon or lime juice

Salt and pepper to taste

1. Combine edamame, bell pepper, corn, and cilantro if desired in a large bowl.

2. Whisk together the olive oil, vinegar, soy sauce, chili powder, and lemon or lime juice and combine with the edamame. Season with salt and pepper, to taste.

3. Chill for at least 1 hour before serving.

Eda-What?

You're probably familiar with the lightly steamed and salted edamame served as an appetizer at Japanese restaurants, but many grocers sell shelled edamame in the frozen foods section. Edamame—baby green soybeans—are a great source of unprocessed soy protein.

SWEET RED SALAD WITH STRAWBERRIES AND BEETS

Colorful and nutritious, this vibrant red salad can be made with roasted or canned beets, or even raw grated beets if you prefer.

INGREDIENTS
Serves 4

3–4 small beets, chopped

Water for boiling

Spinach or lettuce

1 cup sliced strawberries

½ cup chopped pecans

¼ cup olive oil

2 tablespoons red wine vinegar

2 tablespoons agave nectar

2 tablespoons orange juice

Salt and pepper to taste

1. Boil beets in water until soft, about 20 minutes. Allow to cool completely.

2. In a large bowl, combine spinach or lettuce, strawberries, pecans, and cooled beets.

3. In a separate small bowl, whisk together the olive oil, vinegar, agave nectar, and orange juice, and pour over salad, tossing well to coat.

4. Season generously with salt and pepper, to taste.

PESTO AND NEW POTATO SALAD

A simple side dish if served hot, or potato salad if served cold, these creamy pesto potatoes are a lively and creative way to use an elegant ingredient.

INGREDIENTS
Serves 4

½ cup vegan pesto

¼ cup Vegan Mayonnaise (Chapter 3)

2 pounds new potatoes, chopped and cooked

3 scallions, chopped

⅓ cup sliced black olives

Salt and pepper, to taste

1. Whisk together pesto and mayonnaise and toss with potatoes, scallions, and olives.

2. Season generously with salt and pepper, to taste.

CHAPTER 6

SOUPS, STEWS, AND CHILIES

SOUPS

BARLEY VEGETABLE SOUP

Barley Vegetable Soup is an excellent "kitchen sink" recipe, meaning that you can toss in just about any fresh or frozen vegetables or spices you happen to have on hand.

INGREDIENTS

Serves 6

1 onion, chopped

2 carrots, sliced

2 ribs celery, chopped

2 tablespoons olive oil

8 cups Vegetable Broth (this chapter)

1 cup barley, uncooked

1½ cups frozen mixed vegetables

1 (14-ounce) can crushed or diced tomatoes

½ teaspoon parsley

½ teaspoon thyme

2 bay leaves

Salt and pepper to taste

1. In a large soup pot or stockpot, sauté the onion, carrots, and celery in olive oil for 3–5 minutes, just until onions are almost soft.

2. Reduce heat to medium-low, and add remaining ingredients except salt and pepper.

3. Bring to a simmer, cover, and allow to cook for at least 45 minutes, stirring occasionally.

4. Remove cover and allow to cook for 10 more minutes.

5. Remove bay leaves and season with salt and pepper to taste.

BLACK BEAN SOUP

You can use the leftover green bell pepper, red bell pepper, and red onion from this recipe to make Fajita Chili (this chapter).

INGREDIENTS

Serves 6

2 tablespoons olive oil

½ green bell pepper, diced

½ red bell pepper, diced

½ red onion, sliced

2 cloves garlic, minced

2 (15-ounce) cans black beans, drained and rinsed

2 teaspoons cumin, minced

1 teaspoon chipotle powder

1 teaspoon salt

4 cups Vegetable Broth (this chapter)

¼ cup cilantro, chopped

1. In a sauté pan, heat the olive oil over medium heat, then sauté the bell peppers, onion, and garlic for 2–3 minutes.

2. In a 4-quart slow cooker, add the sautéed vegetables, black beans, cumin, chipotle powder, salt, and Vegetable Broth; cover, and cook on low for 6 hours.

3. Let the soup cool slightly, then pour half into a blender. Process until smooth, then pour back into the pot. Add the chopped cilantro, and stir.

CREAMY BROCCOLI SOUP

Broccoli is loaded with vitamins A and C, making it a must-have veggie in your kitchen.

INGREDIENTS

Serves 6

6 cups broccoli florets

2 medium russet potatoes, peeled and diced

½ onion, chopped

4 cups Vegetable Broth (this chapter)

2 tablespoons vegan margarine

2 tablespoons flour

1 cup unsweetened soymilk

Salt, to taste

1. Place the broccoli, potatoes, onion, and Vegetable Broth in a 6-quart slow cooker, cover, and cook over low heat for 6–8 hours or until the potatoes are very tender.

2. Use an immersion blender or traditional blender to purée the soup until smooth.

3. Heat the vegan margarine in a small sauce pan over low heat. Once melted, add the flour and stir to form a roux. Slowly add the soymilk and whisk until smooth.

4. Add the milk mixture to the soup, stir until well combined, and season with salt to taste.

In Season

Broccoli fares better during cooler months than it does during hot summer days. Depending on where you live, broccoli is typically at its best during the fall and winter.

SAVORY BEET SOUP

Shallots have a milder flavor than onions and are a better choice for recipes that have subtle flavors.

INGREDIENTS

Serves 8

2 tablespoons olive oil

2 cloves garlic, minced

2 shallots, diced

4 beets, peeled and chopped

1 Yukon gold potato, peeled and chopped

4 cups Vegetable Broth (this chapter)

½ teaspoon dried thyme

½ teaspoon black pepper

Salt, to taste

1. Heat the olive oil in a sauté pan over medium-low heat. Add the garlic and shallots and sauté for 2 minutes, then transfer to a 6-quart slow cooker.

2. Add the beets, potato, Vegetable Broth, thyme, and pepper. Cover, and cook over low heat for 6 hours or until beets and potatoes are very tender.

3. Use an immersion blender or traditional blender to purée, then season with salt, to taste.

SUMMER BORSCHT

Serve this cooling soup with a dollop of vegan sour cream, such as Tofutti Sour Supreme.

INGREDIENTS

Serves 6

3½ cups cooked beets, shredded

¼ cup onion, diced

½ teaspoon salt

1 teaspoon sugar

¼ cup lemon juice

½ tablespoon celery seed

2 cups Vegetable Broth (this chapter)

2 cups water

1. In a 4-quart slow cooker, place all of the ingredients; cover, and cook on low for 6–8 hours, or on high for 4 hours.

2. Refrigerate the soup for 4 hours or overnight. Serve cold.

Can't Beat Beets
Beets, also known as beetroot, can be peeled, steamed, cooked, pickled, and shredded; they are good hot or cold. They are high in folate, vitamin C, potassium, and fiber. Although they have the highest sugar content of all vegetables, beets are very low in calories; one beet is only 75 calories.

RUSTIC CABBAGE SOUP

This cabbage soup isn't just for dieters! Leave the peels on the potatoes and carrots to enhance the rustic feel.

INGREDIENTS

Serves 6

2 tablespoons olive oil

1 white onion, sliced

½ head of cabbage, shredded

2 russet potatoes, diced

1 celery stalk, sliced

1 carrot, sliced

2 tomatoes, diced

5 cups Vegetable Broth (this chapter)

Salt and pepper, to taste

1. Heat the olive oil in a small sauté pan over medium-low heat. Add the onion and sauté until softened, about 5 minutes, then transfer to a 8-quart slow cooker.

2. Add all remaining ingredients to the slow cooker except the salt and pepper, cover, and cook on low heat for 8 hours.

3. Add salt and pepper, to taste, before serving.

CANNELLINI BEAN AND CORN CHOWDER

This is a filling and textured soup that could easily be a main dish. Some chopped collards or a dash of hot sauce would be a welcome addition. For a lower-fat version, skip the initial sauté and add about 5 minutes to the cooking time.

INGREDIENTS
Serves 4

1 potato, chopped small

1 onion, chopped

2 tablespoons olive oil

3 cups Vegetable Broth (this chapter)

2 ears of corn, kernels cut off, or 1½ cups frozen or canned corn

1 (14-ounce) can cannellini or great northern beans

½ teaspoon thyme

¼ teaspoon black pepper

1½ cups soymilk

1 tablespoon flour

1. In a large soup pot or stockpot, sauté potato and onion in olive oil for 3–5 minutes.

2. Reduce heat and add Vegetable Broth. Bring to a slow simmer, cover, and allow to cook for 15–20 minutes.

3. Uncover, and add corn, beans, thyme, and pepper.

4. Whisk together soymilk and flour, and add to the pot, stirring well to prevent lumps. Reduce heat to prevent soymilk from curdling, and cook uncovered for 5–6 more minutes, stirring frequently.

5. Allow to cool slightly before serving, as soup will thicken as it cools.

Fresh Is Always Best

Cans are convenient, but dried beans are cheaper, need less packaging, and add a fresher flavor. And if you plan in advance, they aren't much work at all to prepare. Place beans in a large pot, cover with water (more than you think you'll need), and allow to sit for at least 2 hours or overnight. Drain the water and simmer in fresh water for about an hour, then you're good to go! One cup dried beans yields about 3 cups cooked.

CASHEW CREAM OF ASPARAGUS SOUP

A dairy-free and soy-free asparagus soup with a rich cashew base brings out the natural flavors of the asparagus without relying on other enhancers.

INGREDIENTS

Serves 4

1 onion, chopped

4 cloves garlic, minced

2 tablespoons olive oil

2 pounds asparagus, trimmed and chopped

4 cups Vegetable Broth (this chapter)

¾ cup raw cashews

¾ cup water

¼ teaspoon sage

½ teaspoon salt

¼ teaspoon black pepper

2 teaspoons lemon juice

2 tablespoons nutritional yeast (optional)

1. In a large soup pot or stockpot, sauté onion and garlic in olive oil for 2–3 minutes until onion is soft. Reduce heat and carefully add asparagus and Vegetable Broth.

2. Bring to a simmer, cover, and cook for 20 minutes. Cool slightly, then purée in a blender, working in batches as needed until almost smooth. Return to pot over low heat.

3. Purée together cashews and water until smooth and add to soup. Add sage, salt, and pepper and heat for a few more minutes, stirring to combine.

4. Stir in lemon juice and nutritional yeast if desired just before serving, and adjust seasonings to taste.

Varieties of Veggie Broths

A basic vegetable broth is made by simmering vegetables, potatoes, and a bay leaf or two in water for at least 30 minutes. While you may be familiar with the canned and boxed stocks available at the grocery store, vegan chefs have a few other tricks up their sleeves to impart extra flavor to recipes calling for vegetable broth. Check your natural grocer for specialty flavored bouillon cubes such as vegetarian "chicken" or "beef" flavor, or shop the bulk bins for powdered vegetable broth mix.

CAULIFLOWER SOUP

Cauliflower's peak season is the fall, so try this soup on a crisp autumn night.

INGREDIENTS

Serves 6

1 small head cauliflower, chopped

½ onion, diced

1 teaspoon salt

1 teaspoon pepper

2 tablespoons vegan margarine

4 cups Vegetable Broth (this chapter)

Zest of ½ lemon

1. In a 4-quart slow cooker, add all ingredients (except lemon zest); cover, and cook on low for 6 hours.

2. Turn off slow cooker and let soup cool about 10 minutes. Using a blender or immersion blender, process until very smooth.

3. Return soup to the slow cooker; add lemon zest, and heat until warm.

Zest Versus Juice

Lemon zest is obtained by grating the outer peel of the lemon. It contains a more intense lemon flavor than the juice of the citrus fruit, although many recipes call for both lemon zest and lemon juice.

CELERY ROOT SOUP

Serve a bowl of this soup topped with green apple crisps.

INGREDIENTS

Serves 6

2 tablespoons vegan margarine

1 small leek (white and light green parts only), chopped

2 cloves garlic, minced

1 large celery root, peeled and cubed

2 medium russet potatoes, peeled and cubed

6 cups Vegetable Broth (this chapter)

1½ teaspoons salt

1 teaspoon pepper

1. In a large sauté pan over medium heat, melt the vegan margarine, then add the leeks and sauté about 4 minutes. Add the garlic and sauté an additional 30 seconds.

2. In a 4-quart slow cooker, add the sautéed leeks and garlic, celery root, potatoes, Vegetable Broth, salt, and pepper. Cover, and cook over low heat for 6–8 hours.

3. Let the soup cool slightly, then process in a blender or with an immersion blender until smooth.

Celery Root

Celery root, also known as celeriac, is not the root of the celery you know. It is similar in texture to a potato, and is cultivated for its root, not its leaves or stalk. It is grown in cool weather and is best in the fall, right after it has been pulled. The roots and crevices have to be trimmed away, so a 1-pound root will only yield about 2 cups after it is peeled and sliced or grated, something to keep in mind when buying for a recipe.

"CHICKEN" NOODLE SOUP

If you're sick in bed, this brothy soup is just as comforting and nutritious as the real thing.

INGREDIENTS

Serves 6

6 cups Vegetable Broth (this chapter)

1 carrot, diced

2 ribs celery, diced

1 onion, chopped

½ cup TVP

2 bay leaves

1½ teaspoons Italian seasoning

Salt and pepper to taste

1 cup vegan noodles, or small pasta

Combine all ingredients in a large soup pot or stockpot. Cover, and simmer for 15–20 minutes. Remove bay leaves before serving.

To Get That Chicken Flavor

Several brands make a vegetarian chicken-flavored broth and vegetarian chicken-flavored bouillon cubes if you want a more genuine flavor. Just about any natural foods store will stock these products. Rarely spotted is the elusive chicken-flavored TVP, so if you can find some, stock up!

CHINESE HOT AND SOUR SOUP

If you can't get enough of old Jackie Chan flicks and Wong Kar-wai films, then this traditional Chinese soup is for you.

INGREDIENTS

Serves 6

2 cups seitan, diced small, or other meat substitute

2 tablespoons vegetable oil

1½ teaspoons hot sauce

6 cups Vegetable Broth (this chapter)

½ head Napa cabbage, shredded

¾ cup sliced shiitake mushrooms

1 small can bamboo shoots, drained

2 tablespoons soy sauce

2 tablespoons white vinegar

¾ teaspoon crushed red pepper flakes

¾ teaspoon salt

2 tablespoons cornstarch

¼ cup water

3 scallions, sliced

2 teaspoons sesame oil

1. Brown seitan in vegetable oil for 2–3 minutes until cooked. Reduce heat to low and add hot sauce, stirring well to coat. Cook over low heat for 1 more minute, then remove from heat and set aside.

2. In a large soup pot or stockpot, combine Vegetable Broth, cabbage, mushrooms, bamboo, soy sauce, vinegar, red pepper, and salt. Bring to a slow simmer and cover. Simmer for at least 15 minutes.

3. In a separate small bowl, whisk together the cornstarch and water, then slowly stir into soup. Heat just until soup thickens.

4. Portion into serving bowl, then top each serving with scallions and drizzle with sesame oil.

Traditional Ingredients

If this Americanized version of hot and sour soup just doesn't satisfy your Szechuan cravings, hit up a specialty Asian grocery store for some exotic ingredients. Replace the cabbage with ½ cup dried lily buds and substitute half of the shiitake with wood ear fungus and add a healthy shake of white pepper and chili oil.

CARROT-COCONUT SOUP

Coconut milk is high in fat so should be used sparingly, but it's also a good source of iron for vegans.

INGREDIENTS

Serves 4

2 tablespoons olive oil

½ onion, diced

3 cloves garlic, minced

1 pound carrots, peeled and chopped

3 cups Vegetable Broth (this chapter)

1 stalk lemongrass, sliced

1 tablespoon soy sauce

Juice of 1 lime

1 cup coconut milk

Salt, to taste

¼ cup fresh basil, chopped

1. Heat the olive oil in a sauté pan over medium-low heat. Add the onion and sauté until translucent, or about 5 minutes. Add the garlic and sauté for an additional 30 seconds.

2. Place the cooked onion and garlic, carrots, Vegetable Broth, lemongrass, soy sauce, and lime juice in a 6-quart slow cooker, cover, and cook on low heat for 4–6 hours or until carrots are very tender.

3. Add the coconut milk, then use an immersion blender or traditional blender and purée the soup until very smooth. Season with salt, to taste, and top with fresh chopped basil.

Choosing Coconut Milk

Coconut milk varies in thickness and fat content—some brands are quite thin and others are more like cream than milk. Most brands of canned coconut milk are very similar but you can usually see the percentage of coconut milk to water in the list of ingredients to help you select the level of thickness you are looking for.

CREAM OF CARROT SOUP WITH COCONUT

This carrot soup will knock your socks off! The addition of coconut milk transforms an ordinary carrot and ginger soup into an unexpected treat.

INGREDIENTS
Serves 6

3 medium carrots, chopped

1 sweet potato, chopped

1 yellow onion, chopped

3½ cups Vegetable Broth (this chapter)

3 cloves garlic, minced

2 teaspoons fresh ginger, minced

1 (14-ounce) can coconut milk

1 teaspoon salt

¾ teaspoon cinnamon (optional)

1. In a large soup pot or stockpot, bring the carrots, sweet potato, and onion to a simmer in the Vegetable Broth. Add garlic and ginger, cover, and heat for 20–25 minutes until carrots and potatoes are soft.

2. Allow to cool slightly, then transfer to a blender and purée until smooth.

3. Return soup to pot. Over very low heat, stir in the coconut milk and salt, stirring well to combine. Heat just until heated through, another 3–4 minutes.

4. Garnish with cinnamon if desired just before serving.

CREAMY CHICKPEA SOUP

Almost any bean can be puréed to make a creamy soup without the cream, but chickpeas work especially well.

INGREDIENTS
Serves 6

1 small onion, diced

2 cloves garlic, minced

2 (15-ounce) cans chickpeas, drained and rinsed

5 cups Vegetable Broth (this chapter)

1 teaspoon salt

½ teaspoon cumin

Juice of ½ lemon

1 tablespoon olive oil

¼ fresh parsley, chopped

1. In a 4-quart slow cooker, add all ingredients except the lemon juice, olive oil, and parsley; cover, and cook over low heat for 4 hours.

2. Allow to cool slightly, then process the soup in a blender or using an immersion blender.

3. Return the soup to the slow cooker, then add the lemon juice, olive oil, and parsley, and heat on low for an additional 30 minutes.

DAL

Yellow split peas are most commonly used to make dal but the green variety will work too.

INGREDIENTS
Serves 6

2 cups dried yellow split peas

8 cups water

2 carrots, peeled and diced

½ onion, diced

2 teaspoons cumin

½ teaspoon turmeric

½ teaspoon coriander

2 teaspoons garam masala

Salt, to taste

1. Combine all of the ingredients except salt in a 6-quart slow cooker; cover, and cook over low heat for 6 hours.

2. Season with salt, to taste, before serving.

FAVA BEAN SOUP

Before cooking fava beans you should first remove them from their pods.

INGREDIENTS
Serves 6

1 cup shelled fava beans

1 small onion, diced

2 carrots, peeled and diced

2 Yukon gold potatoes, peeled and diced

2 cups fresh tomatoes, diced

6 cups Vegetable Broth (this chapter)

¼ cup kalamata olives, pitted and chopped

½ teaspoon red pepper flakes

Salt, to taste

¼ cup fresh flat leaf parsley, chopped

1. Place all of the ingredients except salt and parsley in a 6-quart slow cooker. Cover, and cook on low heat for 4 hours.

2. Before serving, season with salt, to taste, and garnish with fresh parsley.

Flat Leaf Versus Curly Parsley

There is a debate about which of the most commonly used parsleys has more flavor, flat leaf or curly, but there is an undeniable difference in texture. Curly leaf parsley tends to be slightly tougher and maintains a lot of its curl when chopped. Flat leaf, or Italian parsley, is softer.

FRENCH ONION SOUP

Vidalia onions are a sweet variety of onion that work particularly well in French Onion Soup.

INGREDIENTS

Serves 4

¼ cup olive oil

4 Vidalia onions, sliced

4 cloves garlic, minced

1 tablespoon dried thyme

1 cup red wine

4 cups Vegetable Broth (this chapter)

1 teaspoon salt

1 teaspoon pepper

4 slices French bread

4 ounces vegan cheese such as Daiya Mozzarella Style Shreds

1. In a sauté pan, heat the olive oil over medium-high heat and cook the onions until golden brown, about 3 minutes. Add the garlic and sauté for 1 minute.

2. In a 4-quart slow cooker, pour the sautéed vegetables, thyme, red wine, Vegetable Broth, salt, and pepper; cover, and cook on low heat for 4 hours.

3. While the soup is cooking, preheat the oven to the broiler setting. Lightly toast the slices of French bread.

4. To serve, ladle the soup into a broiler-safe bowl, place a slice of the toasted French bread on top of the soup, sprinkle the vegan cheese on top of the bread, and place the soup under the broiler until the cheese has melted.

GARLIC MISO AND ONION SOUP

Boiling miso destroys some of its beneficial enzymes, so be sure to heat this soup to just below a simmer. Use a soft hand when slicing the silken tofu, so it doesn't crumble.

INGREDIENTS

Serves 4

5 cups water

½ cup sliced shiitake mushrooms

3 scallions, chopped

½ onion, chopped

4 cloves garlic, minced

¾ teaspoon garlic powder

2 tablespoons soy sauce

1 teaspoon sesame oil

1 block silken tofu, diced

⅓ cup miso

1 tablespoon chopped seaweed, any kind (optional)

1. Combine all ingredients except the miso and seaweed in a large soup pot or stockpot and bring to a slow simmer. Cook, uncovered, for 10–12 minutes.

2. Reduce heat and stir in miso and seaweed if desired, being careful not to boil.

3. Heat, stirring to dissolve miso, for another 5 minutes until onions and mushrooms are soft.

INDIAN CURRIED LENTIL SOUP

Similar to a traditional Indian lentil dal recipe but with added vegetables to make it into an entrée, this lentil soup is perfect as is or perhaps paired with rice or some warmed Indian flatbread.

INGREDIENTS

Serves 4

1 onion, diced

1 carrot, sliced

3 whole cloves

2 tablespoons vegan margarine

1 teaspoon cumin

1 teaspoon turmeric

1 cup yellow or green lentils, uncooked

2¾ cups Vegetable Broth (this chapter)

2 large tomatoes, chopped

1 teaspoon salt

¼ teaspoon black pepper

1 teaspoon lemon juice

1. In a large soup pot or stockpot, sauté the onion, carrot, and cloves in margarine until onion is just turning soft, about 3 minutes. Add cumin and turmeric and toast for 1 minute, stirring constantly to avoid burning.

2. Reduce heat to medium-low and add lentils, Vegetable Broth, tomatoes, and salt. Bring to a simmer, cover, and cook for 35–40 minutes, until lentils are done.

3. Season with black pepper and lemon juice just before serving.

COLD SPANISH GAZPACHO WITH AVOCADO

This is best enjoyed on an outdoor patio just after sunset on a warm summer evening. But really, anytime you want a simple light starter soup, this will do, no matter the weather. Add some crunch too by topping with homemade croutons.

INGREDIENTS

Serves 6

2 cucumbers, diced

½ red onion, diced

2 large tomatoes, diced

¼ cup fresh chopped cilantro

2 avocadoes, diced

4 cloves garlic

2 tablespoons lime juice

1 tablespoon red wine vinegar

¾ cup Vegetable Broth (this chapter)

1 chili pepper (jalapeño, serrano, or cayenne) or 1 teaspoon hot sauce

Salt and pepper to taste

1. Mix together the cucumbers, red onion, tomatoes, cilantro, and avocado. Set half of the mixture aside. Take the other half and mix in a blender. Add the garlic, lime juice, vinegar, Vegetable Broth, and chili pepper or hot sauce and process until smooth.

2. Transfer to serving bowl and add remaining diced cucumbers, onion, tomatoes, cilantro, and avocado, gently stirring to combine.

3. Season generously with salt and pepper, to taste.

Crunchy Croutons

Slice your favorite vegan artisan bread, focaccia, or whatever you've got into 1" cubes. Toss them in a large bowl with a generous coating of olive oil or a flavored oil, a bit of salt, and some Italian seasoning, garlic powder, a dash of cayenne, or whatever you prefer, then transfer to a baking sheet and bake 15–20 minutes at 275°F, tossing once or twice.

KIDNEY BEAN AND ZUCCHINI GUMBO

This vegetable gumbo uses zucchini instead of okra. Traditional gumbo always calls for filé powder, but if you can't find this anywhere, increase the amounts of the other spices.

INGREDIENTS

Serves 5

1 onion, diced

1 red or green bell pepper chopped

3 stalks celery, chopped

2 tablespoons olive oil

1 zucchini, sliced

1 (14-ounce) can diced tomatoes

3 cups Vegetable Broth (this chapter)

1 teaspoon hot sauce

1 teaspoon filé powder (optional)

¾ teaspoon thyme

1 teaspoon Cajun seasoning

2 bay leaves

1 (15-ounce) can kidney beans, drained

1½ cups rice, cooked

1. In a large soup pot or stock pan, sauté the onion, bell pepper, and celery in olive oil for just 1–2 minutes. Reduce heat and add zucchini, tomatoes, Vegetable Broth, and remaining ingredients except beans and rice.

2. Bring to a simmer, cover, and allow to cook for 30 minutes.

3. Uncover, add beans, and stir to combine. Heat for 5 more minutes. Remove bay leaves before serving. Serve over cooked rice.

Gumbo on the Go

If you don't have some precooked rice on hand, add ⅔ cup instant rice and an extra cup of Vegetable Broth during the last 10 minutes of cooking. For a "meatier texture," quickly brown some vegetarian sausage or ground beef substitute and toss it in the mix.

MUSHROOM BARLEY SOUP

Using three types of mushrooms in this soup adds a more robust, earthier flavor.

INGREDIENTS

Serves 8

1 ounce dried porcini mushrooms

1 cup boiling water

1½ teaspoons vegan margarine

5 ounces fresh shiitake mushrooms, sliced

4 ounces fresh button mushrooms, sliced

1 large onion, diced

1 clove garlic, minced

⅔ cup medium pearl barley

¼ teaspoon ground black pepper

½ teaspoon salt

6 cups Vegetable Broth (this chapter)

1. In a heat-safe bowl, place the dried porcini mushrooms; pour the boiling water over the mushrooms. Soak for 15 minutes.

2. Meanwhile, in a medium sauté pan, melt the vegan margarine. Sauté the fresh mushrooms, onion, and garlic until the onion is soft, about 3 minutes.

3. Drain the porcini mushrooms and discard the water.

4. In a 4-quart slow cooker, add all of the mushrooms, onions, garlic, barley, pepper, salt, and Vegetable Broth. Stir, cover, and cook 6–8 hours on low.

GREEK-STYLE ORZO AND SPINACH SOUP

Lemon zest adds a bright, robust flavor to this simple soup.

INGREDIENTS

Serves 6

2 cloves garlic, minced

3 tablespoons lemon juice

1 teaspoon lemon zest

5 cups Vegetable Broth (this chapter)

1½ teaspoons salt

1 small onion, thinly sliced

1 package extra-firm tofu, cubed

4 cups fresh baby spinach

⅓ cup dried orzo

1. In a 4-quart slow cooker, add the garlic, lemon juice, zest, Vegetable Broth, salt, onion, tofu, and spinach. Cover, and cook on low for 1 hour.

2. Add the orzo, stir, and continue to cook on high for an additional 15 minutes.

Quick Tip: Zesting

There are many tools on the market that are for zesting citrus, but all you really need is a fine grater. Be sure to take off just the outermost part of the peel, where the aromatic essential oils that hold the flavor are located. The white pith underneath is bitter and inedible.

SIMPLE SPLIT PEA SOUP

Split peas break down during cooking and will leave you with a soup that is slightly creamy, but to make your soup very smooth, just blend after removing the bay leaves.

INGREDIENTS

Serves 8

2 cups dried green split peas

7 cups water

2 carrots, peeled and diced

2 stalks celery, sliced

1 white onion, diced

2 bay leaves

½ teaspoon pepper

1 teaspoon salt

3 dashes vegan Worcestershire sauce

1. Place all ingredients in a 6-quart slow cooker, cover, and cook on low for 8 hours.

2. Remove the bay leaves and stir well before serving.

AFRICAN PEANUT AND GREENS SOUP

Cut back on the red pepper flakes to make this soup for kids, or reduce the liquids to turn it into a thick and chunky curry to pour over rice. Although the ingredients are all familiar, this is definitely not a boring meal!

INGREDIENTS

Serves 4

1 onion, diced

3 tomatoes, chopped

2 tablespoons olive oil

2 cups Vegetable Broth (this chapter)

1 cup coconut milk

⅓ cup peanut butter

1 (15-ounce) can chickpeas, drained

½ teaspoon salt

1 teaspoon curry powder

1 teaspoon sugar

⅓ teaspoon red pepper flakes

1 bunch fresh spinach

1. Sauté the onions and tomatoes in olive oil until onions are soft, about 2–3 minutes.

2. Reduce heat to medium-low and add remaining ingredients except spinach, stirring well to combine.

3. Allow to simmer on low heat, uncovered, stirring occasionally for 8–10 minutes.

4. Add spinach and allow to cook for another 1–2 minutes, just until spinach is wilted.

5. Remove from heat and adjust seasonings to taste. Soup will thicken as it cools.

PHO

This Vietnamese noodle soup is easy to make in the slow cooker. Try it instead of vegetable soup on a cold night.

INGREDIENTS

Serves 6

1 tablespoon coriander seeds

1 tablespoon whole cloves

6 star anises

1 cinnamon stick

1 tablespoon fennel seed

1 tablespoon whole cardamom

4 knobs fresh ginger, sliced

1 onion, sliced

1 quart Vegetable Broth (this chapter)

1 teaspoon soy sauce

8 ounces Vietnamese rice noodles

1 cup shredded seitan

½ cup chopped cilantro

½ cup chopped Thai basil

2 cups mung bean sprouts

¼ cup sliced scallions

1. In a dry nonstick skillet, quickly heat the spices, ginger, and onion until the seeds start to pop, about 5 minutes. The onion and ginger should look slightly caramelized. Place them in a cheesecloth packet and tie it securely.

2. In a 4-quart slow cooker, place the cheesecloth packet. Add the Vegetable Broth, soy sauce, noodles, and seitan. Cover, and cook on low for 4 hours.

3. Remove the cheesecloth packet after cooking. Serve each bowl topped with cilantro, basil, sprouts, and scallions.

POTATO AND LEEK SOUP

With simple earthy flavors, this classic soup is a comforting starter.

INGREDIENTS
Serves 6

1 yellow onion, diced

2 cloves garlic, minced

2 tablespoons olive oil

6 cups Vegetable Broth (this chapter)

3 leeks, sliced

2 large potatoes, chopped

2 bay leaves

1 cup soymilk

2 tablespoons vegan margarine

¾ teaspoon salt

⅓ teaspoon black pepper

½ teaspoon sage

½ teaspoon thyme

2 tablespoons nutritional yeast (optional)

1. Sauté onion and garlic in olive oil for a few minutes until onion is soft.

2. Add Vegetable Broth, leeks, potatoes, and bay leaves and bring to a slow simmer.

3. Allow to cook, partially covered, for 30 minutes until potatoes are soft.

4. Remove bay leaves. Working in batches as needed, purée soup in a blender until almost smooth, or desired consistency.

5. Return soup to pot and stir in remaining ingredients. Adjust seasonings and reheat as needed.

Get Your Leeks Ready

Fresh leeks impart an oniony root flavor. To prepare your leeks, chop off the inedible dark green leaves, and use only the white and soft light green stem. Leeks tend to hide bits of dirt inside, so rinse or submerge well, chop, then rinse again, using a colander or salad spinner. Got extras? Toss any leftover bits into a vegetable broth.

CREAM CHEESE AND BUTTERNUT SQUASH SOUP

This isn't a healthy hippie vegetable soup—it's a rich, decadent, stick-to-your-thighs soup. Nonetheless, it's absolutely delicious. Top with a mountain of homemade croutons or serve with crusty French bread.

INGREDIENTS

Serves 4

2 cloves garlic, minced

½ yellow onion, diced

2 tablespoons olive oil

3½ cups Vegetable Broth (this chapter)

1 medium butternut squash, peeled, seeded, and chopped into cubes

1 teaspoon curry powder

¼ teaspoon nutmeg

¼ teaspoon salt

½ (8-ounce) container vegan cream cheese

1. In a large skillet or stockpot, sauté garlic and onion in olive oil until soft, about 3–4 minutes.

2. Reduce heat to medium-low and add Vegetable Broth, squash, curry powder, nutmeg, and salt. Simmer for 25 minutes until squash is soft.

3. Working in batches, purée until almost smooth, or to desired consistency. Or if squash is soft enough, mash smooth with a large fork.

4. Return soup to very low heat and stir in vegan cream cheese until melted, combined, and heated through. Adjust seasonings to taste.

PUMPKIN-ALE SOUP

Use fresh pumpkin in place of the canned pumpkin purée when the ingredient is in season. You'll need 3¾ cups of cooked, puréed fresh pumpkin.

INGREDIENTS

Serves 6

2 (15-ounce) cans pumpkin purée

¼ cup diced onion

2 cloves garlic, minced

2 teaspoons salt

1 teaspoon pepper

¼ teaspoon dried thyme

5 cups Vegetable Broth (this chapter)

1 (12-ounce) bottle pale ale beer

1. In a 4-quart slow cooker, add the pumpkin purée, onion, garlic, salt, pepper, thyme, and Vegetable Broth. Stir well. Cover, and cook over low heat for 4 hours.

2. Allow the soup to cool slightly then process in a blender or with an immersion blender until smooth.

3. Pour the soup back into the slow cooker, add the beer, and cook for 1 hour over low heat.

CURRIED PUMPKIN SOUP

You don't have to wait for fall to make this pumpkin soup, as canned pumpkin purée will work just fine. It's also excellent with coconut milk instead of soymilk.

INGREDIENTS

Serves 4

1 yellow onion, diced

3 cloves garlic, minced

2 tablespoons vegan margarine

1 (15-ounce) can pumpkin purée

3 cups Vegetable Broth (this chapter)

2 bay leaves

1 tablespoon curry powder

1 teaspoon cumin

½ teaspoon ground ginger

1 cup soymilk

¼ teaspoon salt

1. In a large soup pot or stockpot, heat onion and garlic in margarine until onion is soft, about 4–5 minutes.

2. Add pumpkin and Vegetable Broth and stir well to combine. Add bay leaves, curry, cumin, and ginger and bring to a slow simmer.

3. Cover, and allow to cook for 15 minutes.

4. Reduce heat to low and add soymilk, stirring to combine. Heat for just another 1–2 minutes until heated through.

5. Season with salt to taste and remove bay leaves before serving.

Ditch the Can

If you've got the time, there's nothing like fresh roasted pumpkin! Make your own purée to substitute for canned. Carefully chop your pumpkin in half, remove the seeds (save and toast those later!), and roast for 45 minutes to an hour in a 375°F oven. Cool, then peel off the skin and mash or purée until smooth. Whatever you don't use will keep in the freezer for next time.

PUMPKIN, SQUASH, AND SAGE SOUP

Pumpkin and butternut squash have similar flavors, so feel free to adjust the amount of each in this recipe.

INGREDIENTS

Serves 8

3 sprigs fresh sage

3 cups fresh pumpkin, skinned and chopped

2 cups butternut squash, skinned and chopped

1 small white onion, diced

4 cups Vegetable Broth (this chapter)

2 bay leaves

2 teaspoons salt

½ cup unsweetened soymilk

1. Place the sage in a piece of cheesecloth and tie closed.

2. Combine all of the ingredients except the soymilk in a 6-quart slow cooker; cover, and cook over low heat for 4–6 hours, or until the vegetables are very tender.

3. Remove the sage and bay leaves, add the soymilk, and blend until very smooth using an immersion blender.

Cheesecloth

Cheesecloth is a handy kitchen tool that can be used for securing fresh herbs, nuts, beans, or other ingredients you may want the flavor of in a dish, without including the whole thing. It's available at grocery stores and a few yards can usually be purchased for just a couple of dollars.

RED LENTIL SOUP

Store-bought vegetable broth or stock typically contains much more sodium than the homemade variety, so adjust salt accordingly.

INGREDIENTS

Serves 6

3 tablespoons olive oil

1 small onion, sliced

1½ teaspoons fresh ginger, peeled and minced

2 cloves garlic, minced

2 cups red lentils

6 cups Vegetable Broth (this chapter)

Juice of 1 lemon

½ teaspoon paprika

1 teaspoon cayenne pepper

1½ teaspoons salt

1. In a sauté pan, heat the olive oil over medium heat, then sauté the onion, ginger, and garlic for 2–3 minutes.

2. In a 4-quart slow cooker, add the sautéed vegetables and all remaining ingredients; cover, and cook on low for 6–8 hours. Add more salt if necessary, to taste.

Cleaning Lentils

Before cooking lentils, rinse them carefully by placing in a colander and running ample cold water over the lentils. Sort through the bunch to remove any debris that may be lingering behind and discard.

ROASTED RED PEPPER AND CORN SOUP

You can roast your own bell peppers for this recipe or use jarred peppers to save a little time.

INGREDIENTS
Serves 6

6 red bell peppers, halved and seeded

1 cup corn kernels

1 russet potato, peeled and chopped

½ white onion, diced

2 cloves garlic, minced

6 cups Vegetable Broth (this chapter)

2 tablespoons white wine vinegar

2 bay leaves

¼ teaspoon pepper

1 teaspoon salt

⅛ cup cilantro, chopped

1. Preheat your oven's broiler. Place the bell peppers on a baking sheet, skin side up, and broil for 15 minutes or until black spots appear. Place the peppers in a paper or plastic bag, close, and let sit for 5 minutes to loosen the skins. Remove the peppers, peel off the skins, and chop.

2. Place the peppers and all remaining ingredients except cilantro in a 6-quart slow cooker, cover, and cook over low heat for 6 hours. Remove bay leaves when done.

3. Purée using an immersion blender or traditional blender, then add the cilantro before serving.

SHIITAKE AND GARLIC BROTH

Shiitake mushrooms transform ordinary broth into a rich stock with a deep flavor.

INGREDIENTS

Yields 6 cups broth

⅓ cup dried shiitake mushrooms

6 cups water

2 cloves garlic, smashed

1 bay leaf

½ teaspoon thyme

½ onion, chopped

1. Combine all ingredients in a large soup pot or stockpot and bring to a slow simmer.

2. Cover, and allow to cook for at least 30–40 minutes.

3. Strain and remove bay leaf before using.

Vegetarian Dashi

To turn this into a Japanese dashi stock for miso and noodle soups, omit the bay leaf and thyme and add a generous amount of seaweed, preferably kombu if you can find it!

THAI TOM KHA KAI COCONUT SOUP

In Thailand, this soup is a full meal, served alongside a large plate of steamed rice, and the vegetables vary with the season and whim of the chef—broccoli, bell peppers, or mild chilies are common. Don't worry if you can't find lemongrass or galangal, as lime and ginger add a similar flavor.

INGREDIENTS
Serves 4

1 (14-ounce) can coconut milk

2 cups Vegetable Broth (this chapter)

1 tablespoon soy sauce

3 cloves garlic, minced

5 slices fresh ginger or galangal

1 stalk lemongrass, chopped (optional)

1 tablespoon lime juice

1–2 small chilies, chopped

½ teaspoon red pepper flakes, or to taste

1 onion, chopped

2 tomatoes, chopped

1 carrot, sliced thin

½ cup sliced mushrooms, any kind

¼ cup chopped fresh cilantro

1. Combine the coconut milk and Vegetable Broth over medium-low heat. Add soy sauce, garlic, ginger or galangal, lemongrass if desired, lime juice, chilies, and red pepper flakes. Heat, but do not boil.

2. When broth is hot, add onion, tomatoes, carrot, and mushrooms. Cover, and cook on low heat for 10–15 minutes.

3. Remove from heat and top with chopped fresh cilantro.

TOFU NOODLE SOUP

Even firm tofu is quite soft, so for added texture, freeze the tofu and bake before adding to the soup.

INGREDIENTS
Serves 4

2 tablespoons olive oil

1 medium onion, diced

3 cloves garlic, minced

2 ribs celery, sliced in ½" pieces

7 ounces extra-firm tofu, cubed

5 cups Vegetable Broth (this chapter)

1 bay leaf

1 teaspoon salt

Juice of 1 lemon

2 teaspoons fresh parsley, chopped

2 teaspoons fresh thyme, chopped

8 ounces cooked noodles or linguine

1. In a large sauté pan heat the olive oil over medium heat. Add the onion, garlic, and celery and sauté for 3 minutes.

2. Add the tofu and cook 5 additional minutes.

3. In a 4-quart slow cooker, pour the sautéed vegetables, tofu, Vegetable Broth, bay leaf, and salt; cover, and cook on low for 8 hours.

4. Add the lemon juice, parsley, thyme, and pasta. Cover, and cook for an additional 20 minutes. Remove bay leaf before serving.

Herbal Options
A variety of herbs can work well in Tofu Noodle Soup. Try substituting basil, rosemary, or even dill in this recipe.

TORTILLA SOUP

Turn this soup into a complete meal by adding pieces of cooked vegan chicken, such as Morningstar Farms Meal Starters Chik'n Strips or Gardein Seasoned Bites.

INGREDIENTS
Serves 8

2 tablespoons olive oil

1 large onion, chopped

2 cloves garlic, minced

2 tablespoons soy sauce

7 cups Vegetable Broth (this chapter)

12 ounces firm silken tofu, crumbled

2 cups tomato, diced

1 cup corn kernels

1 teaspoon chipotle powder

1 teaspoon cayenne pepper

2 teaspoons ground cumin

2 teaspoons salt

1 teaspoon dried oregano

10 small corn tortillas, sliced

8 ounces shredded vegan cheese, such as Daiya Mozzarella Style Shreds

1. In a sauté pan over medium heat, add the olive oil; sauté the onion until just soft, about 3 minutes. Add the garlic and sauté for an additional 30 seconds.

2. In a 4-quart slow cooker, add all ingredients except tortillas and cheese. Stir, cover, and cook over low heat for 4 hours.

3. While the soup is cooking, Preheat oven to 450°F. Slice the corn tortillas into thin strips and place them on an ungreased baking sheet. Bake for about 10 minutes, or until they turn golden brown. Remove from heat and set aside.

4. After the soup has cooled slightly, use an immersion blender or regular blender to purée the soup.

5. Serve with cooked tortilla strips and 1 ounce of shredded cheese in each bowl of soup.

Chipotle Powder

Chipotle powder is made from ground chipotle peppers, a type of dried jalapeño. They bring a smoky spiciness to dishes, but can be replaced with cayenne pepper or chili powder.

EASY ROASTED TOMATO SOUP

Use the freshest, ripest, juiciest red tomatoes you can find for this super-easy recipe, as there are few other added flavors. If you find that you need a bit more spice, add a spoonful of nutritional yeast, a dash of cayenne pepper, or an extra shake of salt and pepper.

INGREDIENTS

Serves 4

6 large tomatoes

1 small onion

4 cloves garlic

2 tablespoons olive oil

1¼ cups soymilk

2 tablespoons chopped fresh basil

1½ teaspoons balsamic vinegar

¾ teaspoon salt

¼ teaspoon black pepper

1. Preheat oven to 425°F.

2. Slice tomatoes in half and chop onion into quarters. Place tomatoes, onion, and garlic on baking sheet and drizzle with olive oil.

3. Roast in the oven for 45 minutes to 1 hour.

4. Carefully transfer tomatoes, onion, and garlic to a blender, including any juices on the baking sheet. Add remaining ingredients and purée until almost smooth.

5. Reheat over low heat for just 1–2 minutes if needed, and adjust seasonings to taste.

UDON NOODLE BUDDHA BOWL

Say that five times fast! This is a nutritious full meal in a bowl, which might be particularly comforting on the edge of a cold or after an early-morning zazen meditation. For an authentic Japanese flavor, add a large piece of kombu seaweed to the broth or use a vegetarian dashi stock.

INGREDIENTS

Serves 4

2 (8-ounce) packages udon noodles

3½ cups Shiitake and Garlic Broth (this chapter)

1½ teaspoons fresh minced ginger

1 tablespoon sugar

1 tablespoon soy sauce

1 tablespoon rice vinegar

¼ teaspoon red pepper flakes, or to taste

1 baby bok choy, sliced

1 cup mushrooms, any kind, sliced

1 block silken tofu, cubed

¼ cup bean sprouts

1 cup fresh spinach

1 teaspoon sesame oil or hot chili oil

1. Cook noodles in boiling water until soft, about 5 minutes. Drain and divide into 4 serving bowls and set aside.

2. In a large pot, combine the Shiitake and Garlic Broth, ginger, sugar, soy sauce, vinegar, and red pepper flakes and bring to a simmer. Add bok choy, mushrooms, and tofu and cook just until veggies are soft, about 10 minutes.

3. Add bean sprouts and spinach and simmer for 1 more minute until spinach has wilted. Remove from heat and drizzle with sesame oil or chili oil.

4. Divide soup into the 4 bowls containing cooked noodles and serve immediately.

Know Your Noodles: Udon, Sōmen, Soba, Shirataki

Udon noodles have a thick and chewy texture, but you can try this recipe with any noodle you like. Noodles cook quicker than pasta, so they're great when you're super hungry or in a hurry. Many grocery stores even stock shirataki noodles—a high-protein, low-carb noodle that doesn't need to be cooked—perfect for hungry vegans to slurp! Check the refrigerator section for these.

VEGAN VICHYSSOISE

Vichyssoise is traditionally served cold (and is made using cream, too) but this warm vegan version will leave you satisfied on a cold day.

INGREDIENTS

Serves 6

2 tablespoons vegan margarine

3 leeks (white part only), sliced

1 white onion, sliced

3 Idaho potatoes, peeled and diced

4 cups Vegetable Broth (this chapter)

1 bay leaf

½ teaspoon pepper

¼ teaspoon dried thyme

1 cup unsweetened soymilk

Salt, to taste

2 tablespoons chopped chives

1. Melt the vegan margarine in a large pan over medium heat. Add the leeks and onion and sauté for 10 minutes, then transfer to a 6-quart slow cooker.

2. Add the potatoes, Vegetable Broth, bay leaf, pepper, and thyme; cover, and cook over low heat for 6 hours. Remove the bay leaf when done.

3. Add the soymilk, then purée using an immersion blender or traditional blender.

4. Season with salt, to taste, and top with chives before serving.

Earth Balance

Earth Balance is a popular brand of vegan buttery spread that has a delicious flavor and acts similarly to butter in cooking. Many types of margarine contain dairy or have a rubbery texture, but Earth Balance is very creamy and can be used in all types of recipes, including creamy sauces and vegan baked goods.

VEGETABLE BROTH

A versatile vegetable broth can be used as the base for almost any soup or stew. Note that it does not contain salt, so you must add that separately when using this broth in recipes.

INGREDIENTS

Yields 4 cups

2 large onions, peeled and halved

2 medium carrots, cleaned and cut into large pieces

3 stalks celery, cut in half

1 whole bulb garlic, crushed

10 peppercorns

1 bay leaf

6 cups water

1. In a 4-quart slow cooker, add all ingredients; cover, and cook on low heat for 8–10 hours.

2. Strain the broth to remove the vegetables. Remove bay leaf. Store in the refrigerator.

Storing Broth

Homemade broth can be stored in a covered container in the refrigerator for 2–3 days, or frozen for up to 3 months.

WHITE BEAN AND ORZO MINESTRONE

Italian minestrone is a simple and universally loved soup. This version uses tiny orzo pasta, cannellini beans, and plenty of veggies.

INGREDIENTS

Serves 6

3 cloves garlic, minced

1 onion, chopped

2 ribs celery, chopped

2 tablespoons olive oil

5 cups Vegetable Broth (this chapter)

1 carrot, diced

1 cup green beans, chopped

2 small potatoes, chopped small

2 tomatoes, chopped

1 (15-ounce) can cannellini beans, drained

1 teaspoon basil

½ teaspoon oregano

¾ cup orzo

Salt and pepper to taste

1. In a large soup pot, heat garlic, onion, and celery in olive oil until just soft, about 3–4 minutes.

2. Add Vegetable Broth, carrot, green beans, potatoes, tomatoes, beans, basil, and oregano and bring to a simmer. Cover, and cook on medium-low heat for 20–25 minutes.

3. Add orzo and heat another 10 minutes, just until orzo is cooked. Season well with salt and pepper.

STEWS

JAMAICAN RED BEAN STEW

Make your own jerk seasoning by combining thyme, allspice, black pepper, cinnamon, cayenne, onion powder, and nutmeg.

INGREDIENTS

Serves 4

2 tablespoons olive oil

½ onion, diced

2 cloves garlic, minced

1 (15-ounce) can diced tomatoes

3 cups sweet potatoes, peeled and diced

2 (15-ounce) cans red kidney beans, drained

1 cup coconut milk

3 cups Vegetable Broth (this chapter)

2 teaspoons jerk seasoning

2 teaspoons curry powder

Salt and pepper, to taste

1. In a sauté pan over medium heat, add the olive oil, then sauté the onion and garlic for about 3 minutes.

2. In a 4-quart slow cooker, add all ingredients. Cover, and cook on low heat for 6 hours.

WHITE BEAN CASSOULET

The longer you cook this cassoulet, the creamier it will get as the cannellini beans break down.

INGREDIENTS

Serves 8

1 pound dried cannellini beans

2 cups boiling water

1 ounce dried porcini mushrooms

2 leeks, sliced

1 teaspoon canola oil

2 parsnips, diced

2 carrots, diced

2 stalks celery, diced

½ teaspoon ground fennel

1 teaspoon crushed rosemary

1 teaspoon dried chervil

⅛ teaspoon cloves

¼ teaspoon salt

¼ teaspoon freshly ground black pepper

2 cups Vegetable Broth (this chapter)

1. The night before making the soup, place the beans in a 4-quart slow cooker. Fill with water to 1" below the top of the insert. Soak overnight.

2. Drain the beans and return them to the slow cooker.

3. In a heat-proof bowl, pour the boiling water over the dried mushrooms and soak for 15 minutes.

4. Slice only the white and light green parts of the leeks into ¼ rounds. Cut the rounds in ½.

5. In a nonstick skillet, heat the oil; add the parsnips, carrots, celery, and leeks. Sauté for 1 minute, just until the color of the vegetables brightens.

6. Add to the slow cooker along with the spices. Add the mushrooms, their soaking liquid, and the Vegetable Broth; stir. Cook on low for 8–10 hours.

WHITE BEAN RAGOUT

Ragout is another word for stew and can be made with any combination of vegetables, herbs, and liquids.

INGREDIENTS

Serves 4

2 tablespoons olive oil

1 onion, diced

5 cloves garlic, minced

2 (14-ounce) cans navy beans, drained

1 (14-ounce) can diced tomatoes

3 cups water

¼ cup tomato paste

½ cup fresh parsley, chopped

2 tablespoons fresh sage, chopped

¼ teaspoon salt

⅛ teaspoon black pepper

1. Add the olive oil to the slow cooker and sauté the onion on medium-high heat for 3–5 minutes. Add the garlic and sauté for 1 minute more.

2. Add the navy beans, tomatoes, water, tomato paste, parsley, sage, salt, and black pepper and cook on low heat for 4 hours.

BRUNSWICK STEW

Try adding barbecue sauce to this stew to spice things up.

INGREDIENTS

Serves 4

4 cups Vegetable Broth (this chapter)

1 (15-ounce) can diced tomatoes

1 (6-ounce) can tomato paste

1 cup okra, sliced

1 cup corn

1 cup frozen lima beans

2 cups seitan, diced

¼ teaspoon dried rosemary

¼ teaspoon dried oregano

2 teaspoons vegan Worcestershire sauce

Salt and pepper, to taste

In a 4-quart slow cooker, add all ingredients. Cover, and cook on low heat for 5–6 hours.

Debate on Origin

Some claim that Brunswick stew was first served in Brunswick, Georgia, in 1898, while others say it was created in Brunswick County, Virginia, in 1828. Today, Brunswick stew recipe ingredients vary by region.

NEW ENGLAND CORN CHOWDER

This chowder is even better with fresh corn, when it is in season. Just remove the kernels from the husk and use the same amount of corn.

INGREDIENTS

Serves 4

½ cup vegan margarine

1 onion, diced

3 cloves garlic, minced

¼ cup flour

4 cups unsweetened soymilk

3 potatoes, peeled and diced

2 cups frozen corn

2 cups Vegetable Broth (this chapter)

½ teaspoon dried thyme

½ teaspoon salt

1. Add the vegan margarine to the slow cooker and sauté the onion on medium heat for 4–5 minutes. Add the garlic and sauté for 1 minute more.

2. Slowly stir in the flour with a whisk and create a roux. Stir in the soymilk and continue whisking until very smooth.

3. Add the remaining ingredients and cook on low heat for 3–4 hours.

ÉTOUFFÉE

Vegan shrimp can be purchased online at VeganStore.com.

INGREDIENTS

Serves 6

½ cup vegan margarine

1 onion, diced

3 celery ribs, chopped

1 carrot, diced

3 cloves garlic, minced

1 green bell pepper, chopped

¼ cup flour

1 cup water

2 teaspoons Cajun seasoning

1 (8.8-ounce) package vegan shrimp

Juice of 1 lemon

½ teaspoon salt

¼ teaspoon black pepper

4 cups cooked white rice

½ cup parsley, chopped

1. In a sauté pan over medium heat, add the vegan margarine. Sauté the onion, celery, carrot, garlic, and green bell pepper until soft, about 5–7 minutes. Stir in the flour to make a roux.

2. Add the roux to a 4-quart slow cooker. Whisk in the water, Cajun seasoning, vegan shrimp, lemon juice, salt, and pepper. Cover, and cook on low heat for 4–5 hours.

3. Serve over the white rice and garnish with parsley.

Cajun Seasoning

To make your own Cajun seasoning, use a blend of equal parts cayenne pepper, black pepper, paprika, garlic powder, onion powder, salt, and thyme.

GUMBO Z'HERBES

You won't miss the meat with all the delicious flavors in this gumbo. As they say in New Orleans, "Laissez les bons temps rouler!" Or, "Let the good times roll!"

INGREDIENTS

Serves 6

½ cup olive oil

1 onion, chopped

1 green bell pepper, chopped

2 stalks celery, chopped

4 cloves garlic, minced

½ cup flour

4 cups Vegetable Broth (this chapter)

2 cups okra, chopped

½ teaspoon dried thyme

½ teaspoon dried oregano

1 teaspoon salt

½ teaspoon black pepper

¼ teaspoon red pepper flakes

6 cups cooked white rice

1. Add the olive oil to the slow cooker and sauté the onion, bell pepper, and celery on medium heat for 4–5 minutes. Add the garlic and sauté for 1 minute more.

2. Slowly stir in the flour with a whisk and create a roux. Pour in the Vegetable Broth and continue to whisk to remove all lumps.

3. Add the rest of the ingredients except the rice and cook on medium-high heat for 3–4 hours. Serve over the cooked white rice.

The Holy Trinity

The base of some of New Orleans' most well-known dishes is referred to as the "holy trinity." It contains equal parts onions, bell pepper, and celery.

HOPPIN' JOHN STEW

In the South, eating Hoppin' John on New Year's Day is a tradition and thought to bring good luck throughout the year.

INGREDIENTS

Serves 6

2 tablespoons olive oil

1 onion, diced

2 stalks celery, chopped

3 cloves garlic, minced

1 pound dried black-eyed peas

3 cups water

4 cups Vegetable Broth (this chapter)

1 tablespoon soy sauce

1 bay leaf

1 teaspoon hot sauce

½ teaspoon salt

⅛ teaspoon black pepper

6 cups cooked white rice

1. Add the olive oil to the slow cooker and sauté the onion and celery on medium-high heat for 3–5 minutes. Add the garlic and sauté for 1 minute more.

2. Add the rest of the ingredients except the rice, and cook on high heat for 5–6 hours.

3. Remove bay leaf and serve the stew over the cooked white rice in a bowl.

KOREAN-STYLE HOT POT

Serve this hot and spicy main dish with sides of steamed rice and kimchi (a side of fermented vegetables).

INGREDIENTS

Serves 8

3 bunches baby bok choy

8 cups water

8 ounces sliced cremini mushrooms

12 ounces extra-firm tofu, cubed

3 cloves garlic, thinly sliced

¼ teaspoon sesame oil

1 tablespoon crushed red pepper flakes

7 ounces enoki mushrooms

1. Remove the leaves of the baby bok choy. Wash thoroughly.

2. Place the leaves whole in a 4-quart slow cooker. Add the water, cremini mushrooms, tofu, garlic, sesame oil, and crushed red pepper. Stir.

3. Cook on low for 8 hours.

4. Add the enoki mushrooms and stir. Cook an additional ½ hour.

MEDITERRANEAN VEGETABLE STEW

Try serving this stew with large pieces of warm pita bread and a scoop of hummus.

INGREDIENTS

Serves 6

2 tablespoons extra-virgin olive oil

4 garlic cloves, chopped

1 red onion, chopped

1 red bell pepper, seeded and chopped

1 eggplant, chopped

1 (15-ounce) can artichokes, drained and chopped

⅓ cup kalamata olives, pitted and chopped

2 (15-ounce) cans diced tomatoes

4 cups Vegetable Broth (this chapter)

1 teaspoon red pepper flakes

½ teaspoon dried oregano

½ teaspoon dried parsley

1 teaspoon salt

½ teaspoon pepper

In a 4-quart slow cooker, add all ingredients. Cover, and cook on low heat for 4–6 hours.

Preparing Eggplant

Some people salt eggplant prior to cooking in order to remove bitterness, but this step is not required for making delicious recipes using eggplant. The skins can be removed, but this also is not necessary. Eggplants, called aubergine in almost all other parts of the world, can be boiled, steamed, sautéed, stir-fried, deep-fried, braised, baked, grilled, broiled, and microwaved.

WILD MUSHROOM RAGOUT

For a more refined flavor, try substituting shallots for the onion in this recipe.

INGREDIENTS

Serves 4

2 tablespoons olive oil

1 onion, diced

½ pound white button mushrooms, sliced

½ pound shiitake mushrooms, sliced

½ pound oyster mushrooms, sliced

3 cloves garlic, minced

¼ teaspoon salt

⅛ teaspoon black pepper

1 cup red wine

2 cups Vegetable Broth (this chapter)

1. Add the olive oil to the slow cooker and sauté the onion and mushrooms on medium-high heat for 4–5 minutes. Add the garlic, salt, and black pepper and sauté for 1 minute more.

2. Add the red wine and Vegetable Broth and cook over low heat for 2 hours.

Cooking with Alcohol

In recipes like this one, which contain a significant amount of alcohol, you shouldn't expect all of the alcohol to "cook off." If you are pregnant, cooking for a child, or just like to avoid alcohol, you may want to skip this recipe.

CHUNKY MUSHROOM TRIO

All of the delicious mushrooms in this recipe create a very think and chunky stew. You can eat it plain or served over a bed of steamed white rice.

INGREDIENTS

Serves 6

2 tablespoons olive oil

1 onion, chopped

1 pound white button mushrooms, chopped

1 pound shiitake mushrooms, stemmed and chopped

1 pound oyster mushrooms, stemmed and chopped

3 cloves garlic, minced

½ pound red potatoes, chopped into bite-size pieces

4 cups Vegetable Broth (this chapter)

1 tablespoon soy sauce

½ cup red wine (optional)

1 teaspoon dried thyme

¼ teaspoon salt

⅛ teaspoon black pepper

1. Add the olive oil to the slow cooker and sauté the onion and mushrooms on medium-high heat for 3–5 minutes. Add the garlic and sauté for 1 minute more.

2. Add the rest of the ingredients and cook on medium-high heat for 3–4 hours.

Mushroom Varieties

Button mushrooms are a milder type of mushroom with little flavor but they are inexpensive and can be used in combination with more flavorful varieties. Shiitake, oyster, chanterelle, and hen-of-the-woods are more expensive varieties that have wonderful texture and flavor.

POSOLE

This rich-tasting stew just needs a sprinkling of shredded red cabbage to finish it to perfection.

INGREDIENTS

Serves 6

8 large dried New Mexican red chilies

1½ quarts Vegetable Broth (this chapter), divided

3 cloves garlic, minced

2 tablespoons lime juice

1 tablespoon ground cumin

1 tablespoon oregano

1 (7-ounce) package Gardein Chick'n Strips

¾ cup flour

1 teaspoon canola oil

1 large onion, sliced

40 ounces canned hominy

1. Seed the chilies, reserving the seeds.

2. In a dry, hot frying pan, heat the chilies until warmed through and fragrant, about 2–3 minutes. Do not burn or brown them.

3. In a medium pot, place the chilies and seeds, 1 quart Vegetable Broth, garlic, lime juice, cumin, and oregano. Bring to a boil and continue to boil for 20 minutes.

4. Meanwhile, in a plastic bag, toss the Gardein Chick'n Strips with the flour to coat. Heat the oil in a large nonstick skillet and brown the vegan meat on all sides, about 3 minutes.

5. Add the onion and cook about 5 minutes, or until the onion is soft.

6. In a 4-quart slow cooker, pour the unused Vegetable Broth, hominy, the onion, and vegan meat mixture.

7. Strain the chili-stock mixture through a mesh sieve into the slow-cooker insert, mashing down with a wooden spoon to press out the pulp and juice. Discard the seeds and remaining solids. Cook on low for 8 hours.

Citrus Leftovers

If you have a small amount of juice left, pour it into an ice cube tray in your freezer, one well at a time if necessary, and freeze. Leftover zest can also be saved. Place the zest in a freezer bag and refrigerate up to 1 week or freeze in a freezer-safe container up to 1 month.

POTATO AND LENTIL STEW

If you prefer a creamier stew, try using red lentils instead of green because they break down much faster.

INGREDIENTS

Serves 6

2 tablespoons olive oil

1 onion, diced

2 carrots, sliced

2 stalks celery, chopped

3 cloves garlic, minced

½ pound potatoes, chopped into bite-size pieces

1 pound dried green lentils

4 cups water

4 cups Vegetable Broth (this chapter)

1 tablespoon soy sauce

1 bay leaf

½ teaspoon salt

⅛ teaspoon black pepper

1. Add the olive oil to the slow cooker and sauté the onion, carrot, and celery on medium-high heat for 3–5 minutes. Add the garlic and sauté for 1 minute more.

2. Add the rest of the ingredients and cook on low heat for 6 hours. Remove bay leaf before serving.

FALL PUMPKIN STEW

Have some festive fun by serving this soup in small, hollowed-out pumpkins.

INGREDIENTS

Serves 6

3 tablespoons vegan margarine

1 onion, diced

2 carrots, sliced

2 stalks celery, chopped

3 cloves garlic, minced

1 pumpkin, rind and seeds removed,
    flesh cut into ½" chunks

2 sweet potatoes, cut into bite-size pieces

1 (14-ounce) can diced tomatoes

4 cups Vegetable Broth (this chapter)

1 tablespoon soy sauce

1 bay leaf

1 teaspoon dried thyme

¼ teaspoon salt

1. Add the vegan margarine to the slow cooker and sauté the onion, carrots, and celery on medium-high heat for 3–5 minutes. Add the garlic and sauté for 1 minute more.

2. Add the rest of the ingredients and cook on low heat 6 hours. Remove bay leaf before serving.

CURRIED SEITAN STEW

Adding a small amount of soy sauce to a curry dish gives it a richness that is normally achieved with fish sauce in recipes that aren't vegan.

INGREDIENTS

Serves 4

2 tablespoons olive oil

½ onion, chopped

2 cloves garlic, minced

1 teaspoon fresh ginger, minced

2 tablespoons panang curry paste

1 teaspoon paprika

1 teaspoon sugar

½ teaspoon cayenne pepper

1 teaspoon soy sauce

1 (14-ounce) can coconut milk

3 cups Vegetable Broth (this chapter)

2 cups seitan, cubed

½ teaspoon salt

¼ teaspoon pepper

¼ cup cilantro, chopped

1. In a 4-quart slow cooker, add all ingredients except the cilantro. Cover, and cook on low heat for 4 hours.

2. Garnish with cilantro before serving.

SEITAN BOURGUIGNONNE

Better Than Bouillon No Beef Base is a good vegan alternative to beef stock.

INGREDIENTS

Serves 6

2 tablespoons olive oil

1 pound cooked seitan, cut into 2" cubes

2 carrots, sliced

1 onion, sliced

1 teaspoon salt

2 tablespoons flour

2 cups red wine

2 cups vegan beef stock

1 tablespoon tomato paste

2 cloves garlic, minced

½ teaspoon dried thyme

1 bay leaf

¼ teaspoon pepper

1 tablespoon vegan margarine

18 whole pearl onions, peeled

2 cups button mushrooms, sliced

1. Heat the olive oil in a sauté pan over medium heat. Sauté the seitan, carrots, and onion until soft, about 7 minutes. Stir in the salt and flour.

2. In a 4-quart slow cooker, add the vegetables and roux. Whisk in the red wine and vegan beef stock, then add all remaining ingredients.

3. Cover, and cook over low heat for 6–8 hours. Remove bay leaf before serving.

Seitan

Seitan is made from wheat gluten and is often used as a vegetarian substitute for all types of meat. It's one of the easiest meat substitutes to cook with at home; see Chapter 12 for more recipes.

WINTER SEITAN STEW

If you're used to a "meat and potatoes" kind of diet, this hearty seitan and potato stew ought to become a favorite.

INGREDIENTS
Serves 6

2 cups chopped seitan

1 onion, chopped

2 carrots, chopped

2 stalks celery, chopped

2 tablespoons olive oil

4 cups Vegetable Broth (this chapter)

2 potatoes, chopped

½ teaspoon sage

½ teaspoon rosemary

½ teaspoon thyme

2 tablespoons cornstarch

⅓ cup water

Salt and pepper to taste

1. In a large soup pot, heat seitan, onion, carrots, and celery in olive oil for 4–5 minutes, stirring frequently, until seitan is lightly browned.

2. Add Vegetable Broth and potatoes and bring to a boil. Reduce to a simmer, add spices, and cover. Allow to cook for 25–30 minutes until potatoes are soft.

3. In a small bowl, whisk together cornstarch and water. Add to soup, stirring to combine.

4. Cook, uncovered, for another 5–7 minutes until stew has thickened.

5. Season generously with salt and pepper to taste.

SUCCOTASH STEW

Try adding chopped okra to this versatile Southern stew.

INGREDIENTS

Serves 6

1 pound dry lima beans

8 cups water

2 (14-ounce) cans corn, drained

2 (14-ounce) cans diced tomatoes

2 bay leaves

1 teaspoon dried thyme

1 teaspoon dried oregano

¼ teaspoon cayenne pepper

¼ teaspoon salt

⅛ teaspoon black pepper

1. Place the dry lima beans and 7 cups water in a 4-quart slow cooker, cover, and cook on high heat for 4 hours. Drain the lima beans.

2. Place the drained lima beans, 1 cup water, corn, tomatoes, bay leaves, thyme, oregano, cayenne pepper, salt, and black pepper in the slow cooker and cook on low heat for 4 hours. Remove bay leaves before serving.

SUPER GREENS STEW

Kale and Swiss chard can hold up during long cooking times, but a more delicate green, such as spinach, would break down more.

INGREDIENTS

Serves 6

2 cups chopped kale

2 cups chopped Swiss chard

1 (15-ounce) can chickpeas, drained

¼ onion, diced

1 carrot, peeled and sliced

2 cloves garlic, minced

6 cups Vegetable Broth (this chapter)

1½ teaspoons salt

½ teaspoon pepper

1 sprig rosemary

½ teaspoon dried marjoram

In a 4-quart slow cooker, add all ingredients. Cover, and cook on low heat for 6 hours.

SWEET POTATO AND CRANBERRY STEW

You can call it "Thanksgiving in a bowl" because this spiced stew is loaded with holiday flavors such as sweet potato, cranberry, cinnamon, and nutmeg.

INGREDIENTS

Serves 6

2 tablespoons olive oil

1 onion, chopped

3 cloves garlic, minced

2 teaspoons turmeric

1 teaspoon curry powder

1 teaspoon cumin

1 teaspoon cinnamon

¼ teaspoon nutmeg

4 sweet potatoes, peeled and cut into bite-size cubes

2 cups frozen cranberries

6 cups Vegetable Broth (this chapter)

½ teaspoon salt

⅛ teaspoon black pepper

1. Add the olive oil to the slow cooker and sauté the onion on medium heat for 4–5 minutes. Add the garlic and sauté for 1 minute more.

2. Add the rest of the ingredients and cook on low heat for 6 hours.

CHILIES

ACORN SQUASH CHILI

Acorn squash keeps its shape in this chili, giving it a chunky texture.

INGREDIENTS

Serves 8

2 cups acorn squash, cubed

2 (15-ounce) cans petite diced tomatoes

2 stalks celery, diced

1 medium onion, diced

3 cloves garlic, minced

2 carrots, diced

1 teaspoon mesquite liquid smoke

2 teaspoons hot sauce

1 teaspoon chili powder

1 teaspoon paprika

1 teaspoon oregano

1 teaspoon smoked paprika

1 (15-ounce) can kidney beans, drained and rinsed

1 (15-ounce) can cannellini beans, drained and rinsed

1 cup fresh corn kernels

1. In a 4-quart slow cooker, add all ingredients except the corn. Cover, and cook for 8 hours on low.

2. Add the corn and stir. Cover, and continue to cook on low for ½ hour. Stir before serving.

BLACK BEAN AND BUTTERNUT SQUASH CHILI

Squash is an excellent addition to vegetarian chili in this Southwestern-style dish.

INGREDIENTS

Serves 4

1 onion, chopped

3 cloves garlic, minced

2 tablespoons oil

1 medium butternut squash, chopped into chunks

2 (15-ounce) cans black beans, drained

1 (28-ounce) can stewed or diced tomatoes, undrained

¾ cup water or Vegetable Broth (this chapter)

1 tablespoon chili powder

1 teaspoon cumin

¼ teaspoon cayenne pepper, or to taste

½ teaspoon salt

2 tablespoons chopped fresh cilantro (optional)

1. In a large stockpot, sauté onion and garlic in oil until soft, about 4 minutes.

2. Reduce heat and add remaining ingredients except cilantro.

3. Cover, and simmer for 25 minutes. Uncover, and simmer another 5 minutes. Top with fresh cilantro just before serving.

BLACK BEAN, CORN, AND FRESH TOMATO CHILI

Tofutti makes a delicious nondairy sour cream called Sour Supreme, and it can be found in some national grocery store chains.

INGREDIENTS

Serves 4

1 red onion, diced

1 jalapeño, seeded and minced

3 cloves garlic, minced

1 (15-ounce) can black beans, drained

1 (15-ounce) can corn, drained

3 tablespoons chili powder

1 tablespoon paprika

1 teaspoon dried oregano

1 teaspoon ground cumin

½ teaspoon chipotle powder

2 cups Vegetable Broth (this chapter)

½ teaspoon salt

¼ teaspoon black pepper

2 cups tomatoes, diced

¼ cup cilantro, chopped

4 tablespoons vegan sour cream

1. In a 4-quart slow cooker, add all ingredients except tomatoes, cilantro, and sour cream. Cover, and cook on low heat for 5 hours.

2. When the chili is done cooking, mix in the tomatoes and garnish with the cilantro. Top with vegan sour cream.

CHILI CON "CARNE"

Try Boca Ground Crumbles in this fast recipe as a vegan alternative to ground beef.

INGREDIENTS

Serves 4

½ cup onion, diced

½ cup bell pepper, diced

1 (12-ounce) package frozen veggie burger crumbles

2 cloves garlic, minced

1 (15-ounce) can kidney beans, rinsed and drained

2 cups Vegetable Broth (this chapter)

1 tablespoon chili powder

½ tablespoon chipotle powder

½ tablespoon cumin

1 teaspoon thyme

1 tablespoon oregano

2 cups fresh tomatoes, diced

1 tablespoon tomato paste

1 tablespoon cider vinegar

1 teaspoon salt

In a 4-quart slow cooker, add all ingredients. Cover, and cook on low heat for 5 hours.

Vegan Beef

In addition to Boca Ground Crumbles, there are other types of vegan ground beef on the market. Try Gimme Lean Ground Beef Style, Match Ground Beef, or TVP.

CINCINNATI CHILI

Cincinnati chili is native to the state of Ohio and is typically eaten over spaghetti or on hot dogs.

INGREDIENTS

Serves 4

1 onion, chopped

1 (12-ounce) package frozen veggie burger crumbles

3 cloves garlic, minced

1 cup tomato sauce

1 cup water

2 tablespoons red wine vinegar

2 tablespoons chili powder

½ teaspoon cumin

½ teaspoon ground cinnamon

½ teaspoon paprika

½ teaspoon ground allspice

1 tablespoon light brown sugar

1 tablespoon unsweetened cocoa powder

1 teaspoon hot pepper sauce

16 ounces cooked spaghetti

Vegan cheese (optional)

Additional chopped onion for topping (optional)

Pinto beans (optional)

1. In a 4-quart slow cooker, add all ingredients except the spaghetti and optional ingredients. Cover, and cook on low heat for 5 hours.

2. Serve the chili over the spaghetti and top with vegan cheese, onions, and/or pinto beans if desired.

Ways to Serve

Cincinnati chili is known for being served up to five ways: two-way means chili and spaghetti; three-way means chili, spaghetti, and vegan Cheddar cheese; four-way means chili, spaghetti, vegan cheese, and onions or pinto beans; and five-way means all of the above!

FAJITA CHILI

Recreate the flavor of sizzling restaurant fajitas in your own home!

INGREDIENTS

Serves 6

1 red onion, diced

1 jalapeño, seeded and minced

3 cloves garlic, minced

1 (15-ounce) can black beans, drained

1 (15-ounce) can diced tomatoes, drained

1 (7-ounce) package Gardein Chick'n Strips, cut into bite-size pieces

2 cups Vegetable Broth (this chapter)

2 teaspoons chili powder

1 teaspoon sugar

1 teaspoon paprika

¼ teaspoon garlic powder

¼ teaspoon cayenne pepper

¼ teaspoon cumin

1 teaspoon salt

¼ teaspoon black pepper

In a 4-quart slow cooker, add all ingredients. Cover, and cook on low heat for 5 hours.

Simplify This Recipe

One way to simplify this recipe is to use a packet of fajita seasoning (sold in the international aisle in many stores) in place of the chili powder, sugar, paprika, garlic powder, cayenne pepper, cumin, salt, and black pepper.

FIVE-PEPPER CHILI

Sound the alarm! This chili will set mouths aflame.

INGREDIENTS

Serves 8

1 onion, diced

1 jalapeño, seeded and minced

1 habanero pepper, seeded and minced

1 bell pepper, diced

1 poblano pepper, seeded and diced

2 cloves garlic, minced

2 (15-ounce) cans crushed tomatoes

2 cups fresh tomatoes, diced

2 tablespoons chili powder

1 tablespoon cumin

½ tablespoon cayenne pepper

⅛ cup vegan Worcestershire sauce

2 (15-ounce) cans pinto beans

1 teaspoon salt

¼ teaspoon black pepper

In a 4-quart slow cooker, add all ingredients. Cover, and cook on low heat for 5 hours.

Hot, Hot, Hot

Peppers vary greatly with regards to heat and the Scoville scale was designed to measure this heat. Here are the peppers in this recipe, from mildest to hottest: bell, poblano, jalapeño, cayenne, habanero.

GARDEN VEGETABLE CHILI

A true garden vegetable recipe requires some flexibility, since all ingredients aren't available year-round, and you should use what's actually growing in your garden.

INGREDIENTS
Serves 8

1 large onion, diced

3 cloves garlic, minced

1 large green bell pepper, chopped

2 cups zucchini, chopped

1½ cups corn kernels

1 (28-ounce) can diced tomatoes

2 cups Vegetable Broth (this chapter)

1 (15-ounce) can kidney beans, drained

1 (15-ounce) can pinto beans, drained

1 (15-ounce) can cannellini beans, drained

2 tablespoons chili powder

1 teaspoon cumin

1 teaspoon dried oregano

1 teaspoon salt

¼ teaspoon black pepper

In a 4-quart slow cooker, add all ingredients. Cover, and cook on low heat for 6 hours.

Selecting What's in Season

In the summer, corn, green beans, and okra are in season and would be delicious additions to this recipe. In the winter, cauliflower, parsnips, and winter squash may be in season and would be good too.

LENTIL CHILI

Before using dried lentils, rinse them well and pick through to remove any debris or undesirable pieces.

INGREDIENTS

Serves 6

1 cup lentils, uncooked

1 onion, diced

3 cloves garlic, minced

4 cups Vegetable Broth (this chapter)

¼ cup tomato paste

1 cup carrots, chopped

1 cup celery, chopped

1 (15-ounce) can diced tomatoes, drained

2 tablespoons chili powder

½ tablespoon paprika

1 teaspoon dried oregano

1 teaspoon cumin

1 teaspoon salt

¼ teaspoon black pepper

In a 4-quart slow cooker, add all ingredients. Cover, and cook on low heat for 8 hours.

PUMPKIN CHILI

Pumpkin is typically complemented by sugar, cinnamon, and other earthy spices but it also works well with a dash of heat, like chili powder.

INGREDIENTS
Serves 6

2 tablespoons olive oil

1 onion, diced

2 (14-ounce) cans tomatoes

1 cup Vegetable Broth (this chapter)

1 pumpkin, rind and seeds removed, flesh cut into ½" chunks

1 (14-ounce) can white beans, drained

2 tablespoons chili powder

3 teaspoons cumin

1 teaspoon salt

½ teaspoon black pepper

1. Add the oil to the slow cooker and sauté the onion on medium-high heat for 3–5 minutes.

2. Add the rest of the ingredients and cook on low heat for 6 hours.

RED BEAN CHILI

In the United States, "red beans" most commonly refers to kidney beans.

INGREDIENTS

Serves 4

2 (15-ounce) cans red kidney beans, drained

½ cup onion, diced

2 cloves garlic, minced

2 cups Vegetable Broth (this chapter)

1 tablespoon chili powder

½ tablespoon chipotle powder

½ tablespoon cumin

½ tablespoon paprika

1 (15-ounce) can tomatoes, diced

½ teaspoon salt

¼ teaspoon black pepper

In a 4-quart slow cooker, add all ingredients. Cover, and cook on low heat for 5 hours.

The Benefits of Canned Tomatoes

In addition to being inexpensive and always available, canned tomatoes are higher in lycopene than fresh tomatoes, making them a great option for chili and stews.

SHREDDED "CHICKEN" CHILI

There are many vegan chicken substitutes on the market, but you can also use shredded seitan to replace the meat.

INGREDIENTS

Serves 4

½ cup onion, diced

½ cup bell pepper, diced

1 (7-ounce) package Gardein Chick'n Strips, shredded by hand

2 cloves garlic, minced

1 (15-ounce) can kidney beans, rinsed and drained

2 cups Vegetable Broth (this chapter)

1 tablespoon chili powder

½ tablespoon chipotle powder

½ tablespoon cumin

1 teaspoon thyme

1 tablespoon oregano

1 (15-ounce) can diced tomatoes, drained

1 tablespoon tomato paste

1 tablespoon cider vinegar

1 teaspoon salt

In a 4-quart slow cooker, add all ingredients. Cover, and cook on low heat for 5 hours.

SOUTHWEST VEGETABLE CHILI

Southwest cuisine is similar to Mexican food and includes a wide variety of peppers, such as the jalapeños, bell peppers, chipotle, and chili powder found in this recipe.

INGREDIENTS

Serves 4

1 (28-ounce) can diced tomatoes

1 (15-ounce) can red kidney beans

1 onion, chopped

1 green bell pepper, chopped

1 red bell pepper, chopped

1 zucchini, chopped

1 squash, chopped

¼ cup pickled jalapeños, chopped

⅛ cup chili powder

2 tablespoons garlic powder

2 tablespoons cumin

1 teaspoon chipotle powder

⅛ teaspoon dried thyme

¼ teaspoon black pepper

In a 4-quart slow cooker, add all ingredients. Cover, and cook on low heat for 5 hours.

SUMMER CHILI

This chili is full of summer vegetables, and you can add vegan chicken for a heartier dish.

INGREDIENTS
Serves 8

1 bulb fennel, diced

4 radishes, diced

2 stalks celery including leaves, diced

2 carrots, cut into coin-size pieces

1 medium onion, diced

1 shallot, diced

4 cloves garlic, sliced

1 habanero pepper, diced

1 (15-ounce) can cannellini beans, drained and rinsed

1 (12-ounce) can tomato paste

½ teaspoon dried oregano

½ teaspoon black pepper

½ teaspoon crushed rosemary

½ teaspoon cayenne

½ teaspoon ground chipotle

1 teaspoon chili powder

1 teaspoon tarragon

¼ teaspoon cumin

¼ teaspoon celery seed

2 zucchinis, cubed

10 campari tomatoes, quartered

1 cup corn kernels

1. In a 4-quart slow cooker, add the fennel, radishes, celery, carrots, onion, shallot, garlic, habanero pepper, beans, tomato paste, and all spices; stir. Cook on low for 6–7 hours.

2. Stir in the zucchinis, tomatoes, and corn. Cook for an additional 30 minutes on high. Stir before serving.

Campari Tomatoes
Campari is a variety of tomato that is grown on the vine and has a sweet, juicy taste. It is round and on the small side, but not as small as a cherry tomato.

SUPER "MEATY" CHILI WITH TVP

Any mock meat will work well in a vegetarian chili, but TVP is easy to keep on hand and very inexpensive. This is more of a thick, "meaty," Texas chili than a vegetable chili, but chili is easy and forgiving, so if you want to toss in some zucchini, broccoli, or diced carrots, by all means, do!

INGREDIENTS
Serves 6

1½ cups TVP granules

1 cup hot Vegetable Broth (this chapter)

1 tablespoon soy sauce

1 yellow onion, chopped

5 cloves garlic, minced

2 tablespoons olive oil

1 cup corn kernels (fresh, frozen, or canned)

1 bell pepper, any color, chopped

2 (15-ounce) cans beans (black, kidney, or pinto)

1 (15-ounce) can diced tomatoes

1 jalapeño pepper, minced, or ½ teaspoon cayenne pepper (optional)

1 teaspoon cumin

2 tablespoons chili powder

Salt and pepper to taste

1. Cover the TVP with hot Vegetable Broth and soy sauce. Allow to sit for 3–4 minutes only, then drain.

2. In a large soup pot or stockpot, sauté the onion and garlic in olive oil until onion is soft, about 3–4 minutes.

3. Add remaining ingredients and TVP, stirring well to combine. Cover, and allow to simmer over low heat for at least 30 minutes, stirring occasionally.

4. Adjust seasonings to taste.

Rehydrating TVP

Most of the time, TVP needs to be rehydrated in hot water for 8–10 minutes in order to be fully rehydrated, unless it will be hydrated when cooking, such as in a soup with extra liquid. But the secret in this recipe is to only partially rehydrate the TVP, so that it absorbs some of the spices from the chili and the liquid from the tomatoes.

SWEET POTATO CHILI

Sweet potatoes are great sources of fiber and beta carotene, making this chili healthy and delicious.

INGREDIENTS

Serves 4

1 red onion, diced

1 jalapeño, seeded and minced

3 cloves garlic, minced

1 (15-ounce) can black beans, drained

1 sweet potato, peeled and diced

3 tablespoons chili powder

1 tablespoon paprika

1 teaspoon dried oregano

1 teaspoon ground cumin

½ teaspoon chipotle powder

1 (28-ounce) can diced tomatoes, drained

2 cups Vegetable Broth (this chapter)

¼ teaspoon black pepper

1 lime, juiced

¼ cup cilantro, chopped

1. In a 4-quart slow cooker, add all ingredients except the lime and cilantro. Cover, and cook on low heat for 8 hours.

2. When the chili is done cooking, mix in the lime juice and garnish with the cilantro.

What Is Chili Powder?

Chili powder is made from grinding dried chilies, and may be created from a blend of different types of chilies or just one variety. The most commonly used chilies are red peppers and cayenne peppers.

TEN-MINUTE CHEATER'S CHILI

No time? No problem! This is a quick and easy way to get some veggies and protein on the table with no hassle. Instead of veggie burgers, you could toss in a handful of TVP flakes if you'd like, or any other mock meat you happen to have on hand.

INGREDIENTS

Serves 4

1 (12-ounce) jar salsa

1 (14-ounce) can diced tomatoes

2 (14-ounce) cans kidney beans or black beans, drained

1½ cups frozen veggies

4 veggie burgers, crumbled (optional)

2 tablespoons chili powder

1 teaspoon cumin

½ cup water

In a large pot, combine all ingredients. Simmer for 10 minutes, stirring frequently.

THREE-BEAN CHILI

Using dried beans will save you a little money on this recipe, but be sure to soak the beans overnight to save a little cooking time.

INGREDIENTS
Serves 8

1 (15-ounce) can pinto beans, drained

1 (15-ounce) can black beans, drained

1 (15-ounce) can great northern white beans, drained

1 onion, diced

3 cloves garlic, minced

3 cups Vegetable Broth (this chapter)

1 tablespoon chili powder

½ tablespoon chipotle powder

½ tablespoon cumin

½ tablespoon paprika

1 (15-ounce) can dice tomatoes

¼ teaspoon black pepper

In a 4-quart slow cooker, add all ingredients. Cover, and cook on low heat for 5 hours.

CHAPTER 7

VEGETABLES, STIR-FRIES, AND SIDES

ORANGE AND GINGER MIXED-VEGGIE STIR-FRY

Rice vinegar can be substituted for the apple cider vinegar if you prefer. As with most stir-fry recipes, the vegetables are merely a suggestion; use your favorites or whatever looks like it's been sitting too long in your crisper.

INGREDIENTS

Serves 4

3 tablespoons orange juice

1 tablespoon apple cider vinegar

2 tablespoons soy sauce

2 tablespoons water

1 tablespoon maple syrup

1 teaspoon powdered ginger

2 cloves garlic, minced

2 tablespoons oil

1 bunch broccoli, chopped

½ cup sliced mushrooms

½ cup snap peas, chopped

1 carrot, sliced

1 cup chopped cabbage or bok choy

1. Whisk together the orange juice, vinegar, soy sauce, water, maple syrup, and ginger.

2. Heat garlic in oil and add veggies. Allow to cook, stirring frequently, over high heat for 2–3 minutes until just starting to get tender.

3. Add sauce and reduce heat. Simmer, stirring frequently, for another 3–4 minutes, or until veggies are cooked.

Oodles of Noodles

When stir-frying a saucy veggie dish, you can add quick-cooking Asian-style noodles right into the pan. Add some extra sauce ingredients and ¼–⅓ cup of water. Add the noodles, stir up the sauce, reduce the heat so the veggies don't scald, and keep covered for just a few minutes.

MAPLE GLAZED ROAST VEGGIES

These easy roast veggies make an excellent holiday side dish. The vegetables can be roasted in advance and reheated with the glaze to save on time if needed. If parsnips are too earthy for you, substitute one large potato.

INGREDIENTS
Serves 4

3 carrots, chopped

2 small parsnips, chopped

2 sweet potatoes, chopped

2 tablespoons olive oil

Salt and pepper to taste

⅓ cup maple syrup

2 tablespoons Dijon mustard

1 tablespoon balsamic vinegar

½ teaspoon hot sauce

Extra salt and pepper (optional)

1. Preheat oven to 400°F.

2. On a large baking sheet, spread out chopped carrots, parsnips, and sweet potatoes. Drizzle with olive oil and season generously with salt and pepper. Roast for 40 minutes, tossing once.

3. In a small bowl, whisk together maple syrup, Dijon mustard, balsamic vinegar, and hot sauce.

4. Transfer the roasted vegetables to a large bowl and toss well with the maple syrup mixture. Add more salt and pepper to taste.

Root Haven

This tangy and sweet glaze will lend itself well to a variety of roasted vegetables and combinations. Try it with roasted Brussels sprouts, beets, baby new potatoes, butternut or acorn squash, or even with roasted turnips or daikon radish.

MOROCCAN ROOT VEGETABLES

The Moroccan Root Vegetables recipe is good served with couscous and a yogurt or vegan side salad.

INGREDIENTS

Serves 8

1 pound parsnips, peeled and diced

1 pound turnips, peeled and diced

2 medium onions, chopped

1 pound carrots, peeled and diced

6 dried apricots, chopped

4 pitted prunes, chopped

1 teaspoon ground turmeric

1 teaspoon ground cumin

½ teaspoon ground ginger

½ teaspoon ground cinnamon

¼ teaspoon ground cayenne pepper

1 tablespoon dried parsley

1 tablespoon dried cilantro

2 cups Vegetable Broth (Chapter 6)

1 teaspoon salt

1. Add the parsnips, turnips, onions, carrots, apricots, prunes, turmeric, cumin, ginger, cinnamon, cayenne pepper, parsley, and cilantro to a 4-quart slow cooker.

2. Pour in the Vegetable Broth and salt.

3. Cover, and cook on low for 9 hours, or until the vegetables are cooked through.

RATATOUILLE

Ratatouille made in the slow cooker comes out surprisingly crisp-tender.

INGREDIENTS
Serves 4

1 onion, roughly chopped

1 eggplant, sliced horizontally

2 zucchinis, sliced

1 cubanelle pepper, sliced

3 tomatoes, cut into wedges

2 tablespoons fresh basil, minced

2 tablespoons fresh Italian parsley, minced

¼ teaspoon salt

½ teaspoon freshly ground black pepper

3 ounces tomato paste

¼ cup water

1. Place the onion, eggplant, zucchinis, pepper, and tomatoes into a 4-quart slow cooker. Sprinkle with basil, parsley, salt, and pepper.

2. In a small bowl, whisk the tomato paste and water together. Pour the mixture over the vegetables. Stir.

3. Cook on low for 4 hours, or until the eggplant and zucchinis are fork-tender.

Cubanelle Peppers

Cubanelles look very similar to banana peppers and are similar in taste and heat, but they are two different varieties. Cubanelles can be mild to somewhat spicy and, like banana peppers, are often pickled.

SAUCY CHINESE VEGGIES WITH SEITAN OR TEMPEH

This is a simple and basic stir-fry recipe with Asian ingredients, suitable for a main dish. Serve over noodles or rice.

INGREDIENTS

Serves 6

1½ cups Vegetable Broth (Chapter 6)

3 tablespoons soy sauce

1 tablespoon rice vinegar

1 teaspoon minced ginger

1 teaspoon sugar

1 (18-ounce) block tempeh, cubed, or about 1 cup chopped seitan

2 tablespoons olive oil

1 red bell pepper, chopped

1 cup snow peas

½ cup sliced water chestnuts (optional)

¼ cup sliced bamboo shoots (optional)

2 scallions, sliced

1 tablespoon cornstarch

1. In a small bowl, whisk together the Vegetable Broth, soy sauce, rice vinegar, ginger, and sugar.

2. In a large skillet, brown the tempeh or seitan in olive oil on all sides, about 3–4 minutes.

3. Add bell pepper, snow peas, water chestnuts and bamboo shoots if desired, and scallions, and heat just until vegetables are almost soft, about 2–3 minutes, stirring constantly.

4. Reduce heat and add the Vegetable Broth mixture. Whisk in cornstarch. Bring to a slow simmer and cook until thickened, stirring to prevent lumps.

SAUCY VAISHNAVA VEGGIES

These simple, low-fat veggies will fill your kitchen with the smells and dreams of India as they simmer. Why not pick up a Bollywood movie to accompany your dinner?

INGREDIENTS
Serves 4

1 (28-ounce) can diced tomatoes, undrained

2 potatoes, chopped small

½ teaspoon chili powder

2 teaspoons curry powder

1½ teaspoons cumin

½ teaspoon turmeric (optional)

1 head cauliflower, chopped

1 carrot, diced

¾ cup green peas

¾ teaspoon crushed red pepper flakes

¼ teaspoon salt, or to taste

1. Combine the tomatoes, potatoes, chili powder, curry powder, cumin, and turmeric if desired in a large pot. Cover, and cook for 10 minutes.

2. Add chopped cauliflower, carrot, green peas, and red pepper flakes and cook, covered, for 15 more minutes until potatoes and vegetables are soft, stirring occasionally.

3. Season with salt, to taste.

Indian Vegan Options
In India, many vegetarians forswear eggs as well as onions and garlic for religious purposes, making Indian food an excellent choice for vegans. When eating at Indian restaurants, be sure to ask about ghee (Indian butter), which is a traditional ingredient, but easily and frequently substituted for with oil.

MARINATED ARTICHOKES

Marinated artichokes can be stored in the refrigerator for about a week or if you jar them, about two months.

INGREDIENTS

Serves 4

2 (9-ounce) boxes fresh artichoke hearts

½ cup olive oil

¼ cup cider vinegar

2 tablespoons lemon juice

3 bay leaves

1 teaspoon dried oregano

½ teaspoon salt

½ teaspoon crushed red pepper flakes

Combine all ingredients in a 2-quart slow cooker and stir well. Cover, and cook over low heat for 2 hours. Remove bay leaves before serving.

SESAME SOY ASPARAGUS AND MUSHROOMS

Fresh asparagus in season has such a vibrant taste, it needs very little enhancement. If you can't find fresh asparagus, don't bother trying this with the canned variety; it's not the same at all!

INGREDIENTS

Serves 4

1 pound fresh asparagus, trimmed and chopped

¾ cup chopped mushrooms

2 teaspoons sesame oil

1 teaspoon soy sauce

½ teaspoon sugar

2 tablespoons sesame seeds (optional)

1. Preheat oven to 350°F.

2. Place asparagus and mushrooms on a baking pan and roast for 10 minutes.

3. Remove pan from oven; drizzle with sesame oil, soy sauce, and sugar and toss gently to coat.

4. Roast in oven for 5–6 more minutes.

5. Remove from oven and toss with sesame seeds, if desired.

CITRUSY BEETS

Beets can be served as a warm side dish or a chilled salad over a bed of greens.

INGREDIENTS

Serves 4

12 baby beets, halved, ends trimmed

1 cup orange juice

Juice of ½ lime

¼ red onion, sliced

½ teaspoon pepper

Add all ingredients to a 2-quart or 4-quart slow cooker and cook on low for 4 hours.

BABY BOK CHOY

Dark, leafy bok choy is a highly nutritious vegetable that can be found in well-stocked groceries. Keep an eye out for light green baby bok choy, which is a bit more tender but carries a similar flavor.

INGREDIENTS

Serves 6

2 tablespoons soy sauce

2 tablespoons apple cider vinegar

2 tablespoons sesame oil

½ teaspoon garlic powder

1 teaspoon crushed red pepper flakes

3 heads baby bok choy, halved lengthwise

1. In a small bowl, whisk together all ingredients except the bok choy.

2. Place the bok choy in a 4-quart slow cooker and pour the soy sauce mixture over the bok choy. Cover, and cook on low heat for 3 hours.

GINGERED BOK CHOY AND TOFU STIR-FRY

Bok choy, sometimes called "Chinese cabbage," has deep significance in Chinese culture, where it symbolizes wealth.

INGREDIENTS

Serves 3

3 tablespoons soy sauce

2 tablespoons lemon or lime juice

1 tablespoon fresh ginger, minced

1 block firm or extra-firm tofu, well pressed

2 tablespoons olive oil

1 head bok choy or 3–4 small baby bok choys

½ teaspoon sugar

½ teaspoon sesame oil

1. Whisk together soy sauce, lemon or lime juice, and ginger in a shallow pan. Cut tofu into cubes and marinate for at least 1 hour. Drain, reserving marinade.

2. In a large skillet or wok, sauté tofu in olive oil for 3–4 minutes.

3. Carefully add reserved marinade, bok choy, and sugar, stirring well to combine.

4. Cook, stirring, for 3–4 more minutes, or until bok choy is done.

5. Drizzle with sesame oil and serve over rice.

It's Easy Being Green!

Learn to love your leafy greens! Pound for pound and calorie for calorie, dark, leafy green vegetables are the most nutritious foods on the planet! Try a variety of greens: bok choy, collard greens, spinach, kale, mustard greens, Swiss chard, or watercress. When you find one or two that you like, sneak it in as many meals as you can!

SESAME BOK CHOY

Mirin is a sweet rice wine that is commonly used in Asian recipes. Most recipes don't call for much because of the strong flavor but it shouldn't be skipped because it adds sweetness and depth to the dish.

INGREDIENTS

Serves 6

3 tablespoons sesame oil

1 tablespoon soy sauce

1 teaspoon mirin

1 clove garlic, minced

1 teaspoon lime juice

1 head bok choy, cut into 1" strips

1. In a small bowl, whisk together all ingredients except the bok choy.

2. Place the bok choy in a 4-quart slow cooker and pour the soy sauce mixture over the bok choy. Cover, and cook on low heat for 3 hours.

BASIC BRUSSELS SPROUTS

Overcooking Brussels sprouts is a common culprit for ruining the flavor. Be sure to cook until just done and don't use more liquid than is needed.

INGREDIENTS

Serves 6

1 pound Brussels sprouts, trimmed and halved

2 tablespoons vegan margarine

3 tablespoons water

½ teaspoon salt

¼ teaspoon pepper

Place all ingredients in a 2-quart slow cooker, cover, and cook on high heat for 2½ hours.

ROASTED BRUSSELS SPROUTS WITH APPLES

Brussels sprouts are surprisingly delicious when prepared properly, so if you have bad memories of being force-fed soggy, limp baby cabbages as a child, don't let it stop you from trying this recipe!

INGREDIENTS

Serves 4

2 cups Brussels sprouts, chopped into quarters

8 whole cloves garlic, peeled

2 tablespoons olive oil

2 tablespoons balsamic vinegar

¾ teaspoon salt

½ teaspoon black pepper

2 apples, cored and chopped

1. Preheat oven to 425°F.

2. Arrange Brussels sprouts and garlic on a single layer on a baking sheet. Drizzle with olive oil and balsamic vinegar and season with salt and pepper. Roast for 10–12 minutes, tossing once.

3. Remove tray from oven and add apples, tossing gently to combine. Roast for 10 more minutes or until apples are soft, tossing once again.

Reuse and Recycle!

Recycle this basic recipe by adding an extra garnish or two each time you make it: a touch of fresh rosemary, a couple of shakes of a vegan Parmesan cheese, or some chopped toasted nuts or vegetarian bacon bits for crunch. For a Thanksgiving side dish, toss in some rehydrated dried cranberries.

SLOW-COOKED CABBAGE

Cabbage is an easy and inexpensive side dish that goes well with barbecued seitan or tempeh.

INGREDIENTS
Serves 6

1 cup cabbage, shredded

½ white onion, sliced

4 cloves garlic, minced

2 tablespoons olive oil

½ teaspoon salt

¼ teaspoon pepper

Add all ingredients to a 6-quart slow cooker and toss. Cover, and cook over low heat for 4 hours.

In Season
Cabbage is at its peak during fall and winter months. That makes it a suitable addition to hearty dishes such as root-vegetable stews or potato dishes.

CARAMELIZED BABY CARROTS

Baby carrots have a natural sweetness when cooked, and this recipe turns them into a treat even the pickiest veggie-hater will gobble up.

INGREDIENTS
Serves 4

4 cups baby carrots

1 teaspoon lemon juice

2 tablespoons vegan margarine

2 tablespoons brown sugar

¼ teaspoon sea salt

1. Simmer carrots in water until just soft, about 8–10 minutes; do not overcook. Drain and drizzle with lemon juice.

2. Heat together carrots, margarine, brown sugar, and sea salt, stirring frequently until glaze forms and carrots are well coated, about 5 minutes.

COCONUT CAULIFLOWER CURRY

To save time chopping, substitute a bag of mixed frozen veggies or toss some leftover cooked potatoes into this tropical yellow curry recipe.

INGREDIENTS

Serves 4

¾ cup Vegetable Broth (Chapter 6)

1 cup coconut milk

1½ cups green peas

1 cauliflower, chopped

2 carrots, chopped small

2 teaspoons fresh ginger, minced

3 cloves garlic, minced

2 teaspoons curry powder

½ teaspoon turmeric

1 teaspoon brown sugar

¼ teaspoon salt

¼ teaspoon nutmeg

1 cup diced pineapple

2 tablespoons chopped fresh cilantro (optional)

1. Whisk together the Vegetable Broth and coconut milk in a large saucepan.

2. Add remaining ingredients except the pineapple and cilantro, stirring well to combine. Bring to a slow simmer, cover, and cook for 8–10 minutes, stirring occasionally. Add pineapple and heat for 2 more minutes.

3. Top with fresh cilantro if desired, and serve hot over rice or another whole grain.

INDIAN-SPICED CHICKPEAS WITH SPINACH (CHANA MASALA)

This is a mild recipe, suitable for the whole family, but if you want to turn up the heat, toss in some fresh minced chilies or a hearty dash of cayenne pepper. It's enjoyable as is for a side dish or piled on top of rice or another grain for a main meal.

INGREDIENTS

Serves 3

1 onion, chopped

2 cloves garlic, minced

2 tablespoons vegan margarine

¾ teaspoon coriander

1 teaspoon cumin

1 (15-ounce) can chickpeas, undrained

3 tomatoes, puréed, or ⅔ cup tomato paste

½ teaspoon curry

¼ teaspoon turmeric

¼ teaspoon salt

1 tablespoon lemon juice

1 bunch fresh spinach

1. In a large skillet, sauté onion and garlic in margarine until almost soft, about 2 minutes.

2. Reduce heat to medium-low and add coriander and cumin. Toast the spices, stirring, for 1 minute.

3. Add the chickpeas with liquid in can, tomatoes or tomato paste, curry, turmeric, and salt and bring to a slow simmer. Allow to cook until most of the liquid has been absorbed, about 10–12 minutes, stirring occasionally, then add lemon juice.

4. Add spinach and stir to combine. Cook just until spinach begins to wilt, about 1 minute. Serve immediately.

CAJUN COLLARD GREENS

Like Brussels sprouts and kimchi, collard greens are one of those foods folks tend to either love or hate. They're highly nutritious, so hopefully this recipe will turn you into a lover if you're not already.

INGREDIENTS

Serves 4

1 onion, diced

3 cloves garlic, minced

1 pound collard greens, chopped

2 tablespoons olive oil

¾ cup water or Vegetable Broth (Chapter 6)

1 (14-ounce) can diced tomatoes, drained

1½ teaspoons Cajun seasoning

½ teaspoon hot sauce (or to taste)

¼ teaspoon salt

1. In a large skillet, sauté onion, garlic, and collard greens in olive oil for 3–5 minutes until onion is soft.

2. Add water or Vegetable Broth, tomatoes, and Cajun seasoning. Bring to a simmer, cover, and allow to cook for 20 minutes, or until greens are soft, stirring occasionally.

3. Remove lid, stir in hot sauce and salt, and cook, uncovered, for another 1–2 minutes to allow excess moisture to evaporate.

How to Prepare Collards

Give your collards a good rinse, then tear the leaves off the middle stem. Fold or roll all the leaves together, then run a knife through them to create thin strips, similar to a chiffonade cut used for herbs. The stems can be added to a vegetable broth or your compost pile.

CHIPOTLE CORN ON THE COB

Corn husks can be dried out and reused as a tamale casing.

INGREDIENTS

Serves 6

6 ears corn, shucked

Water, as needed

3 tablespoons vegan margarine

½ teaspoon chipotle powder

½ teaspoon salt

1. Place the corn in a 4-quart slow cooker and cover with water until it is 1" from the top of the slow cooker.

2. Cook on high heat for 2 hours.

3. While the corn is cooking, combine the vegan margarine, chipotle powder, and salt in a small bowl. When the corn is done cooking, rub a small spoonful of the vegan margarine mixture on each cob and then serve.

CREAMED CORN

For this recipe, choose frozen corn that is free of salt or added flavors.

INGREDIENTS

Serves 4

1 (16-ounce) bag frozen corn kernels

½ cup unsweetened soymilk

¼ cup vegan margarine

½ teaspoon salt

¼ teaspoon pepper

1. Add all ingredients to a 4-quart slow cooker. Cover, and cook on high heat for 3 hours.

2. Allow to cool slightly, then pour ¼ of the corn into a blender and pulse 1–2 times. Return to the slow cooker and stir before serving.

CRANBERRY APPLE STUFFING

Why wait for Thanksgiving? Stuffing is a fabulous side dish anytime. All the fresh herbs will flavor your kitchen with a home-cooked and nostalgic aroma.

INGREDIENTS

Serves 6

3 tablespoons vegan margarine

1 yellow onion, diced

2 ribs celery, diced

⅔ cup sliced mushrooms

¾ teaspoon sage

¾ teaspoon thyme

½ teaspoon marjoram

12 slices dry bread, chopped into cubes

1 cup dried cranberries

1 apple, diced

½ cup apple juice

2 cups Vegetable Broth (Chapter 6)

Salt and pepper to taste

1. Preheat oven to 375°F.

2. In a pan, melt margarine over low heat and add onion, celery, and mushrooms, heating and stirring just until mushrooms and onion are soft, about 4–5 minutes. Add sage, thyme, and marjoram and heat 1 more minute.

3. Combine onion and celery mixture with bread, cranberries, apple, apple juice, and Vegetable Broth, adding just enough Vegetable Broth to moisten well. You may need a little more or less than 2 cups. Season generously with salt and pepper.

4. Transfer to a large casserole or baking dish and bake for 20–25 minutes.

For an Extra Moist and Sweet Stuffing

Rehydrate your dried cranberries first in juice. Simply cover them with apple, orange, or even pineapple juice and allow them to sit until fat and plumped, about 15 minutes. If you want to get fancy, use a fruit liqueur instead of juice for a subtly gourmet flavor.

FIERY BASIL AND EGGPLANT STIR-FRY

Holy basil, called tulsi, is revered in Vishnu temples across India and is frequently used in ayurvedic healing. It lends a fantastically spicy flavor, but regular basil will also do.

INGREDIENTS

Serves 3

3 cloves garlic, minced

3 small fresh chili peppers, minced

1 block firm or extra-firm tofu, pressed and diced

2 tablespoons olive oil

1 eggplant, chopped

1 red bell pepper, chopped

⅓ cup sliced mushrooms

3 tablespoons water

2 tablespoons soy sauce

1 teaspoon lemon juice

⅓ cup fresh Thai basil or holy basil

1. Sauté the garlic, chili peppers, and tofu in olive oil for 4–6 minutes until tofu is lightly golden.

2. Add eggplant, bell pepper, mushrooms, water, and soy sauce and heat, stirring frequently, for 5–6 minutes, or until eggplant is almost soft.

3. Add lemon juice and basil and cook for another 1–2 minutes, just until basil is wilted.

Types of Basil

Sweet Italian basil may be the most common, but other varieties can add a layer of sensually enticing flavor. Lemon basil is identifiable by its lighter green color and fresh, citrusy scent. For this recipe, look for spicy holy basil or Thai basil with a purplish stem and jagged leaf edge for a delightfully scorching flavor.

EGGPLANT CAPONATA

Serve this on small slices of Italian bread as an appetizer or use as a filling in sandwiches or wraps.

INGREDIENTS

Serves 8

2 (1-pound) eggplants

1 teaspoon olive oil

1 red onion, diced

4 cloves garlic, minced

1 stalk celery, diced

2 tomatoes, diced

2 tablespoons nonpareil capers

2 tablespoons toasted pine nuts

1 teaspoon red pepper flakes

¼ cup red wine vinegar

1. Pierce the eggplants with a fork. Cook on high in a 4- or 6-quart slow cooker for 2 hours.

2. Allow to cool. Peel off the skin. Slice each in half and remove the seeds. Discard the skin and seeds.

3. Place the pulp in a food processor. Pulse until smooth. Set aside.

4. Heat the oil in a nonstick skillet. Sauté the onion, garlic, and celery until the onion is soft, about 5 minutes.

5. Add the eggplant and tomatoes. Sauté 3 minutes.

6. Return to the slow cooker and add the capers, pine nuts, red pepper flakes, and vinegar. Stir. Cook on low 30 minutes. Stir prior to serving.

Capers

Capers are found on a flowering bush and the flower bud is what is commonly called the "caper." They are often pickled and used in a variety of sauces and salads.

EGGPLANT "LASAGNA"

This no-noodle dish makes for a hearty meal and is perfect served with a light side salad.

INGREDIENTS
Serves 8

2 (1-pound) eggplants

1 tablespoon kosher salt

2 teaspoons olive oil, divided use

1 medium onion, diced

3 cloves garlic, minced

1 tablespoon fresh, minced Italian parsley

1 tablespoon fresh, minced basil

1 (28-ounce) can crushed tomatoes

1 shallot, diced

4 ounces fresh spinach

1 tablespoon dried mixed Italian seasoning

¼ teaspoon salt

½ teaspoon freshly ground black pepper

30 ounces Tofu Ricotta (see recipe in sidebar)

1. Slice the eggplant lengthwise into ¼"-thick slices. Set aside.

2. Heat 1 teaspoon olive oil in a nonstick pan. Sauté the onion and garlic until just softened, about 1–2 minutes.

3. Add the parsley, basil, and crushed tomatoes. Sauté until the sauce thickens and the liquid has evaporated, about 20 minutes.

4. In a second nonstick pan, heat the remaining oil. Sauté the shallot and spinach until the spinach has wilted, about 30 seconds–1 minute. Drain off any extra liquid.

5. Stir the shallot-spinach mixture, Italian seasoning, salt, and pepper into the Tofu Ricotta. Set aside.

6. Preheat the oven to 375°F. Place the eggplant slices on baking sheets. Bake for 10 minutes. Cool slightly.

7. Pour ⅓ of the sauce onto the bottom of a 4-quart slow cooker. Top with a single layer of eggplant. Top with ½ of the cheese mixture. Add ⅓ of the sauce. Top with the rest of the cheese mixture.

8. Layer the remaining eggplant on top, then top with remaining sauce. Cover, and cook for 4 hours on low, then uncovered 30 minutes on high.

Tofu Ricotta

You can make your own Tofu Ricotta by crumbling one package of drained tofu, then adding 1 tablespoon lemon juice, 1 teaspoon salt, 1 teaspoon dried parsley, and ½ teaspoon pepper. Or you can use store-bought vegan ricotta.

SPICED "BAKED" EGGPLANT

Serve this as a main dish over rice or as a side dish as is.

INGREDIENTS

Serves 4

1 pound eggplant, cubed

⅓ cup onion, sliced

½ teaspoon red pepper flakes

½ teaspoon crushed rosemary

¼ cup lemon juice

Place all ingredients in a 1½- to 2-quart slow cooker. Cook on low for 3 hours, or until the eggplant is tender.

Cold Snap

Take care not to put a cold ceramic slow cooker insert directly into the slow cooker. The sudden shift in temperature can cause it to crack. If you want to prepare your ingredients the night before use, refrigerate them in reusable containers, not in the insert.

STUFFED EGGPLANT

This easy vegan dish is a complete meal in itself.

INGREDIENTS

Serves 2

1 (1-pound) eggplant

½ teaspoon olive oil

2 tablespoons red onion, minced

1 clove garlic, minced

⅓ cup cooked rice

1 tablespoon fresh parsley

¼ cup corn kernels

¼ cup diced cremini mushrooms

1 (15-ounce) can diced tomatoes

1. Preheat oven to 375°F.

2. Slice the eggplant in 2 equal halves, lengthwise. Use an ice cream scoop to take out the seeds. Place on a baking sheet, skin-side down. Bake for 8 minutes. Allow to cool slightly.

3. In a small skillet, heat the oil. Add the onion and garlic and sauté until softened, about 3 minutes.

4. In a medium bowl, stir the onion, garlic, rice, parsley, corn, and mushrooms. Divide evenly between the eggplant halves.

5. Pour the tomatoes onto the bottom of an oval 4- or 6-quart slow cooker. Place the eggplant halves side by side on top of the tomatoes. Cook on low for 3 hours.

6. Remove the eggplants and plate. Drizzle with tomato sauce.

CLASSIC GREEN BEAN CASSEROLE

Shop for a vegan cream of mushroom soup to use in your traditional holiday recipe, or try this easy homemade vegan version. Delish!

INGREDIENTS

Serves 4

1 (12-ounce) bag frozen green beans

¾ cup sliced mushrooms

2 tablespoons vegan margarine

2 tablespoons flour

1½ cups soymilk

1 tablespoon Dijon mustard

½ teaspoon garlic powder

½ teaspoon salt

¼ teaspoon sage

¼ teaspoon oregano

¼ teaspoon black pepper

1½ cups french-fried onions

1. Preheat oven to 375°F. Place green beans and mushrooms in a large casserole dish.

2. Melt vegan margarine over low heat. Stir in flour until pasty and combined. Add soymilk, mustard, garlic powder, salt, sage, oregano, and black pepper, stirring continuously to combine until thickened.

3. Pour sauce over mushrooms and green beans and top with french-fried onions.

4. Bake for 16–18 minutes until onions are lightly browned and toasted.

Cut the Fat

For a slightly healthier version, top your green bean casserole with bread crumbs, crushed crackers, or a vegan cornflake cereal instead of the crispy fried onions.

GARLIC AND GINGERED GREEN BEANS

Afraid of vampires? This garlicky recipe ought to scare them away.

INGREDIENTS

Serves 4

1 pound fresh green beans, trimmed and chopped

2 tablespoons olive oil

4 cloves garlic, minced

1 teaspoon fresh minced ginger

½ teaspoon crushed red pepper flakes

Salt and pepper to taste

1. Boil green beans in water for just 3–4 minutes; do not overcook. Or steam for 4–5 minutes. Drain and rinse under cold water.

2. Heat olive oil in a skillet with garlic, ginger, green beans, and red pepper flakes. Cook, stirring frequently, for 3–4 minutes until garlic is soft.

3. Taste, and season lightly with salt and pepper.

GREEN BEAN AMANDINE

Fresh green beans are so much tastier than the frozen or canned variety! Try preparing them with almonds and mushroom with this easy, rhyming Green Bean Amandine.

INGREDIENTS

Serves 4

1 pound fresh green beans, trimmed and chopped

2 tablespoons olive oil

⅓ cup sliced almonds

¾ cup sliced mushrooms

½ yellow onion, chopped

½ teaspoon lemon juice

1. Boil green beans in water for just 3–4 minutes; do not overcook. Or steam for 4–5 minutes. Drain and rinse under cold water.

2. In olive oil heat almonds, mushrooms, and onion over medium heat for 3–4 minutes, stirring frequently. Add green beans and lemon juice and heat for another 1–2 minutes.

LEMONY GREEN BEANS

This dish can be served warm or for a summery treat, chill for two hours and serve cold.

INGREDIENTS
Serves 4

¼ cup water

2 tablespoons olive oil

Juice of 1 lemon

½ teaspoons salt

1 pound green beans, trimmed

1. Add the water, olive oil, lemon juice, and salt to a 4-quart slow cooker and stir.

2. Add the green beans and toss until well coated. Cover, and cook over low heat for 2 hours.

How to Trim
Green beans have one tougher end and one pretty tapered end. To trim a pile of beans quickly, line up the beans with the tough ends all pointing in the same direction and use a large knife to cut them off all at the same time. Leave the pretty tapered end intact.

ROSEMARY-THYME GREEN BEANS

In this recipe, the slow cooker acts like a steamer, resulting in tender, crisp green beans.

INGREDIENTS
Serves 4

1 pound green beans

1 tablespoon fresh minced rosemary

1 teaspoon fresh minced thyme

2 tablespoons lemon juice

2 tablespoons water

1. Place all ingredients into a 2-quart slow cooker. Stir to distribute the spices evenly.

2. Cook on low for 1½ hours, or until the green beans are tender. Stir before serving.

WARM JICAMA SLAW

Jicama is a crunchy root vegetable that is typically served cold but also works well in warm dishes because it retains its crunchy texture.

INGREDIENTS

Serves 6

¼ cup lime juice

¼ cup water

¼ cup orange juice

2 tablespoons vegetable oil

1 teaspoon vinegar

1 teaspoon red pepper flakes

2 cups jicama, peeled and shredded

1 cup cabbage, shredded

1 cup carrots, peeled and shredded

1. Combine the lime juice, water, orange juice, oil, vinegar, and red pepper flakes in a small bowl and stir until well combined.

2. Add the jicama, cabbage, and carrots to a 4-quart slow cooker, add the liquid, and stir. Cover, and cook over low heat for 1 hour.

MEATLESS MOUSSAKA

If you get your eggplant at the supermarket and suspect that it's been waxed, peel it before dicing it and adding it to the slow cooker.

INGREDIENTS
Serves 8

¾ cup dry brown or yellow lentils, rinsed and drained

2 large potatoes, peeled and diced

1 cup water

1 stalk celery, diced fine

1 medium sweet onion, peeled and diced

3 cloves garlic, minced

½ teaspoon salt

¼ teaspoon ground cinnamon

Pinch freshly ground nutmeg

¼ teaspoon freshly ground black pepper

¼ teaspoon dried basil

¼ teaspoon dried oregano

¼ teaspoon dried parsley

1 medium eggplant, diced

12 baby carrots, each cut into 3 pieces

2 cups Roma tomatoes, diced

1 (8-ounce) package vegan cream cheese, softened

1. Add the lentils, potatoes, water, celery, onion, garlic, salt, cinnamon, nutmeg, pepper, basil, oregano, and parsley to a 4-quart slow cooker. Stir. Top with eggplant and carrots.

2. Cover, and cook on low for 6 hours, or until the lentils are cooked through.

3. Stir in the tomatoes and add a dollop of vegan cream cheese over lentil mixture. Cover, and cook on low for an additional ½ hour.

Traditional Moussaka

Moussaka is traditionally made with minced meat but you can easily veganize the Greek and Arabic dish by using an abundance of vegetables instead. It can be served either warm or cold.

MUSHROOM AND OLIVE BLEND

Try serving on top of toasted baguette slices or on pasta or as a savory side dish.

INGREDIENTS

Serves 6

2 tablespoons vegan margarine

1 clove garlic, minced

½ cup sliced shiitake mushrooms

½ cup sliced oyster mushrooms

½ cup chopped hen-of-the-woods mushrooms

¼ cup pitted and sliced kalamata olives

½ teaspoon salt

¼ teaspoon pepper

Add all ingredients to a 2-quart slow cooker, cover, and cook on low heat for 2 hours. Stir occasionally to make sure the margarine is coating the mushrooms.

Mushroom Varieties

Hen-of-the-woods mushrooms are also called maitake mushrooms, and grow in clusters. If you can't find this variety, you can substitute ½ cup more shiitake or oyster mushrooms.

CARAMELIZED ONIONS

Caramelized onions are a great addition to roasts, dips, and sandwiches.

INGREDIENTS

Serves 8

4 pounds Vidalia or other sweet onions

3 tablespoons vegan margarine

1 tablespoon balsamic vinegar

1. Peel and slice the onions in ¼" slices. Separate them into rings.

2. Place the onions into a 4-quart slow cooker. Scatter chunks of the vegan margarine over top of the onions and drizzle with balsamic vinegar. Cover, and cook on low for 10 hours.

3. If after 10 hours the onions are wet, turn the slow cooker up to high and cook uncovered for an additional 30 minutes, or until the liquid evaporates.

Storing Caramelized Onions

Store the onions in an airtight container. They will keep up to 2 weeks refrigerated or up to 6 months frozen. If frozen, defrost overnight in the refrigerator before using.

MANGO AND BELL PEPPER STIR-FRY

Add some marinated tofu to make it a main dish, or enjoy just the mango and veggies for a light lunch. Use thawed frozen cubed mango if you can't find fresh.

INGREDIENTS

Serves 4

2 tablespoons lime juice

2 tablespoons orange juice

1 tablespoon hot chili sauce

3 tablespoons soy sauce

2 cloves garlic, minced

2 tablespoons oil

1 red bell pepper

1 yellow or orange bell pepper

1 bunch broccoli, chopped

1 mango, cubed

3 scallions, chopped

1. Whisk together the lime juice, orange juice, hot sauce, and soy sauce.

2. Heat garlic in oil for just 1–2 minutes, then add bell peppers and broccoli and cook, stirring frequently, for another 2–3 minutes.

3. Add juice and soy sauce mixture, reduce heat, and cook for another 2–3 minutes until broccoli and bell peppers are almost soft.

4. Reduce heat to low and add mango and scallions, gently stirring to combine. Heat for just another 1–2 minutes until mango is warmed.

STUFFED BELL PEPPERS

The cuisine of Mexico inspired this version of stuffed bell peppers but you can prepare the versatile peppers with an Italian twist instead.

INGREDIENTS

Serves 4

1 cup crumbled soy chorizo

1 cup Roma tomatoes, diced

¼ teaspoon garlic powder

1 teaspoon chili powder

½ teaspoon salt

½ cup red onion, diced

3 cups plain dry bread crumbs

4 green bell peppers

½ cup shredded vegan Cheddar cheese

1. Combine all of the ingredients except the bell peppers and vegan cheese in a medium bowl and stir until well combined.

2. To prepare the bell peppers, cut the tops off of each and scoop out the pulp and seeds. Stuff each pepper with ¼ of the bread crumb mixture.

3. Arrange the bell peppers so they are standing upright in a 4-quart slow cooker. Sprinkle with the vegan cheese, cover, and cook on low heat for 4–6 hours.

"BAKED" POTATOES

This dish is so easy that it takes less than 5 minutes of prep time and is perfect for a busy morning.

INGREDIENTS

Serves 6

6 medium potatoes, stabbed with a fork

Wrap each potato with tin foil and place in the slow cooker. Cook on low heat for 8–10 hours, or until the potatoes are tender.

CHEESY PEASY POTATOES

Cheese, potatoes, and peas are a classic dinner combo! Use whatever variety of potato you like most, and if you don't like mushrooms, feel free to use cream of celery soup instead.

INGREDIENTS

Serves 4

8 cups potatoes, cubed

1 (14½-ounce) can vegan cream of mushroom soup

3 cups vegan "chicken" broth

2 cups frozen peas

1 cup chopped vegan "bacon"

1 cup shredded vegan Cheddar cheese

1 teaspoon salt

¼ teaspoon black pepper

Add all ingredients to a 4-quart slow cooker, cover, and cook on medium-high heat for 4–5 hours.

Vegan Bacon

There are different types of veggie bacon for sale in most major supermarkets but not all are vegan. One great vegan option is Lightlife Smart Bacon, or you can make your own with strips of tempeh.

DILL RED POTATOES

Fresh dill is the perfect herb to season a summer dish. If you can't find it in your supermarket, substitute with one tablespoon of dried dill.

INGREDIENTS

Serves 6

2 tablespoons extra-virgin olive oil

1½ pounds red potatoes

1 teaspoon salt

¼ teaspoon black pepper

2 tablespoons fresh dill, chopped

½ teaspoon lemon pepper

1. Add the olive oil, potatoes, salt, and pepper to a 4-quart slow cooker. Cover, and cook on low heat for 3–4 hours.

2. Remove the cover and mix in the dill and lemon pepper.

GERMAN POTATO SALAD

It's potato salad with a twist—this unique version has a bold, sweet and sour taste, and is served warm.

INGREDIENTS

Serves 6

¼ cup olive oil

1 onion, diced

2 tablespoons flour

⅓ cup vinegar

⅓ cup sugar

1 cup water

¼ cup whole grain mustard

3 pounds red potatoes, cut into ¼" slices

1 teaspoon salt

¼ teaspoon black pepper

1. Add the olive oil to a 4-quart slow cooker and sauté the onion on medium-high heat for 5 minutes. Mix in the flour to create a roux and then add the rest of the ingredients.

2. Cover the slow cooker and cook on high heat for 4 hours, or until the potatoes are tender. Serve warm.

HERBED POTATOES

Any combination of herbs will work in this potato dish. Rosemary, thyme, dill, and coriander are great alternatives.

INGREDIENTS

Serves 4

2 tablespoons olive oil

1 onion, diced

8 cups red potatoes, quartered

1 teaspoon dried oregano

1 teaspoon dried basil

1 teaspoon salt

¼ teaspoon black pepper

1. Add the olive oil to a 4-quart slow cooker and sauté the onion on high heat until translucent, about 3–5 minutes.

2. Add the remaining ingredients to the slow cooker. Cover, and cook on medium heat for 4 hours.

LEMON MINT NEW POTATOES

Potatoes are an easy standby side that goes with just about any entrée, and this version with fresh mint adds a twist to the usual herb-roasted version.

INGREDIENTS

Serves 4

10–12 small new potatoes, chopped

4 cloves garlic, minced

1 tablespoon olive oil

¼ cup chopped mint

Salt and pepper to taste

2 teaspoons lemon juice

1. Preheat oven to 350°F. Line or lightly grease a baking sheet.

2. In a large bowl, toss together the potatoes with the garlic, olive oil, and mint, coating potatoes well.

3. Arrange potatoes on a single layer on baking sheet. Roast for 45 minutes.

4. Season with salt and pepper and drizzle with lemon juice just before serving.

Got Leftovers?

Make a double batch to have "planned-overs." Turn this into a Greek-inspired potato salad for lunch the next day. Cool the potatoes, then combine with ¼ cup vegan yogurt, green peas, diced red onions or celery, and some extra fresh mint for garnish and flavor.

MEXICAN SPICE POTATOES

If you like things spicy, really kick it up by adding an extra teaspoon of cayenne to these potatoes!

INGREDIENTS

Serves 4

6 cups red potatoes, cubed

1 teaspoon chili powder

½ teaspoon sugar

½ teaspoon paprika

⅛ teaspoon cayenne pepper

⅛ teaspoon garlic powder

¼ teaspoon cumin

½ teaspoon salt

⅛ teaspoon black pepper

½ cup water

Add all ingredients to a 4-quart slow cooker. Cover, and cook on high heat for 4 hours.

POT ROAST–STYLE POTATOES

Add large pieces of chopped seitan to this dish to take it from pot roast–style to full-on veggie pot roast!

INGREDIENTS

Serves 6

1 onion, chopped

4 carrots, peeled and chopped

2 stalks celery, chopped

5 cloves garlic

5 medium potatoes, cut into 1" cubes

3 cups Vegetable Broth (Chapter 6)

1 tablespoon vegan Worcestershire sauce

1 teaspoon salt

¼ teaspoon black pepper

Add all ingredients to a 4-quart slow cooker, cover, and cook on low heat for 4–6 hours.

Traditional Pot Roast

A more traditional pot roast recipe would contain braised beef that is cooked for a long period of time over low heat. Veggies, such as carrots and potatoes, are typically thrown in the same pot and absorb the cooking liquid, which leads to their delicious flavor and soft texture. Vegan versions recreate the flavor nicely by adding vegan Worcestershire sauce to the broth.

POTATO HOT POT

This dish is a bit labor-intensive, but the taste will leave you saying that it was worth it!

INGREDIENTS
Serves 6

2 tablespoons olive oil

1 onion, diced

1 cup mushrooms, sliced

5 cloves garlic, minced

⅛ teaspoon salt

⅛ teaspoon black pepper

¼ cup vegan margarine

¼ cup flour

2 cups plain unsweetened soymilk

¼ cup nutritional yeast

1 tablespoon soy sauce

5 potatoes, peeled and thinly sliced

1. Add the olive oil to a sauté pan and sauté the onion, mushrooms, and garlic for 5 minutes. Add the salt and pepper to the mixture and set aside.

2. In another pan, melt the vegan margarine and stir in the flour to make a roux. Slowly add the soymilk until the sauce has thickened, stirring often. Mix in the nutritional yeast and soy sauce and set aside.

3. Grease the bottom of the slow cooker with olive oil and layer the potatoes. Then, pour the onion and mushroom mixture on top of the potatoes. Next, pour the nutritional yeast sauce on top of the mushroom mixture.

4. Cover the slow cooker and cook on low heat for 4 hours, or until the potatoes are tender.

British Cuisine
Potato hot pots are similar to scalloped potatoes but this dish hails from England. One of the main differences between scalloped potatoes and a hot pot is that hot pots can be more like a pie with a potato topping.

POTATO PICCATA

"Piccata" typically means a dish that contains butter, lemon, and herbs, but you can veganize it by replacing butter with vegan margarine. Italian parsley, capers, garlic, and shallots are also commonly used.

INGREDIENTS

Serves 4

2 tablespoons vegan margarine

1 onion, julienned

1 red bell pepper, sliced

4 russet potatoes, sliced

¼ cup Vegetable Broth (Chapter 6)

2 tablespoons fresh lemon juice

1 teaspoon salt

¼ teaspoon black pepper

¼ cup parsley, chopped

1. Add the vegan margarine to a 2-quart slow cooker and sauté the onion and bell pepper on high heat until they are golden brown, about 5–7 minutes.

2. Add the rest of the ingredients except the parsley. Cover, and cook on medium heat for 4 hours. Mix in the parsley.

Varieties of Garlic

Most people think of garlic as just "garlic," but there are actually two different subspecies—hard-neck and soft neck—and many different varieties. The type most commonly found in grocery stores is artichoke garlic, which is of the softneck variety.

POTATO RISOTTO

Finely diced potato replaces arborio rice in this spin on a classic. You can replace the spinach with peas if you like.

INGREDIENTS

Serves 4

2 leeks (white part only)

¼ cup olive oil

3 sprigs fresh thyme, chopped

3 pounds russet potatoes, peeled and finely diced

2 cups dry white wine

5 cups Vegetable Broth (Chapter 6)

1 teaspoon salt

¼ teaspoon black pepper

4 cups fresh spinach

1. Thinly slice the leeks crosswise into semicircles and rinse.

2. Add the olive oil to a 4-quart slow cooker and sauté the leeks on high heat until translucent, about 5–7 minutes.

3. Add the rest of the ingredients except the spinach. Cover, and cook on medium-high heat for 4 hours.

4. Mix the spinach into the risotto and continue cooking for 1 more hour.

POTATOES AND LEEKS

Nothing pairs better with potatoes than the buttery taste of leeks.

INGREDIENTS

Serves 6

2 tablespoons olive oil

2 leeks, diced

4 potatoes, cut into 1" chunks

½ cup Vegetable Broth (Chapter 6)

½ teaspoon salt

¼ teaspoon black pepper

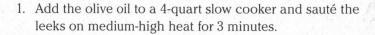

1. Add the olive oil to a 4-quart slow cooker and sauté the leeks on medium-high heat for 3 minutes.

2. Add the rest of the ingredients to the slow cooker, cover, and cook on high heat for 4 hours or until the potatoes are tender.

In Season

Leeks are in season during autumn months but in some parts of the country, you can buy them nearly year-round. Depending on when you buy them, the flavor and size may differ slightly.

POTATOES "AU GRATIN" CASSEROLE

You'll never miss the boxed version after trying these easy potatoes!

INGREDIENTS

Serves 4

4 potatoes

1 onion, chopped

1 tablespoon vegan margarine

2 tablespoons flour

2 cups unsweetened soymilk

2 teaspoons onion powder

1 teaspoon garlic powder

2 tablespoons nutritional yeast

1 teaspoon lemon juice

½ teaspoon salt

¾ teaspoon paprika

½ teaspoon pepper

¾ cup bread crumbs or french-fried onions (optional)

1. Preheat oven to 375°F.

2. Slice potatoes into thin coins and arrange half the slices in a casserole or baking dish. Layer half of the onions on top of the potatoes.

3. Melt the margarine over low heat and add flour, stirring to make a roux. Add soymilk, onion powder, garlic powder, nutritional yeast, lemon juice, and salt, stirring to combine. Stir over low heat until sauce has thickened, about 2–3 minutes.

4. Pour half of sauce over potatoes and onions, then layer the remaining potatoes and onions on top of the sauce. Pour the remaining sauce on top.

5. Sprinkle with paprika and black pepper and top with bread crumbs or french-fried onions if desired.

6. Cover, and bake for 45 minutes and then an additional 10 minutes uncovered.

POTATOES PAPRIKASH

This Hungarian classic is the perfect spicy side dish to serve with a seitan roast.

INGREDIENTS

Serves 8

1½ teaspoons olive oil

1 medium onion, halved and sliced

1 shallot, minced

4 cloves garlic, minced

½ teaspoon salt

½ teaspoon caraway seeds

¼ teaspoon freshly ground black pepper

1 teaspoon cayenne

3 tablespoons paprika

2 pounds red skin potatoes, thinly sliced

2 cups Vegetable Broth (Chapter 6)

2 tablespoons tomato paste

½ cup vegan sour cream

1. In a nonstick pan, heat the oil. Add the onion, shallot, and garlic and sauté for 1–2 minutes, or until they begin to soften. Add the salt, caraway seeds, pepper, cayenne, and paprika, and stir. Immediately remove from heat.

2. Add the onion mixture, potatoes, Vegetable Broth, and tomato paste to a 4-quart slow cooker. Stir to coat the potatoes evenly.

3. Cover, and cook on high for 2½ hours, or until the potatoes are tender.

4. Turn off the heat and stir in the vegan sour cream.

Hungarian Cuisine

Hungarian food is very aromatic and can be quite heavy. Its most famous dishes are goulash—a meat and vegetable soup or stew—and paprikash.

ROASTED GARLIC MASHED POTATOES

In the absence of milk and butter, load up your mashed potatoes with a full head of roasted garlic for a flavor blast.

INGREDIENTS

Serves 4

1 whole head garlic

2 tablespoons olive oil

6 potatoes, cooked

¼ cup vegan margarine

½ cup soy creamer or soymilk

Sea salt and pepper to taste

1. Heat oven to 400°F.

2. Remove outer layer of skin from garlic head. Drizzle generously with olive oil, wrap in aluminum foil and place on a baking sheet. Roast in oven for 30 minutes.

3. Gently press cloves out of the skins, and mash smooth with a fork.

4. Using a mixer or a potato masher, combine roasted garlic with potatoes, margarine, and creamer or soymilk until smooth or desired consistency.

5. Season generously with salt and pepper.

Vegan Mashed Potato Tricks

There's nothing wrong with just switching the butter and milk for vegan versions in your favorite potato recipe, but half a container of nondairy sour cream or cream cheese, a few teaspoons of fresh crumbled sage, or some chopped artichoke hearts will make your spuds come alive. Or simply add a shake of nutmeg or rosemary.

ROSEMARY FINGERLING POTATOES

Fingerling potatoes are small, long potatoes that look a little like fingers.

INGREDIENTS
Serves 6

2 tablespoons extra-virgin olive oil

1½ pounds fingerling potatoes

1 teaspoon salt

¼ teaspoon black pepper

2 tablespoons fresh rosemary, chopped

1 tablespoon fresh lemon juice

1. Add the olive oil, potatoes, salt, and pepper to a 4-quart slow cooker. Cover, and cook on low heat for 3–4 hours.

2. Remove the cover and mix in the rosemary and lemon juice.

Time Saver
To save on time when cooking potatoes, always cut them into the smallest pieces the recipe will allow and cook at the highest temperature. For this recipe, you can quarter the potatoes and cook on high heat.

SCALLOPED POTATOES

Silken tofu can be used as a substitute for vegan cream cheese if you have difficulty finding the product at your local grocery store.

INGREDIENTS

Serves 6

2 tablespoons olive oil

1 onion, diced

1 cup mushrooms, sliced

5 cloves garlic, minced

8 ounces Tofutti Cream Cheese

¼ teaspoon salt

¼ teaspoon black pepper

8 red potatoes, peeled and thinly sliced

1. Add the olive oil to a sauté pan and sauté the onion, mushrooms, and garlic for 5 minutes. Pour the vegetables into a bowl and mix in the cream cheese and salt and pepper.

2. Grease the bottom of the slow cooker with olive oil and layer it with ⅓ of the potatoes. Spread half of the cream cheese mixture on top of the potatoes. Next, make another layer of potatoes, 1 more layer of cream cheese mixture, and finally, 1 more layer of potatoes.

3. Cover the slow cooker and cook on low heat for 4 hours, or until the potatoes are tender.

Which Potato Is Best?

You could practically write a book on how to determine which type of potato is best suited for a particular recipe. To avoid any confusion, remember this general rule: Potatoes with a high starch content are better for recipes that call for mashing or whipping potatoes, and a lower starch content is preferred if you want a potato to hold its shape, like in this recipe.

SOUTHWESTERN CASSEROLE

Serve it up taco-style! You can scoop this casserole into warmed corn tortillas for an easy, handheld serving option.

INGREDIENTS
Serves 6

4 large red potatoes, diced

1 (15-ounce) can black beans, drained

1 large onion, diced

1 jalapeño, seeded and diced

1 tablespoon vegan margarine

1 (15-ounce) can diced tomatoes

4 ounces button mushrooms, sliced

¼ teaspoon salt

¼ teaspoon pepper

¼ cup shredded vegan Cheddar cheese

1. In a 4-quart slow cooker, stir all ingredients together except the vegan cheese.

2. Cover, and cook on low for 8–9 hours.

3. Stir in the cheese shortly before serving.

Vegan Cheddar Cheese
There are several varieties of vegan Cheddar cheese for sale in grocery stores around the country, but the one that melts, stretches, and tastes the best is Daiya Cheddar Style Shreds.

ULTIMATE MASHED POTATOES

These aren't called ultimate potatoes because of a long list of fancy ingredients, but because they get the classic combo of margarine, garlic, and milk just right!

INGREDIENTS
Serves 6

¼ cup vegan margarine

1 onion, small dice

5 cloves garlic, minced

8 medium potatoes, peeled and cut into 1" pieces

1½ cups water

½ cup unsweetened soymilk

1 teaspoon salt

¼ teaspoon black pepper

1. Add the vegan margarine, onion, garlic, potatoes, and water to a 4-quart slow cooker, cover, and cook on high heat for 4 hours, or until the potatoes are tender.

2. Add the rest of the ingredients and mash with a potato masher until the desired consistency is reached.

CHILLED POTATO SALAD

Vegenaise is the best vegan mayo option for this classic Southern dish.

INGREDIENTS

Serves 8

6 potatoes, peeled and cubed

2 stalks celery, chopped

½ cup sweet relish

¾ cup vegan mayonnaise

3 tablespoons mustard

1 teaspoon salt

¼ teaspoon black pepper

1. Add the potatoes to the slow cooker and add water to just cover the potatoes. Cover, and cook the potatoes on high heat for 4 hours, or until tender.

2. Drain the potatoes and allow them to cool completely before continuing.

3. In a large mixing bowl, add the cooled potatoes and remaining ingredients, then stir until just combined. Cover, and chill for 2 hours before serving.

BAKED SWEET POTATO FRIES

Brown sugar adds a sweet touch to these yummy sweet potato fries. If you like your fries with a kick, add some crushed red pepper flakes or a dash of cayenne pepper to the mix.

INGREDIENTS

Serves 3

2 large sweet potatoes, sliced into fries

2 tablespoons olive oil

¼ teaspoon garlic powder

½ teaspoon paprika

½ teaspoon brown sugar

½ teaspoon chili powder

¼ teaspoon sea salt

1. Preheat oven to 400°F.

2. Spread sweet potatoes on a large baking sheet and drizzle with olive oil, tossing gently to coat.

3. In a small bowl, combine remaining ingredients. Sprinkle over potatoes, coating evenly and tossing as needed.

4. Bake in oven for 10 minutes, turning once. Taste, and sprinkle with a bit more sea salt if needed.

CANDIED APPLE AND SWEET POTATO SALAD

If you're looking to add texture and protein to this salad, try tossing in a handful of toasted and chopped walnuts.

INGREDIENTS

Serves 6

4 sweet potatoes, peeled and cut into 1" pieces

2 green apples, peeled and diced

1 cup apple juice

1 teaspoon cinnamon

⅛ cup brown sugar

½ orange, peel grated

½ lemon, peel grated

½ cup raisins

Add all the ingredients to a slow cooker, cover, and cook on high for 3–4 hours, or until the sweet potatoes are tender.

GINGERED AND PRALINED SWEET POTATOES

Keep this recipe handy during the holiday season. Who needs marshmallows anyway?

INGREDIENTS

Serves 4

4 sweet potatoes, baked

¼ cup soy creamer or soymilk

¼ cup orange juice

½ teaspoon salt

½ cup chopped pecans

2 tablespoons vegan margarine

⅓ cup maple syrup

⅓ cup flour

⅓ cup crystallized (candied) ginger

1. Preheat oven to 350°F.

2. Mash together the sweet potatoes, soy creamer or soymilk, orange juice, and salt until smooth and creamy. Transfer to a lightly greased casserole dish.

3. In a small bowl, combine together the remaining ingredients, and spread over the top of the sweet potatoes.

4. Bake for 30 minutes.

Why Aren't Marshmallows Vegan?

They aren't even technically vegetarian! Marshmallows contain gelatin, which is extracted from boiled animal bones or hides. Online specialty stores and some natural foods stores may stock vegan marshmallows, but candied ginger adds an elegant twist to this holiday favorite!

SWEET POTATO CASSEROLE

If you'd like to use fresh sweet potatoes in this casserole, steam or roast them before using in the dish.

INGREDIENTS
Serves 4

2 (18-ounce) cans sweet potatoes, drained and slightly mashed

1 cup unsweetened soymilk

½ cup vegan margarine, melted

½ cup white sugar

1 teaspoon cinnamon

½ teaspoon nutmeg

½ cup pecans, chopped

½ cup brown sugar

2 tablespoons flour

1. Add the mashed sweet potatoes, soymilk, ¼ cup of vegan margarine, sugar, cinnamon, and nutmeg to a 4-quart slow cooker.

2. In a bowl, mix the pecans, brown sugar, flour, and remaining ¼ cup of vegan margarine.

3. Pour the mixture over the top of the casserole. Cover, and cook on low heat for 3–4 hours.

PARSNIP PURÉE

Parsnips are long white root vegetables related to carrots. Due to the starchiness of their texture, they can frequently be used in place of potatoes.

INGREDIENTS
Serves 6

5 medium parsnips, peeled and chopped

½ cup Vegetable Broth (Chapter 6)

½ cup unsweetened soymilk

1 teaspoon salt

1 tablespoon vegan margarine

1. Add the parsnips, Vegetable Broth, soymilk, and salt to a 4-quart slow cooker, cover, and cook over low heat for 4 hours.

2. Allow the parsnips to cool slightly, then use an immersion blender to process, or use a blender or food processor and blend in batches.

3. Return to the slow cooker, add the vegan margarine, and heat until melted.

SWEET PINEAPPLE CABBAGE STIR-FRY

Toss in a can of pineapple for the last 1–2 minutes of just about any stir-fry recipe for a sweet treat, or try this recipe with a sweet and salty sauce.

INGREDIENTS
Serves 6

1 (15-ounce) can diced pineapple

2 tablespoons red wine vinegar

1 tablespoon soy sauce

1 tablespoon brown sugar

2 teaspoons cornstarch

¼ teaspoon crushed red pepper flakes

2 cloves garlic, minced

1 onion, chopped

2 tablespoons olive oil

1 head broccoli, chopped

1 head Napa cabbage or ½ head green cabbage, chopped

1 batch Easy Fried Tofu (Chapter 11), optional

1. Drain pineapple, reserving juice. Whisk together juice, vinegar, soy sauce, sugar, cornstarch, and red pepper flakes.

2. In a large skillet, heat garlic and onion in olive oil just until soft, about 3–4 minutes. Add broccoli, pineapple, and cabbage, stirring quickly to combine, and cook for another minute.

3. Reduce heat to medium and add pineapple juice mixture. Bring to a slow simmer and heat just until mixture has thickened, stirring frequently.

4. Stir in fried tofu if desired and serve over rice or whole grains.

LIME SOAKED POBLANOS

Simple and fresh, this easy recipe can be used as the filling for tacos or burritos, or as a topping on a nopalitos (cactus) salad.

INGREDIENTS
Serves 4

¼ cup lime juice

¼ cup water

2 cloves garlic, minced

2 tablespoons fresh cilantro, chopped

½ teaspoon salt

4 poblano peppers, seeded and sliced

Combine all of the ingredients in a 4-quart slow cooker and stir until well combined. Cover, and cook on low heat for 4 hours.

CREAMED SPINACH

Fresh spinach reduces greatly when cooked, so to get a bigger bang for your buck, use frozen spinach when possible.

INGREDIENTS
Serves 6

1 tablespoon vegan margarine

1 clove garlic, minced

1 tablespoon flour

1 cup unsweetened soymilk

½ teaspoon salt

½ crushed teaspoon red pepper

¼ teaspoon dried sage

1 (12-ounce) package frozen spinach, thawed

1. Melt the vegan margarine in a 2-quart slow cooker over medium heat. Add the garlic, and cook for 2 minutes before stirring in the flour.

2. Slowly pour in the soymilk and whisk until all lumps are removed.

3. Add all remaining ingredients. Stir, and cook over low heat for 1–2 hours.

Variations
You can simplify this recipe by going with a simple butter or margarine sauce that is flavored with salt, pepper, and sage or make this savory dish even richer by adding a sprinkling of vegan cheese such as Daiya Mozzarella Style Shreds.

CREAMED SPINACH AND MUSHROOMS

The combination of greens and nutritional yeast is simply delicious and provides an excellent jolt of nutrients that vegans need. Don't forget that spinach will shrink when cooked, so use lots!

INGREDIENTS

Serves 4

½ onion, diced

2 cloves garlic, minced

1½ cups sliced mushrooms

2 tablespoons olive oil

1 tablespoon flour

2 bunches fresh spinach, trimmed

1 cup soymilk

1 tablespoon vegan margarine

¼ teaspoon nutmeg (optional)

2 tablespoons nutritional yeast (optional)

Salt and pepper, to taste

1. Sauté onion, garlic, and mushrooms in olive oil for 3–4 minutes. Add flour and heat, stirring constantly, for 1 minute.

2. Reduce heat to medium-low and add spinach and soymilk. Cook uncovered for 8–10 minutes until spinach is soft and liquid has reduced.

3. Stir in remaining ingredients (nutmeg and yeast if desired) and season with salt and pepper to taste.

MASHED KABOCHA SQUASH

Kabocha is a type of Japanese squash that mashes very easily when cooked and becomes quite fluffy.

INGREDIENTS

Serves 6

1 kabocha squash, peeled and cubed

1 cup water

3 tablespoons vegan margarine

1 teaspoon salt

¼ teaspoon black pepper

1. Add all ingredients to a 6-quart slow cooker, cover, and cook over low heat for 6–8 hours.

2. Mash the squash using a fork or masher and stir until creamy.

SUMMER SQUASH CASSEROLE

The cornstarch, water, and soymilk act as the binding agent in this casserole and the nutritional yeast gives it a hint of cheesy flavor.

INGREDIENTS
Serves 8

2 tablespoons vegan margarine

½ white onion, diced

2 cloves garlic, minced

2 teaspoons cornstarch

2 tablespoons water

4 cups yellow squash, diced

½ cup button mushrooms, diced

1 cup unsweetened soymilk

¼ cup nutritional yeast

½ teaspoon salt

¼ teaspoon black pepper

30 Ritz crackers, crushed

1. Melt the vegan margarine in a 4-quart slow cooker over high heat. Add the onion and sauté for 3 minutes. Add the garlic and sauté for an additional minute. Reduce heat to low.

2. Combine the cornstarch and water in a small bowl and whisk until all lumps have been removed.

3. Add cornstarch mixture, squash, mushrooms, soymilk, nutritional yeast, salt, pepper, and half of the crackers to the slow cooker and stir until well combined. Top with the remaining crackers, cover, and cook on low heat for 4 hours.

Butter Crackers
Golden, round crackers are often called "butter" crackers but one of the most popular brands, Ritz, contains no butter at all. There are several vegan butter crackers available in stores. Just be sure to read the label before purchasing.

SUMMER SQUASH SAUTÉ

Green zucchini and yellow squash absorb flavors like magic, though little enhancement is needed with their fresh natural flavor. Toss these veggies with some cooked orzo or linguini to make it a main dish.

INGREDIENTS
Serves 2

1 onion, chopped

2 cloves garlic, minced

2 tablespoons olive oil

2 zucchinis, sliced into coins

2 yellow squash, sliced thin

1 large tomato, diced

2 teaspoons Italian seasoning

1 tablespoon nutritional yeast

2 teaspoons hot chili sauce (optional)

1. Sauté onion and garlic in olive oil for 1–2 minutes, then add zucchinis, yellow squash, and tomato. Heat, stirring frequently, for 4–5 minutes until squash is soft.

2. Season with Italian seasoning and heat for 1 more minute.

3. Stir in nutritional yeast and hot sauce if desired.

SWEETENED ROAST SQUASH

Naturally sweet squash is delicious in this simple, quick side. Serve as is, scooping out of the skin, or remove the soft flesh and give it a quick mash.

INGREDIENTS
Serves 4

1 butternut, acorn, or spaghetti squash

1 teaspoon sea salt

4 tablespoons orange juice

4 tablespoons maple syrup

Nutmeg or ginger to taste

1. Preheat oven to 400°F.

2. Cut squash into quarters and scrape out seeds. Place in a large casserole dish. Sprinkle each chunk of squash with a bit of sea salt, 1 teaspoon of orange juice, and 1 tablespoon maple syrup, then a shake of nutmeg or ginger.

3. Cover with foil and bake for 40–45 minutes until squash is soft, basting with any extra sauce once or twice.

Easy Roasted Squash Sides

Tossing squash in the oven couldn't be easier. A drizzle of olive oil and a dash of garlic powder, salt, nutritional yeast, and perhaps a touch of cayenne will also produce a satisfying roasted squash for a side dish you don't need to sweat over.

HERB-STUFFED TOMATOES

Serve these Italian-influenced stuffed tomatoes with a simple salad for an easy, light meal.

INGREDIENTS
Serves 4

4 large tomatoes

1 cup cooked quinoa

1 stalk celery, minced

1 tablespoon fresh garlic, minced

2 tablespoons fresh oregano, minced

2 tablespoons fresh Italian parsley, minced

1 teaspoon dried chervil

1 teaspoon fennel seeds

¾ cup water

1. Cut out the core of each tomato and discard. Scoop out the seeds, leaving the walls of the tomato intact.

2. In a small bowl, stir together the quinoa, celery, garlic, and spices. Divide evenly among the 4 tomatoes.

3. Place the filled tomatoes in a single layer in an oval 4-quart slow cooker. Pour the water into the bottom of the slow cooker. Cook on low for 4 hours.

STEWED TOMATOES

For an Italian variation, add basil and Italian parsley.

INGREDIENTS
Serves 6

4 cups Roma tomatoes, diced

1 tablespoon minced onion

1 stalk celery, diced

½ teaspoon oregano

½ teaspoon thyme

Place all ingredients into a 2-quart slow cooker. Stir. Cook on low up to 8 hours.

Tomato Varieties

Small tomatoes used in sauces, such as Roma tomatoes or cherry tomatoes, are best for this recipe. Avoid large tomatoes that are used for their large slices, such as beefsteak.

ROASTED GARLIC, ZUCCHINI, AND ONIONS

Roasting veggies brings out their natural flavors, so little additional seasoning is needed.

INGREDIENTS

Serves 4

6 whole cloves garlic

4 zucchinis, chopped

1 onion, chopped into rings

1 tablespoon balsamic vinegar

1 tablespoon olive oil

Salt and pepper, to taste

1 teaspoon fresh thyme

2 teaspoons nutritional yeast (optional)

1. Preheat oven to 400°F.

2. Arrange the garlic, zucchinis, and onions on a baking sheet. Drizzle with vinegar and oil and season with salt and pepper, tossing to coat well.

3. Roast in oven for 20–25 minutes, then toss with fresh thyme, nutritional yeast if desired, and additional salt and pepper to taste.

ZUCCHINI RAGOUT

A ragout is either a main-dish stew or a sauce. This one can be served as either.

INGREDIENTS

Serves 6

5 ounces fresh spinach

3 zucchinis, diced

½ cup diced red onion

2 stalks celery, diced

2 carrots, diced

1 parsnip, diced

3 tablespoons tomato paste

¼ cup water

1 teaspoon freshly ground black pepper

¼ teaspoon kosher salt

1 tablespoon minced fresh basil

1 tablespoon minced fresh Italian parsley

1 tablespoon minced fresh oregano

Place all ingredients into a 4-quart slow cooker. Stir. Cook on low for 4 hours. Stir before serving.

Saving on Herbs

The cost of herbs can add up quickly, but you can save a little money by shopping at an international farmers' market or buying a blend of spices (an Italian blend would work well in this recipe) instead of buying each individually.

CHAPTER 8

RICES AND WHOLE GRAINS

RICES

BAKED MEXICAN RICE CASSEROLE

A quick and easy side dish you can get into the oven in just a few minutes.

INGREDIENTS

Serves 4

1 (15-ounce) can black beans

¾ cup salsa

2 teaspoons chili powder

1 teaspoon cumin

½ cup corn kernels

2 cups rice, cooked

⅓ cup sliced black olives

½ cup grated vegan cheese (optional)

1. Preheat oven to 350°F.

2. Combine the beans, salsa, chili powder, and cumin in a large pot over low heat, and partially mash beans with a large fork.

3. Remove from heat and stir in corn and rice. Transfer to a casserole dish.

4. Top with sliced olives and vegan cheese if desired and bake for 20 minutes.

Is Your Soy Cheese Vegan?

Many nondairy products do actually contain dairy, even if it says "nondairy" right there on the package! Nondairy creamer and soy cheeses are notorious for this. Look for casein or whey on the ingredients list, particularly if you suffer from dairy allergies, and if you're allergic to soy, look for nut- or rice-based vegan cheeses.

CARIBBEAN RED BEANS AND RICE

Cook the beans from scratch and use the cooking liquid instead of the Vegetable Broth if you've got the time.

INGREDIENTS

Serves 4

3 cloves garlic

1 small onion, chopped

3 ribs celery, chopped

2 tablespoons chopped fresh parsley

2 tablespoons olive oil

½ teaspoon rosemary

½ teaspoon thyme

¼ teaspoon cloves

1 (15-ounce) can kidney beans, drained

3 cups Vegetable Broth (Chapter 6)

2 bay leaves

1½ cups rice, uncooked

Dash salt and pepper to taste

1. Use a food processor to process the garlic, onion, celery, and parsley until finely grated or minced.

2. Heat onion mixture in olive oil, stirring frequently, for a few minutes until soft. Add rosemary, thyme, cloves, and beans, stirring to combine well. Cook for a few more minutes until fragrant.

3. Reduce heat and add Vegetable Broth, bay leaves, and rice. Bring to a slow simmer, cover, and cook for 30 minutes.

4. Reduce heat to low, uncover, and cook for 10 more minutes, or until most of the liquid is absorbed.

5. Remove bay leaves before serving. Season to taste.

"CHEESY" BROCCOLI AND RICE CASSEROLE

If you're substituting frozen broccoli, there's no need to cook it first, just thaw and use about 1¼ cups. Serve with ketchup for kids.

INGREDIENTS

Serves 4

1 head broccoli, chopped small

1 onion, chopped

4 cloves garlic, minced

2 tablespoons olive oil

2 tablespoons flour

2 cups unsweetened soymilk

½ cup Vegetable Broth (Chapter 6)

2 tablespoons nutritional yeast

1 tablespoon vegan margarine

¼ teaspoon nutmeg

¼ teaspoon mustard powder

½ teaspoon salt

3½ cups rice, cooked

⅔ cup bread crumbs or crushed vegan crackers

1. Preheat oven to 325°F.

2. Steam or microwave broccoli until just barely soft; do not overcook.

3. Sauté onion and garlic in olive oil until soft, about 3–4 minutes. Reduce heat and add flour, stirring continuously to combine.

4. Add soymilk and Vegetable Broth and heat, stirring, until thickened. Remove from heat and stir in nutritional yeast, margarine, nutmeg, mustard powder, and salt.

5. Combine sauce, steamed broccoli, and cooked rice and transfer to a large casserole or baking dish. Sprinkle the top with bread crumbs or vegan crackers.

6. Cover, and bake for 25 minutes. Uncover, and cook for another 10 minutes.

CHINESE FRIED RICE WITH TOFU AND CASHEWS

On busy weeknights, pick up some plain white rice from a Chinese takeout restaurant and turn it into a home-cooked meal in a jiffy. Garnish with fresh lime wedges and a sprinkle of sea salt and fresh black pepper on top.

INGREDIENTS

Serves 3

2 cloves garlic, minced

1 (12-ounce) block silken tofu, mashed with a fork

3 tablespoons olive oil, divided

3 cups leftover rice, cooked

½ cup frozen mixed diced veggies

3 tablespoons soy sauce

1 tablespoon sesame oil

2 tablespoons lime juice

3 scallions (greens and whites), sliced

⅓ cup chopped cashews (optional)

1. In a large skillet or wok, sauté the garlic and tofu in 2 tablespoons of olive oil over medium-high heat, stirring frequently, until tofu is lightly browned, about 6–8 minutes.

2. Add remaining 1 tablespoon of olive oil, rice, and veggies, stirring well to combine.

3. Add soy sauce and sesame oil and combine well.

4. Allow to cook, stirring constantly, for 3–4 minutes.

5. Remove from heat and stir in remaining ingredients.

Quick Healthy Meals

Like stir-fries and an easy pasta recipe, fried rice is a quick and easy meal you can turn to again and again. The formula is always the same: rice, oil, and seasonings, but the variations are endless. Besides tofu, try adding tempeh, seitan, or store-bought mock meats to fried rice. Add kimchi for a Korean spice, or season with a mixture of cumin, curry, ginger, and turmeric for an Indian-inspired dish.

CUBAN BLACK BEANS, SWEET POTATOES, AND RICE

Stir some plain steamed rice right into the pot, or serve it alongside these well-seasoned beans.

INGREDIENTS

Serves 4

3 cloves garlic, minced

2 large sweet potatoes, chopped small

2 tablespoons olive oil

2 (15-ounce) cans black beans, drained

¾ cup Vegetable Broth (Chapter 6)

1 tablespoon chili powder

1 teaspoon paprika

1 teaspoon cumin

1 tablespoon lime juice

Hot sauce, to taste

2 cups rice, cooked

1. In a large skillet or pot, sauté garlic and sweet potatoes in olive oil for 2–3 minutes.

2. Reduce heat to medium-low and add beans, Vegetable Broth, chili powder, paprika, and cumin. Bring to a simmer, cover, and allow to cook for 25–30 minutes until sweet potatoes are soft.

3. Stir in lime juice and hot sauce, to taste. Serve hot over rice.

COCONUT RICE

Serve coconut rice as a simple side dish or pair it with spicy Thai and Indian curries or stir-fries.

INGREDIENTS

Serves 4

1 cup water

1 (14-ounce) can coconut milk

1½ cups white rice

⅓ cup coconut flakes

1 teaspoon lime juice

½ teaspoon salt

1. In a large pot, combine the water, coconut milk, and rice and bring to a simmer. Cover, and allow to cook 20 minutes, or until rice is done.

2. In a separate skillet, toast the coconut flakes over low heat until lightly golden, about 3 minutes. Gently stir constantly to avoid burning.

3. Combine coconut flakes with cooked rice and stir in lime juice and salt.

Toasted Coconut Flakes

Quickly toasting coconut flakes will help bring out their nutty bounty of flavor. Place the flakes directly onto a dry, ungreased skillet over low heat. Stirring constantly, heat the coconut just until you see the slightest bit of golden brown, then remove the pan from the heat. Use your toasted coconut to top vegan ice cream, cakes, or even a bowl of oatmeal or Maple Cinnamon Breakfast Quinoa (this chapter).

CRANBERRY APPLE WILD RICE

To speed up the cooking time, soak the wild rice for 15–20 minutes before boiling.

INGREDIENTS
Serves 4

1 rib celery, diced

1 red onion, diced

2 tablespoons olive oil

1 cup wild rice

3 cups water or Vegetable Broth (Chapter 6)

⅓ cup orange juice

½ cup dried cranberries or raisins

½ cup pine nuts or sliced almonds

2 scallions, chopped

1 apple, diced

Salt and pepper to taste

1. In a large soup pot or stockpot, sauté celery and onion in olive oil for 3–4 minutes until soft.

2. Reduce heat and add wild rice and water or Vegetable Broth. Bring to a simmer, cover, and cook for 30 minutes. Add orange juice and simmer for another 10–15 minutes, or until rice is cooked.

3. Remove from heat and add cranberries or raisins. Cover, and let sit for 5 minutes.

4. Toss with remaining ingredients and serve hot or cold.

A High-Protein Rice?
Wild rice is not actually rice, but rather a seed. With almost 7 grams of protein per cup when cooked, wild rice can be an excellent source of protein. Add ¼ cup wild rice per cup of white rice to any recipe that calls for regular white rice for an extra protein boost.

CURRIED RICE AND LENTILS

With no added fat, this is a very simple one-pot side dish starter recipe. Personalize it with some chopped greens, browned seitan, or a veggie mix.

INGREDIENTS
Serves 4

1½ cups white or brown rice, uncooked

1 cup lentils

2 tomatoes, diced

3½ cups water or Vegetable Broth (Chapter 6)

1 bay leaf (optional)

1 tablespoon curry powder

½ teaspoon cumin

½ teaspoon turmeric

½ teaspoon garlic powder

Salt and pepper, to taste

1. Combine all ingredients except salt and pepper in a large soup pot or stockpot. Bring to a slow simmer, then cover, and cook for 20 minutes, stirring occasionally, until rice is done and liquid is absorbed.

2. Taste, then add a bit of salt and pepper if needed. If used, remove bay leaf before serving.

Stuff It!
Rice makes excellent stuffing for poblano or green bell peppers. Carefully remove the tops of the bell peppers, or, for poblanos, slice down the middle. Fill with cooked curried rice and lentils, Mexican Rice with Corn and Peppers (this chapter) or leftover Spanish Artichoke and Zucchini Paella rice (this chapter) and bake at 375°F for 25 minutes or 15 minutes for poblano peppers.

GARLIC-PECAN BROWN RICE

Roasting garlic before using it in recipes brings out a whole new flavor. To enhance this dish even further, try toasting the pecans in a dry skillet for 3–4 minutes before adding to the slow cooker.

INGREDIENTS

Serves 4

1 head garlic

1 tablespoon olive oil

½ cup pecans, finely chopped

1 teaspoon dried parsley

¾ teaspoon salt

2 cups brown rice

3 cups water

1. Preheat the oven to 400°F. Cut the top quarter off the head of garlic, place in aluminum foil, and drizzle with the olive oil. Seal the aluminum foil at the top (like a small pouch) and cook for 30–45 minutes, or until soft.

2. Allow the garlic to cool completely, then remove each clove from the paper husk.

3. Place all of the roasted garlic and all remaining ingredients in a 4-quart slow cooker, cover, and cook on high heat for 2½–3 hours.

GREEK LEMON RICE WITH SPINACH

Greek "spanakorizo" is seasoned with fresh lemon, herbs, and black pepper. Serve with Lemon Basil Tofu (Chapter 11) for a citrusy meal.

INGREDIENTS
Serves 4

1 onion, chopped

4 cloves garlic, minced

2 tablespoons olive oil

¾ cup rice, uncooked

2½ cups water or Vegetable Broth (Chapter 6)

1 (8-ounce) can tomato paste

2 bunches fresh spinach, trimmed

2 tablespoons chopped fresh parsley

1 tablespoon chopped fresh mint or dill (optional)

2 tablespoons lemon juice

½ teaspoon salt

½ teaspoon fresh ground black pepper

1. Sauté onion and garlic in olive oil for just 1–2 minutes, then add rice, stirring to lightly toast.

2. Add water or Vegetable Broth, cover, and heat for 10–12 minutes.

3. Add tomato paste, spinach, and parsley. Cover, and cook for another 5 minutes, or until spinach is wilted and rice is cooked.

4. Stir in fresh mint or dill if desired, lemon juice, salt, and pepper.

HAWAIIAN PINEAPPLE AND MINT RICE SALAD

Pineapple and mint are a cooling combination, so this is perfect for a hot day.

INGREDIENTS

Serves 6

4 cups white rice, cooked

2 ribs celery, diced

1 cup diced pineapple (fresh or canned)

⅓ cup chopped macadamia nuts or cashews

¼ cup dried papaya or raisins (optional)

⅓ cup pineapple juice

2 tablespoons olive or safflower oil

2 tablespoons red wine vinegar

¼ cup toasted coconut flakes (see sidebar in Coconut Rice, this chapter)

2 tablespoons chopped fresh mint

1. Combine the cooked rice, celery, pineapple, macadamia nuts or cashews, and dried papaya or raisins if desired together in a large bowl.

2. In a separate small bowl, whisk together the pineapple juice, oil, and vinegar. Toss together with rice and coat well. Chill for at least 1 hour.

3. Gently toss with coconut flakes and mint just before serving.

INDIAN LEMON RICE PILAF

With an unexpected blend of flavors, lemon rice is a popular favorite to serve to the gods and their devotees in South Indian temples. Kick up the heat by adding a couple of green chilies, or if you can find them at an Indian grocer, heat some dried curry leaves with the mustard seeds.

INGREDIENTS

Serves 4

1½ teaspoons black mustard seeds

2 tablespoons olive oil

½ teaspoon turmeric

1 cup rice, uncooked

1¾ cups Vegetable Broth (Chapter 6) or water

½ cup frozen peas

2 tablespoons lemon juice

¼ cup yellow raisins

2 tablespoons scallions, chopped

2 tablespoons chopped fresh cilantro (optional)

1. Heat mustard seeds in olive oil over medium heat for about 1 minute.

2. Add turmeric and rice and stir well to combine. Toast rice, stirring, for 1–2 minutes until lightly golden brown.

3. Add Vegetable Broth or water and bring to a slow simmer. Cover, and allow to cook for about 15 minutes until rice is done.

4. Reduce heat to medium-low and add peas and lemon juice, cooking for another 1–2 minutes until peas are heated through.

5. Remove from heat and combine remaining ingredients.

INDONESIAN FRIED RICE (NASI GORENG)

The kids might like some diced veggie dogs in this recipe instead of or alongside the tempeh. Like any fried rice recipe, the vegetables you use are really up to you.

INGREDIENTS

Serves 6

2 teaspoons molasses

2 tablespoons soy sauce

1 block tempeh, cubed

1 onion, diced

3 cloves garlic, minced

1 small chili, minced

3–4 tablespoons vegetable oil or peanut oil

3 cups rice, cooked

1 tablespoon sesame oil

2 tablespoons ketchup

2 tablespoons hot chili sauce

2 scallions, chopped

1 carrot, sliced thin

1 red or yellow bell pepper, diced

Dash Chinese five-spice powder (optional)

1. Whisk together the molasses and soy sauce, and set aside.

2. In a large skillet, sauté the tempeh, onion, garlic, and chili in oil for a few minutes until tempeh is lightly browned. Add rice and sesame oil, stirring to combine.

3. Add remaining ingredients to molasses and soy sauce, and quickly stir to combine.

4. Cook for just a few minutes, stirring constantly, only until heated through.

A Warung Favorite

In "warungs" (restaurants) across Indonesia, nasi goreng is guaranteed to be on the menu, as it's a favorite of visitors and locals alike. Top it off with some extra hot sauce to spice it up and some sliced cucumbers to cool it back down. Browse an Asian grocery store for kecap manis, a sugary sauce you can use in place of the soy sauce and molasses mixture for a more authentic taste.

ITALIAN RICE SALAD

Double this marinated rice salad recipe for a potluck or picnic.

INGREDIENTS

Serves 4

⅓ cup red wine vinegar

1 tablespoon balsamic vinegar

2 teaspoons Dijon mustard

½ cup olive oil

4 cloves garlic, minced

1 teaspoon basil

⅓ cup chopped fresh parsley

2 cups rice, cooked

1 cup green peas

1 carrot, grated

½ cup roasted red peppers, chopped

½ cup green olives, sliced

Salt and pepper to taste

1. Whisk or shake together the red wine vinegar, balsamic vinegar, Dijon mustard, olive oil, garlic, basil, and parsley.

2. Combine rice with remaining ingredients in a large bowl. Toss with dressing mixture and coat well.

3. Taste, and season with just a bit of salt and pepper.

4. Chill for at least 30 minutes before serving to allow flavors to set, and gently toss again just before serving.

ITALIAN WHITE BEANS AND RICE

This is a quick, inexpensive, and hearty meal that will quickly become a favorite standby on busy nights. It's nutritious, filling, and can easily be doubled for a crowd.

INGREDIENTS

Serves 4

½ onion, diced

2 ribs celery, diced

3 cloves garlic, minced

2 tablespoons olive oil

1 (12-ounce) can diced or crushed tomatoes

1 (15-ounce) can cannellini or great northern beans, drained

½ teaspoon parsley

½ teaspoon basil

1 cup rice, cooked

1 tablespoon balsamic vinegar

1. Sauté onion, celery, and garlic in olive oil for 3–5 minutes until onion and celery are soft.

2. Reduce heat to medium-low and add tomatoes, beans, parsley, and basil. Cover, and simmer for 10 minutes, stirring occasionally.

3. Stir in cooked rice and balsamic vinegar and cook, uncovered, for a few more minutes until liquid is absorbed.

JASMINE RICE

This white rice gets its name from its fragrant, long grains, and it's most commonly used in Thai cuisine.

INGREDIENTS

Serves 8

2 cups jasmine rice

3 cups water

1 teaspoon salt

Combine all ingredients in a 4-quart slow cooker, cover, and cook on high heat for 1 hour, or until rice is tender.

To Rinse or Not to Rinse

Many people like to rinse jasmine thoroughly before cooking. To do this, place the rice in a colander and run cold water over the rice until it runs clear. However, this step isn't crucial so if you're pressed for time, just skip.

MACRO-INSPIRED VEGGIE BOWL

Truly nourishing, this is a full meal in a bowl, inspired by macrobiotic cuisine.

INGREDIENTS

Serves 6

2 cups brown rice, cooked

1 batch Sesame Baked Tofu (Chapter 11), chopped into cubes

1 head broccoli, steamed and chopped

1 red or yellow bell pepper, sliced thin

1 cup bean sprouts

1 cup You Are a Goddess Dressing (Chapter 5)

½ cup pumpkin seeds or sunflower seeds

2 teaspoons dulse or kelp seaweed flakes (optional)

1. Divide brown rice into 6 bowls.

2. Top each bowl with Sesame Baked Tofu, broccoli, bell pepper, and bean sprouts.

3. Drizzle with dressing and sprinkle with seeds and seaweed flakes, if desired.

Live Long and Prosper

Although a macrobiotic diet includes seafood, it is an otherwise vegan diet originally from Japan. Macrobiotics combines a balance of nutrients with Japanese ingredients such as miso, plum vinegar, and seaweed, and lots of organic grains and veggies, while minimizing oils and fruits. A healthy diet, the philosophy goes, will lead to happiness and longevity. For more information see *The Everything® Guide to Macrobiotics*.

MEXICAN RICE WITH CORN AND PEPPERS

Although Mexican rice is usually just a filling for burritos or served as a side dish, this recipe loads up the veggies, making it hearty enough for a main dish. Use frozen or canned veggies if you need to save time.

INGREDIENTS
Serves 4

2 cloves garlic, minced

1 cup rice, uncooked

2 tablespoons olive oil

3 cups Vegetable Broth (Chapter 6)

1 cup tomato paste (or 4 large tomatoes, puréed)

1 green bell pepper, chopped

1 red bell pepper, chopped

Kernels from 1 ear of corn

1 carrot, diced

1 teaspoon chili powder

½ teaspoon cumin

⅓ teaspoon oregano

⅓ teaspoon cayenne pepper (or to taste)

⅓ teaspoon salt

1. Add garlic, rice, and olive oil to a large skillet and heat on medium-high heat, stirring frequently. Toast the rice until just golden brown, about 2–3 minutes.

2. Reduce heat and add Vegetable Broth and remaining ingredients.

3. Bring to a simmer, cover, and allow to cook until liquid is absorbed and rice is cooked, about 20–25 minutes, stirring occasionally.

4. Adjust seasonings to taste.

Vegan Burritos
Brown some vegan chorizo or mock sausage crumbles and wrap in tortillas, perhaps topped with some shredded vegan cheese, to make vegan burritos. Or, combine with TVP Taco "Meat" (Chapter 12) to turn this into a "meaty" Mexican main.

MUSHROOM AND ROSEMARY WILD RICE

Top this rice off with some Lemon Basil Tofu slices (Chapter 11) for an herb-infused main dish.

INGREDIENTS

Serves 4

1 tablespoon chopped fresh rosemary

1 yellow onion, diced

2 tablespoons olive oil

1 cup sliced mushrooms

1½ cups wild rice, uncooked

4½ cups Vegetable Broth (Chapter 6)

2 tablespoons vegan margarine

½ teaspoon lemon juice

¼ teaspoon ground sage

2 tablespoons nutritional yeast (optional)

1. In a large pan, heat rosemary and onion in olive oil until onion is just soft, about 3 minutes. Add mushrooms and heat for another minute.

2. Add wild rice and Vegetable Broth and bring to a simmer. Cover, and cook 40–45 minutes until rice is done and liquid is absorbed.

3. Remove from heat and stir in remaining ingredients.

PINEAPPLE LIME RICE

Fresh cubed mango would also add a sweet flavor to this simple zesty side, instead of the pineapple.

INGREDIENTS

Serves 4

2 tablespoons vegan margarine

2 cups rice, cooked

1½ tablespoon lime juice

⅓ cup chopped fresh cilantro

1 (16-ounce) can pineapple tidbits, drained

Dash sea salt

1. Stir vegan margarine into hot rice until melted and combined.

2. Add remaining ingredients, tossing gently to combine. Season to taste.

SESAME SNOW PEA RICE PILAF

The leftovers from this rice pilaf can be enjoyed chilled the next day as a cold rice salad.

INGREDIENTS

Serves 4

4 cups rice, cooked

2 tablespoons olive or safflower oil

1 tablespoon sesame oil

2 tablespoons soy sauce

3 tablespoons apple cider vinegar

1 teaspoon sugar

1 cup snow peas, chopped

¾ cup baby corn, chopped

3 scallions, chopped

2 tablespoons chopped fresh parsley

½ teaspoon sea salt

1. In a large pot over low heat, combine the rice, olive or safflower oil, sesame oil, soy sauce, vinegar, and sugar, stirring well to combine.

2. Add snow peas, baby corn, and scallions and heat until warmed through and vegetables are lightly cooked, stirring frequently so the rice doesn't burn.

3. While still hot, stir in fresh parsley and season well with sea salt.

SPANISH ARTICHOKE AND ZUCCHINI PAELLA

Traditional Spanish paellas are always cooked with saffron, but this version with zucchinis, artichokes, and bell peppers uses turmeric instead for the same golden hue.

INGREDIENTS

Serves 4

3 cloves garlic, minced

1 yellow onion, diced

2 tablespoons olive oil

1 cup white rice, uncooked

1 (15-ounce) can diced or crushed tomatoes

1 green bell pepper, chopped

1 red or yellow bell pepper, chopped

½ cup artichoke hearts, chopped

2 zucchinis, sliced

2 cups Vegetable Broth (Chapter 6)

1 tablespoon paprika

½ teaspoon turmeric

¾ teaspoon parsley

½ teaspoon salt

1. In the largest skillet you can find, heat garlic and onion in olive oil for 3–4 minutes until onion is almost soft. Add rice, stirring well to coat, and heat for another minute, stirring to prevent burning.

2. Add tomatoes, bell peppers, artichokes, and zucchinis, stirring to combine. Add Vegetable Broth and remaining ingredients, cover, and simmer for 15–20 minutes, or until rice is done.

SPICY SOUTHERN JAMBALAYA

Make this spicy and smoky Southern rice dish a main meal by adding in some browned mock sausage or sautéed tofu.

INGREDIENTS

Serves 6

1 onion, chopped

1 bell pepper, any color, chopped

1 rib celery, diced

2 tablespoons olive oil

1 (14-ounce) can diced tomatoes, undrained

3 cups water or Vegetable Broth (Chapter 6)

2 cups rice

1 bay leaf

1 teaspoon paprika

½ teaspoon thyme

½ teaspoon oregano

½ teaspoon garlic powder

1 cup corn or frozen mixed diced veggies (optional)

½ teaspoon cayenne or hot Tabasco sauce to taste

1. In a large skillet or stockpot, heat onion, bell pepper, and celery in olive oil until almost soft, about 3 minutes.

2. Reduce heat and add remaining ingredients except corn or frozen veggies and cayenne or hot sauce. Cover, bring to a low simmer, and cook for 20 minutes until rice is done, stirring occasionally.

3. Add corn or frozen veggies if desired and cayenne or hot sauce and cook just until heated through, about 3 minutes. Adjust seasonings to taste. Remove bay leaf before serving.

Got Leftovers?

Heat up some refried beans and wrap up your leftover jambalaya in tortillas with some salsa and shredded lettuce to make vegan burritos!

SQUASH AND SAGE RISOTTO

Risotto is easy to make, but it does take a bit of effort with all the stirring! This earthy recipe works well with just about any kind of squash. If you're in a hurry, use canned puréed pumpkin instead of fresh acorn squash or look for precooked butternut squash in your grocer's freezer section.

INGREDIENTS

Serves 4

3 cloves garlic, minced

½ yellow onion, diced

2 tablespoons olive oil

1½ cups arborio rice, uncooked

5 cups Vegetable Broth (Chapter 6), divided

2 whole cloves

1½ cups roasted puréed pumpkin, acorn, or butternut squash

1½ teaspoons sage

⅓ teaspoon salt

¼ teaspoon pepper

1. In a large skillet, sauté the garlic and onion in olive oil for 3 minutes over medium-high heat. Add uncooked rice and cook for 2 more minutes, stirring frequently to lightly toast the rice.

2. Add ¾ cup Vegetable Broth and cloves and stir well. When most of the liquid has been absorbed, add another ½ cup Vegetable Broth, stirring frequently. Continue adding Vegetable Broth ½ cup at a time until rice is just tender and sauce is creamy, about 20–25 minutes.

3. Reduce heat to medium-low and stir in puréed pumpkin or squash and ¼ cup Vegetable Broth. Continue to stir well and allow to cook for 4–5 more minutes.

4. Stir in sage and season with salt and pepper.

5. Allow to cool, stirring occasionally, for at least 5 minutes. Risotto will thicken slightly as it cools. Remove cloves before serving.

Quicker and Creamier

To save time, keep your Vegetable Broth simmering on the stove next to your risotto as it cooks. Adding hot liquid will help the rice cook faster and ensures an evenly cooked rice with a creamy sauce.

SUN-DRIED TOMATO RISOTTO WITH SPINACH AND PINE NUTS

The tomatoes carry the flavor in this easy risotto—no butter, cheese, or wine is needed. But if you're a gourmand who keeps truffle, hazelnut, pine nut, or another gourmet oil on hand, now's the time to use it, instead of the margarine.

INGREDIENTS

Serves 4

1 yellow onion, diced

4 cloves garlic, minced

2 tablespoons olive oil

1½ cups arborio rice, uncooked

5–6 cups Vegetable Broth (Chapter 6)

⅔ cup rehydrated sun-dried tomatoes, sliced

½ cup fresh spinach

1 tablespoon chopped fresh basil (optional)

2 tablespoons vegan margarine (optional)

2 tablespoons nutritional yeast

Salt and pepper to taste

¼ cup pine nuts

1. Heat onion and garlic in olive oil until just soft, about 2–3 minutes. Add rice and toast for 1 minute, stirring constantly.

2. Add ¾ cup Vegetable Broth and stir to combine. When most of the liquid has been absorbed, add another ½ cup, stirring constantly. Continue adding liquid ½ cup at a time until rice is cooked, about 20 minutes.

3. Add another ½ cup Vegetable Broth, tomatoes, spinach, and basil if desired and reduce heat to low. Stir to combine well. Heat for 3–4 minutes until tomatoes are soft and spinach is wilted.

4. Stir in margarine if desired and nutritional yeast. Taste, then season lightly with a bit of salt and pepper.

5. Allow to cool slightly, then top with pine nuts. Risotto will thicken a bit as it cools.

Sun-Dried Tomatoes

If you're using dehydrated tomatoes, rehydrate them first by covering in water for at least 10 minutes, and add the soaking water to the broth. If you're using tomatoes packed in oil, add 2 tablespoons of the oil to risotto at the end of cooking, instead of the vegan margarine.

TOMATILLO RICE

This recipe is similar to jambalaya, in that you cook the rice in a tomato-based sauce so the flavors are completely absorbed.

INGREDIENTS

Serves 4

2 tablespoons olive oil

½ red onion, diced

½ red bell pepper, diced

2 cloves garlic, minced

Juice of 1 lime

1 cup tomatillo salsa

1 cup water

1 teaspoon salt

1 cup long-grain white rice

½ cup cilantro, chopped

1. Heat the olive oil in a sauté pan over medium heat. Add the onion, bell pepper, and garlic and sauté about 5 minutes.

2. Transfer to a 4-quart slow cooker. Add all the remaining ingredients except the cilantro.

3. Cover, and cook on high heat for 2½ hours. Check the rice periodically to make sure the liquid hasn't been absorbed too quickly and the rice is not drying out.

4. Stir in the cilantro before serving.

Tomatillos

Tomatillos are small, green, tomato-like fruit that are used in many Latin-inspired dishes. They come with a papery husk that surrounds the edible fruit, which must first be removed. Try to find tomatillos with an intact, tight-fitting, light brown husk; if it is dry or shriveled, the tomatillos are probably not good.

WILD MUSHROOM RISOTTO

This makes a great side dish, but you can also try it as a main course, paired with a green salad.

INGREDIENTS

Serves 6

1 teaspoon olive oil

1 shallot, minced

2 cloves garlic, minced

8 ounces sliced assorted wild mushrooms

2 cups arborio rice

2 cups Vegetable Broth (Chapter 6)

3 cups water

½ teaspoon salt

1. Heat the oil in a nonstick pan. Sauté the shallot, garlic, and mushrooms until soft, about 4–5 minutes.

2. Add the rice and ½ cup Vegetable Broth and cook until the liquid is fully absorbed, about 5 minutes.

3. Scrape the rice mixture into a 4-quart slow cooker. Add the water, salt, and remaining Vegetable Broth.

4. Cover, and cook on low for 2 hours. Stir before serving.

WHITE BEANS AND RICE

This one-pot dish is somewhere between a stew and a more traditional entrée, and you can adjust the consistency to your liking by adding more or less water one hour before it's done cooking.

INGREDIENTS

Serves 8

2 cups dried great northern beans

8 cups water

1 white onion, diced

1 carrot, peeled and sliced

2 tablespoons ketchup

1 tablespoon vegan Worcestershire sauce

2 bay leaves

1 teaspoon dried thyme

1 teaspoon salt

½ teaspoon pepper

¾ cup rice

1. Add all ingredients except the rice to a 6- or 8-quart slow cooker, cover, and cook over low heat for 6 hours.

2. Add the rice, cover, and cook on high heat for an additional 2–3 hours, or until the rice is tender. Remove bay leaves before serving.

WHOLE GRAINS

BARLEY AND BELL PEPPER CHILI

With all the flavors and ingredients of traditional vegetarian chili, this recipe just adds a bit of whole-grain goodness to the mix.

INGREDIENTS
Serves 6

3 cloves garlic, minced

1 onion, chopped

1 green bell pepper, chopped

1 red bell pepper, chopped

2 tablespoons olive oil

½ cup barley

2½ cups water or Vegetable Broth (Chapter 6)

1 (15-ounce) can diced tomatoes

1 (15-ounce) can black beans or kidney beans

2 tablespoons chili powder

1 teaspoon cumin

½ teaspoon oregano

2 tablespoons chopped fresh cilantro (optional)

1. In a large stockpot, heat the garlic, onion, and bell peppers in olive oil for 2–3 minutes. Add barley and toast, stirring frequently, for just 1 minute.

2. Reduce heat to medium-low and add water or Vegetable Broth, tomatoes, beans, chili powder, cumin, and oregano. Bring to a slow simmer, cover, and heat for at least 35 minutes, stirring occasionally.

3. Uncover, and adjust seasonings to taste, then top with fresh chopped cilantro if desired.

Whole-Grain Chili

Tossing in some cooked whole grains is a great way to stretch out your leftover chili, or just to add some healthy fiber and a touch of homemade goodness to canned chili or even canned baked beans. Although barley has a great texture for pairing with beans, leftover quinoa or millet would also work.

BARLEY AND MUSHROOM PILAF

This has an earthy-flavored pilaf with mushrooms and nutty toasted barley. This one will really stick to your ribs!

INGREDIENTS

Serves 4

1 cup sliced porcini mushrooms

1 cup sliced shiitake mushrooms

2 ribs celery, diced

½ onion, chopped

3 tablespoons vegan margarine or olive oil, divided

1¼ cups barley

3¾ cups Vegetable Broth (Chapter 6)

1 bay leaf

¼ teaspoon sage

½ teaspoon parsley

½ teaspoon thyme

1. In a large skillet or stockpot, sauté mushrooms, celery, and onion in 2 tablespoons margarine or olive oil until almost soft, about 2–3 minutes. Add barley and remaining 1 tablespoon of margarine and allow to toast for 1–2 minutes, stirring frequently.

2. When barley starts to turn brown, add Vegetable Broth and seasonings. Bring to a simmer, cover, and allow to cook for 20–25 minutes, stirring occasionally, until liquid is absorbed and barley is cooked. Remove bay leaf before serving.

Cooking Barley

Be sure you pick up either pearl or quick-cooking barley, and not the hulled variety, which takes ages to cook. Pearl barley is done in 20–25 minutes, and quick-cooking barley is done in about 10, so adjust the cooking times as needed. Barley can also be cooked in your rice steamer with about 2½ cups liquid for each cup of barley.

BARLEY BAKED BEANS

If you prefer to use your slow cooker, you can just dump all the ingredients in, give it a quick stir, and cook it on a medium setting for about 6 hours.

INGREDIENTS

Serves 8

2 cups cooked barley

2 (15-ounce) cans pinto or navy beans, drained

1 onion, diced

1 (28-ounce) can crushed or diced tomatoes

½ cup water

¼ cup brown sugar

⅓ cup barbecue sauce

2 tablespoons molasses

2 teaspoons mustard powder

1 teaspoon garlic powder

1 teaspoon salt

1. Preheat oven to 300°F.

2. Combine all ingredients and transfer to a large casserole or baking dish. Cover, and bake for 2 hours, stirring occasionally.

3. Uncover, and bake for 15 more minutes or until thick and saucy.

BARLEY PILAF WITH EDAMAME AND ROASTED RED PEPPERS

Don't forget! Fresh ground sea salt and hand-cracked pepper will give the best flavor to all your recipes, including this one. Serve chilled like a salad, or heat the edamame lightly first for a warmed and high-protein pilaf.

INGREDIENTS
Serves 6

2 cups frozen shelled edamame, thawed and drained

2 cups cooked barley

½ cup chopped roasted red peppers

⅔ cup green peas

⅔ cup corn (fresh, canned, or frozen)

1½ tablespoons Dijon mustard

2 tablespoons lemon or lime juice

¾ teaspoon garlic powder

2 tablespoons olive oil

Salt and pepper, to taste

¼ cup chopped fresh cilantro

1 avocado, diced (optional)

1. Combine the edamame, barley, peppers, peas, and corn in a large bowl.

2. In a separate small bowl, whisk together the mustard, lemon or lime juice, garlic powder, and olive oil, then drizzle over barley mixture, tossing gently to coat well.

3. Season generously with salt and pepper and toss lightly with cilantro and avocado if desired.

Whole-Grain Bean Salads
If you like bean salads, try adding a portion of cooked barley or quinoa to your favorite recipe. Stretch leftover bean salads by tossing in some extra dressing and cooked whole grains.

BLACK BEAN AND BARLEY TACO SALAD

Adding barley to a taco salad gives a bit of a whole-grain and fiber boost to this low-fat recipe.

INGREDIENTS
Serves 2

1 (15-ounce) can black beans, drained

½ teaspoon cumin

½ teaspoon oregano

2 tablespoons lime juice

1 teaspoon hot chili sauce (optional)

1 cup cooked barley

1 head iceberg lettuce, shredded

¾ cup salsa

Handful tortilla chips, crumbled

2 tablespoons vegan Italian dressing (optional)

1. Mash together the beans, cumin, oregano, lime juice, and hot sauce if desired until beans are mostly mashed, then combine with barley.

2. Layer lettuce with beans and barley and top with salsa and tortilla chips. Drizzle with Italian dressing if desired.

CONFETTI "RICE" WITH TVP

If the kids like Mexican rice, try this whole-grain version with barley and TVP.

INGREDIENTS

Serves 6

1 onion, chopped

2 cloves garlic, minced

2 tablespoons olive oil

1 cup barley

1 (15-ounce) can diced tomatoes

2 cups Vegetable Broth (Chapter 6)

1 teaspoon chili powder

½ teaspoon cumin

¾ cup TVP

1 cup hot water or Vegetable Broth (Chapter 6)

1 tablespoon soy sauce

1 cup frozen veggie mix (peas, corn, and carrots)

1 teaspoon parsley

½ teaspoon salt

1. In a large skillet, heat the onion and garlic in olive oil for 1–2 minutes, then add barley. Toast for 1 minute, stirring constantly.

2. Add canned tomatoes including liquid, Vegetable Broth, chili powder, and cumin. Cook until barley is almost soft, about 15 minutes.

3. While barley is cooking, combine TVP with hot water or Vegetable Broth and soy sauce and allow to sit for 8–10 minutes until TVP is rehydrated. Drain any excess liquid.

4. When barley is almost done cooking, add rehydrated TVP, veggies, parsley, and salt. Heat for another 5 minutes, or until done.

Turn It Into Tacos

Use this "meaty" Mexican "rice" instead of meat as a base for burritos or crunchy tacos, along with some shredded lettuce, vegan cheese, and nondairy sour cream. Or, serve alongside some cooked beans for a healthy Mexican meal.

PORTOBELLO BARLEY

This method of cooking barley makes it as creamy as risotto, but with the bonus of being high in fiber.

INGREDIENTS
Serves 8

1 teaspoon olive oil

2 shallots, minced

2 cloves garlic, minced

3 portobello mushroom caps, sliced

1 cup pearl barley

3¼ cups water

¼ teaspoon salt

½ teaspoon freshly ground black pepper

1 teaspoon crushed rosemary

1 teaspoon dried chervil

¼ cup grated vegan Parmesan cheese

1. Heat the oil in a nonstick skillet. Sauté the shallots, garlic, and mushrooms until softened, about 3–4 minutes.

2. Place the mushroom mixture into a 4-quart slow cooker. Add the barley, water, salt, pepper, rosemary, and chervil. Stir.

3. Cover, and cook on low for 8–9 hours or on high for 4 hours.

4. Turn off the slow cooker and stir in the vegan Parmesan cheese. Serve immediately.

Chervil
Chervil is an herb of the parsley family. It has delicate, curly leaves almost like carrot tops. Its mild flavor, which includes hints of anise, is easily overwhelmed by stronger flavors. Fresh parsley, tarragon, or a combination of both can easily substitute for chervil.

SUMMER SQUASH AND BARLEY RISOTTO

A smooth and saucy risotto with barley instead of rice. Fresh asparagus instead of squash would also be lovely in this nontraditional risotto. Top it off with some vegan Parmesan cheese if you happen to have some on hand.

INGREDIENTS
Serves 4

4 cloves garlic, minced

½ onion, diced

1 zucchini, chopped

1 yellow squash, chopped

2 tablespoons olive oil

1 cup pearled barley

3–4 cups Vegetable Broth (Chapter 6)

2 tablespoons chopped fresh basil

2 tablespoons nutritional yeast

2 tablespoons vegan margarine

Salt and pepper, to taste

1. Sauté garlic, onion, zucchini, and yellow squash in olive oil until soft, about 3–4 minutes. Add barley and heat for 1 minute, stirring to coat well with oil and to prevent burning.

2. Add 1 cup Vegetable Broth and bring to a simmer. Cover, and allow to cook for a few minutes until almost absorbed.

3. Add another cup of Vegetable Broth and continue cooking until barley is soft, about 20–25 minutes, adding more Vegetable Broth as needed.

4. When barley is done, add an additional ¼ cup Vegetable Broth and basil, stirring well to combine just until heated through.

5. Stir in nutritional yeast and vegan margarine and season generously with salt and pepper, to taste.

VEGETARIAN "BEEF" AND BARLEY STEW

Classic and comforting, you can't go wrong with this warming "beef" and barley stew on a cold night.

INGREDIENTS

Serves 6

1 onion, chopped

2 ribs celery, chopped

1 carrot, chopped

1 green bell pepper, chopped

2 tablespoons olive oil

1 cup water

2½ cups tomato or mixed vegetable juice

⅓ cup barley

1½ teaspoons chili powder

1½ teaspoons parsley or Italian seasoning

2 bay leaves

4 veggie burgers, crumbled

Salt and pepper, to taste

1. Heat the onion, celery, carrot, and bell pepper in olive oil in a large soup pot or stockpot, just until veggies are almost soft, about 4–5 minutes.

2. Add water, tomato or vegetable juice, and barley, stirring well to combine, then add chili powder, parsley or Italian seasoning, and bay leaves.

3. Cover, and cook over medium-low heat for 20 minutes. Add veggie burgers and cook for another 5 minutes, uncovered, or until barley is soft.

4. Season with salt and pepper to taste; remove bay leaves before serving.

Bean and Barley Stew

TVP or a store-bought meat substitute could work in this stew, but the chewiness of the veggie burgers provides a nice complement to the equally chewy barley. If you don't have any of these on hand, add some beans instead for a thick and hearty meal.

BULGUR WITH BROCCOLI AND CARROT

This filling and delicious dish makes a comforting meal on a cold day. Make it complete with a salad or a light soup from Chapter 6.

INGREDIENTS
Serves 4

2 cups bulgur, uncooked

2 tablespoons vegan margarine

1 cup carrots, diced

1 cup broccoli, chopped

2 cups Vegetable Broth (Chapter 6)

1 teaspoon salt

1. Add all ingredients to a 4-quart slow cooker. Cover, and cook on low heat for 6 hours.

2. Check the bulgur to see if it is tender and if not, cook for 1 more hour.

Bulgur, the World's Oldest Cooked Cereal
Bulgur was being eaten as a warm cooked cereal by Early Neolithic Bulgarians from between 5920 B.C. to 5730 B.C. It is a type of whole-wheat grain that has been cleaned, parboiled, dried, ground into particles, and sifted into size. It is high in fiber, B vitamins, iron, phosphorus, and manganese. Its pleasant, nutty flavor makes it not just healthy but delicious too.

BULGUR WHEAT TABBOULEH SALAD WITH TOMATOES

Though you'll need to adjust the cooking time, of course, you can try this tabbouleh recipe with just about any whole grain. Bulgur wheat is traditional, but quinoa, millet, or amaranth would also work.

INGREDIENTS

Serves 4

1¼ cups boiling water or Vegetable Broth (Chapter 6)

1 cup bulgur wheat

3 tablespoons olive oil

¼ cup lemon juice

1 teaspoon garlic powder

½ teaspoon sea salt

½ teaspoon pepper

3 scallions, chopped

½ cup chopped fresh mint

½ cup chopped fresh parsley

1 (15-ounce) can chickpeas, drained (optional)

3 large tomatoes, diced

1. Pour boiling water or Vegetable Broth over bulgur wheat. Cover, and allow to sit for 30 minutes, or until bulgur wheat is soft.

2. Toss bulgur wheat with olive oil, lemon juice, garlic powder, and salt, stirring well to coat. Combine with remaining ingredients, adding in tomatoes last.

3. Allow to chill for at least 1 hour before serving.

Leftover Tabbouleh Sandwiches

Spread a slice of bread or a tortilla with some hummus, then layer leftover tabbouleh, sweet pickle relish, thinly sliced cucumbers, and some lettuce and make a quick sandwich or wrap for lunch.

TWO-GRAIN CAULIFLOWER

If you have the time, enhance this dish by roasting the cauliflower before adding to the slow cooker.

INGREDIENTS

Serves 6

2 cups cauliflower, small dice

1 cup dried bulgur

1 cup dried quinoa

4 cups water

1 lemon, juiced

½ cup mint, chopped

1 teaspoon salt

¼ teaspoon black pepper

Olive oil for garnish

1. Place the cauliflower, bulgur, quinoa, and water in the slow cooker and cook on high heat for 1–2 hours or until the grains are tender and the water absorbed.

2. Place the grains in a bowl and allow to cool. Add the remaining ingredients except olive oil, stir, and drizzle a little olive oil over each individual plate before serving.

TROPICAL BREAKFAST COUSCOUS

This recipe is like having a piña colada for breakfast. What could be better? Stick a flower behind your ear and enjoy this breakfast barefoot in the sun.

INGREDIENTS

Serves 2

1 cup coconut milk

1 cup pineapple juice or orange juice

1 cup couscous

½ teaspoon vanilla

2 tablespoons maple syrup or agave nectar

Sliced fresh fruit (optional)

1. In a small saucepan, heat coconut milk and juice until just about to simmer. Do not boil.

2. Add couscous and heat for 1 minute. Stir in vanilla, cover, and turn off heat. Allow to sit, covered, for 5 minutes, until couscous is cooked.

3. Fluff couscous with a fork and stir in maple syrup or agave nectar. Garnish with fresh fruit if desired.

Couscous for Breakfast

Couscous is an excellent choice for breakfast, as it is much quicker to cook than grains and doesn't need to be watched. Boil some water, add your couscous, turn off the stove and cover the couscous, then go brush your teeth and tie your shoes. By the time you finish, breakfast is ready!

BELL PEPPERS STUFFED WITH COUSCOUS

Baked stuffed peppers are always a hit with those who appreciate presentation, and this recipe takes very little effort.

INGREDIENTS

Serves 4

4 cups water or Vegetable Broth (Chapter 6)

3 cups couscous

2 tablespoons olive oil

2 tablespoons lemon or lime juice

1 cup frozen peas or corn, thawed

2 green onions, sliced

½ teaspoon cumin

½ teaspoon chili powder

4 green bell peppers

1. Preheat oven to 350°F.

2. Bring water or Vegetable Broth to a boil and add couscous. Cover, turn off heat, and let sit for 10–15 minutes until couscous is cooked. Fluff with a fork.

3. Combine couscous with olive oil, lemon or lime juice, peas or corn, green onions, cumin, and chili powder.

4. Cut the tops off the bell peppers and remove seeds.

5. Stuff couscous into bell peppers and place the tops back on, using a toothpick to secure if needed.

6. Transfer to a baking dish and bake for 15 minutes.

COUSCOUS AND BEAN PILAF

A quick side or lunch that can be served hot or cold. With a few veggies tossed in, this could also be a full meal.

INGREDIENTS

Serves 2

2 cups water or Vegetable Broth (Chapter 6)

2 cups couscous

2 tablespoons olive oil

2 tablespoons red wine vinegar

½ teaspoon crushed red pepper flakes

1 (15-ounce) can great northern or cannellini beans, drained

2 tablespoons minced pimiento peppers

2 tablespoons chopped fresh parsley

Salt and pepper to taste

1. Bring the water or Vegetable Broth to a simmer and add couscous. Cover, turn off heat, and allow to sit for at least 15 minutes to cook couscous. Fluff with a fork.

2. Whisk together the olive oil, red wine vinegar, and red pepper flakes and toss with cooked couscous.

3. Combine beans, pimiento peppers, and parsley with couscous, tossing gently to combine. Season generously with salt and pepper.

LEMON CILANTRO COUSCOUS

This flavorful couscous is a light and easy side dish, or top it off with a vegetable stew or some stir-fried or roasted veggies.

INGREDIENTS

Serves 4

2 cups Vegetable Broth (Chapter 6)

1 cup couscous

⅓ cup lemon juice

½ cup chopped fresh cilantro

¼ teaspoon sea salt, or to taste

1. Bring Vegetable Broth to a simmer and add couscous. Cover, and let stand for 10 minutes, until soft, then fluff with a fork.

2. Stir in lemon juice and cilantro, and season generously with sea salt.

What Is Couscous?

Couscous isn't technically a whole grain but rather whole-wheat semolina pasta. But its small size and grainy texture gives it more in common with whole grains than pasta.

SPICED COUSCOUS SALAD WITH BELL PEPPER AND ZUCCHINI

A full meal for lunch or dinner, or a side salad, depending on how hungry you are!

INGREDIENTS

Serves 4

2 cups Vegetable Broth (Chapter 6)

2 cups couscous

1 teaspoon cumin

½ teaspoon turmeric

½ teaspoon paprika

¼ teaspoon cayenne pepper

1 tablespoon lemon juice

2 zucchinis, sliced

1 red bell pepper, chopped

1 yellow bell pepper, chopped

3 cloves garlic, minced

2 tablespoons olive oil

2 tablespoons chopped fresh parsley

Salt and pepper to taste

1. Combine Vegetable Broth and couscous and bring to a boil. Add cumin, turmeric, paprika, and cayenne pepper, and stir to combine.

2. Turn off heat, cover, and allow to sit for at least 15 minutes, until couscous is soft and liquid is absorbed. Fluff couscous with a fork and add lemon juice.

3. Sauté zucchinis, bell peppers, and garlic in olive oil just until soft; combine with couscous.

4. Add parsley, taste, and season lightly with salt and pepper.

ORANGE AND RAISIN CURRIED COUSCOUS

Another whole-grain salad or pilaf that can be served either hot or cold. Cranberries, currants, or dates may be used instead of raisins.

INGREDIENTS

Serves 4

2 cups water or Vegetable Broth (Chapter 6)

1½ cups couscous

½ cup orange juice

1 onion, chopped

2 tablespoons olive oil

½ teaspoon coriander powder

1 teaspoon curry powder

2 scallions, chopped

¾ cup golden raisins

¾ cup sliced almonds or pine nuts

1. Bring water or Vegetable Broth to a boil. Add couscous and remove from heat. Stir in orange juice, cover, and allow to sit for 15 minutes until most of the liquid is absorbed and couscous is soft.

2. Heat onion in olive oil for 1–2 minutes, then add spices and heat for 1 more minute until fragrant.

3. Combine couscous with spices, and add scallions, raisins, and nuts.

FARRO AND KALE

Farro is a type of wheat that is often used like small pasta or a hearty rice.

INGREDIENTS

Serves 4

5 cloves garlic, minced

1 tablespoon olive oil

1 cup pearled farro

2 cups kale, chopped

2 cups Vegetable Broth (Chapter 6)

2 tablespoons red wine vinegar

½ teaspoon salt

¼ teaspoon black pepper

1. In a sauté pan over medium heat, sauté the garlic in the olive oil for 30 seconds–1 minute. Remove from heat and place in a 4-quart slow cooker.

2. Add all remaining ingredients, cover, and cook on high heat for 2–3 hours.

WARM FARRO AND HERB SALAD

Farro has a nice chewy texture and a flavor similar to barley or spelt, so you could try using a combination of the grains in this salad.

INGREDIENTS
Serves 6

3 cups dried farro

7 cups water

1 teaspoon salt

1 lemon, juiced

1 bunch parsley, chopped

¼ teaspoon black pepper

1. Add the farro, water, and salt to the slow cooker and cook on high heat for 2–3 hours, or until the farro is tender and the water absorbed.

2. Stir in the remaining ingredients and serve warm.

Time-Saving Tip
If you'd like to save a little time and prepare a grain dish the night before serving, just cover and refrigerate. A few minutes before serving, remove from the fridge, add a little water, and microwave for 2–3 minutes. Adding a small amount of water (up to ¼ cup) will prevent the grains from drying out and will make the dish taste more like it was just prepared.

BAKED MILLET PATTIES

Serve these nutty whole grain patties topped with Mushroom Gravy (Chapter 3), You Are a Goddess Dressing (Chapter 5), or another dressing or sauce.

INGREDIENTS

Yields 8 patties

1½ cups cooked millet

½ cup tahini

1 cup bread crumbs

1 teaspoon parsley

¾ teaspoon garlic powder

½ teaspoon onion powder (optional)

⅓ teaspoon salt

1. Preheat oven to 350°F.

2. Combine all ingredients together in a bowl, mashing to mix well.

3. Use your hands to press firmly into patties, about 1" thick, and place on a baking sheet.

4. Bake for 10–12 minutes on each side.

For the Birds?

In the United States, millet is most frequently spotted being used as a bird-friendly rice alternative at weddings and as a filler in bird feeders. But it's also a healthy whole grain used in one form or another across much of Africa. With a longer cooking time and harder texture than other grains, it tends to be less popular than other whole-grain options, but this recipe uses it well.

MILLET AND BUTTERNUT SQUASH CASSEROLE

Slightly sweet, slightly savory, top this millet medley with some Easy Fried Tofu (Chapter 11) to make it a main meal.

INGREDIENTS

Serves 4

1 cup millet

2 cups Vegetable Broth (Chapter 6)

1 small butternut squash, peeled, seeded, and chopped

½ cup water

1 teaspoon curry powder

½ cup orange juice

2 tablespoons nutritional yeast

½ teaspoon sea salt

1. In a small pot, cook millet in Vegetable Broth until done, about 20–30 minutes.

2. In a separate pan, heat butternut squash in water. Cover, and allow to cook for 10–15 minutes until squash is almost soft. Remove lid and drain extra water.

3. Combine millet with squash over low heat and add curry and orange juice, stirring to combine well. Heat for 3–4 more minutes, add nutritional yeast, and season with sea salt.

MEDITERRANEAN MILLET

The combination of onion, artichokes, and tomatoes are reminiscent of the Mediterranean in this healthy grain dish.

INGREDIENTS

Serves 4

¼ cup onion, diced

2 tablespoons olive oil

½ cup marinated artichoke hearts, quartered

½ cup Roma tomatoes, diced

1 cup millet

2 cups water

Juice of 1 lemon

½ teaspoon salt

1. In a sauté pan over medium heat, sauté the onion in the olive oil for 3 minutes. Remove from heat and place in a 4-quart slow cooker.

2. Add all remaining ingredients, cover, and cook on high heat for 1–2 hours, checking for doneness after one hour.

CHOCOLATE PEANUT BUTTER BREAKFAST QUINOA

Chocolate and peanut butter is a flavor combination from heaven. Even with a bit of cocoa and sweetener, this breakfast cereal is still much more nutritious than the sugar-packed processed and refined cardboard-box brands in the supermarket.

INGREDIENTS
Serves 1

½ cup quinoa

1½ cups soymilk

2 tablespoons peanut butter

1½ tablespoons cocoa

1½ tablespoons maple syrup or brown rice syrup (optional)

1. Combine the quinoa and soymilk over medium-low heat. Cover, and cook for 15 minutes or until quinoa is done, stirring frequently.

2. While still hot, stir in peanut butter, cocoa, and sweetener if desired.

Try Quinoa Flakes

If you discover you like eating quinoa for breakfast, try quinoa flakes instead of whole quinoa. The flakes are quicker to cook, like oatmeal, but provide the same protein and amino acids that make quinoa such a great choice for vegans.

LEMON QUINOA VEGGIE SALAD

If you prefer to use fresh veggies, any kind will do. Steamed broccoli or fresh tomatoes would work well.

INGREDIENTS
Serves 4

1½ cups quinoa

4 cups Vegetable Broth (Chapter 6)

1 cup frozen mixed veggies, thawed

¼ cup lemon juice

¼ cup olive oil

1 teaspoon garlic powder

½ teaspoon sea salt

¼ teaspoon black pepper

2 tablespoons chopped fresh cilantro or parsley (optional)

1. In a large pot, simmer quinoa in Vegetable Broth for 15–20 minutes, stirring occasionally, until liquid is absorbed and quinoa is cooked. Add mixed veggies and stir to combine.

2. Remove from heat and combine with remaining ingredients. Serve hot or cold.

EASY GARLIC QUINOA

A simple way to spruce up plain quinoa to serve as a side dish, or to top with cooked veggies, a stir-fry, or some baked tofu.

INGREDIENTS
Serves 4

1 yellow onion, diced

4 cloves garlic, minced

2 tablespoons olive oil or vegan margarine

3 cups Vegetable Broth (Chapter 6)

1½ cups quinoa

½ teaspoon salt

3 tablespoons nutritional yeast

1. In a large skillet, heat onion and garlic in oil or margarine for 3–4 minutes until onion is soft.

2. Add Vegetable Broth and quinoa and bring to a simmer. Allow to cook for 15 minutes until liquid is absorbed.

3. Fluff quinoa with a fork and stir in salt and nutritional yeast.

FRUITED FALL QUINOA

Cranberries and apricots make a sweet combo; add some sage and thyme to give it some more warming flavors and it would make an excellent Thanksgiving entrée.

INGREDIENTS

Serves 4

1 cup quinoa

2 cups apple juice

1 cup water

½ onion, diced

2 ribs celery, diced

2 tablespoons vegan margarine

½ teaspoon nutmeg

½ teaspoon cinnamon

¼ teaspoon cloves

½ cup dried cranberries

½ cup dried apricots, chopped

1 teaspoon parsley

¼ teaspoon salt

1. In a large pot, combine quinoa, apple juice, and water. Cover, and simmer for 15 minutes or until done.

2. In a large skillet, heat onion and celery in margarine, stirring frequently, until soft.

3. Over low heat, combine onion and celery with quinoa and add remaining ingredients, tossing gently to combine. Heat for 3–4 more minutes.

MAPLE CINNAMON BREAKFAST QUINOA

Quinoa is a filling and healthy breakfast and has more protein than regular oatmeal. This is a deliciously sweet and energizing way to kick off your day.

INGREDIENTS

Serves 2

1 cup quinoa

2–2½ cups water

1 teaspoon vegan margarine

⅔ cup soymilk

½ teaspoon cinnamon

2 tablespoons maple syrup

2 tablespoons raisins (optional)

2 bananas, sliced (optional)

1. Heat the quinoa and water in a small saucepan and bring to a boil. Reduce to a simmer and allow to cook, covered, for 15 minutes, until liquid is absorbed.

2. Remove from heat and fluff the quinoa with a fork. Cover, and allow to sit for 5 minutes.

3. Stir in the margarine and soymilk, then remaining ingredients.

QUINOA AND FRESH HERB STUFFING

Substitute dried herbs if you have to, but fresh is best in this nontraditional stuffing recipe.

INGREDIENTS
Serves 6

1 yellow onion, chopped

2 ribs celery, diced

¼ cup vegan margarine

1 teaspoon chopped fresh rosemary

2 teaspoons chopped fresh marjoram

1½ tablespoons chopped fresh thyme

1 tablespoon chopped fresh sage

6 slices dried bread, cubed

1¼ cups Vegetable Broth (Chapter 6)

2 cups cooked quinoa

¾ teaspoon salt

½ teaspoon pepper

1. Preheat oven to 400°F.

2. Heat onion and celery in vegan margarine and cook until soft, about 6–8 minutes. Add fresh herbs and heat for another minute, just until fragrant.

3. Remove from heat and add bread, combining well. Add Vegetable Broth to moisten bread; you may need a bit more or less than 1¼ cups.

4. Add cooked quinoa, salt, and pepper, and combine well.

5. Cover, and bake for 30 minutes.

Stuffed-Up Stuffing

Stuffing works best with dried bread to better absorb all that flavor and moisture. Leave your bread out for a couple of days, or lightly toast in a 275°F oven for 20 minutes on each side. For a more textured stuffing, add in ¾ cup chopped dried apricots, ¾ cup chopped nuts (walnuts, cashews, or pecans), or sauté some mushrooms or a grated carrot along with the onion and celery.

QUINOA AND HUMMUS SANDWICH WRAP

Lunch is the perfect time to fill up on whole grains. If you've got leftover tabbouleh from the Bulgur Wheat Tabbouleh Salad with Tomatoes (this chapter), use that in place of the cooked quinoa.

INGREDIENTS

Serves 1

1 tortilla or flavored wrap, warmed

3 tablespoons hummus

⅓ cup cooked quinoa

½ teaspoon lemon juice

2 teaspoons Italian or vinaigrette salad dressing

1 roasted red pepper, sliced into strips

¼ cup sprouts

Salt and pepper, to taste

1. Spread a warmed tortilla or wrap with a layer of hummus, then quinoa, and drizzle with lemon juice and salad dressing.

2. Layer red pepper and sprouts on top, season with salt and pepper, and wrap.

QUINOA "MAC 'N' CHEESE" CASSEROLE

Craving mac and cheese but don't want the carbs—or the cheese, for that matter? Try this filling whole-grain substitute.

INGREDIENTS

Serves 4

1½ cups quinoa

3 cups Vegetable Broth (Chapter 6)

1 onion, chopped

3 cloves garlic, minced

2 tablespoons olive oil

1 bunch broccoli, diced small

1 large tomato, diced

1 tablespoon flour

¾ cup soymilk

½ teaspoon sea salt

1 cup shredded vegan cheese

½ teaspoon dried parsley

1 cup seasoned bread crumbs (optional)

¼ teaspoon nutmeg (optional)

1. Preheat oven to 350°F.

2. Cook quinoa in Vegetable Broth until done and liquid is absorbed, about 15 minutes.

3. In a medium skillet or saucepan, heat onion and garlic in olive oil and add broccoli and tomato. Heat, stirring frequently, for 3–4 minutes.

4. Add flour, stirring to coat well, then add soymilk and sea salt, stirring until thick, about 3 minutes.

5. Combine quinoa, broccoli, tomato, and soymilk mixture, and half of the vegan cheese in a large casserole. Sprinkle the other half of the cheese on top, along with parsley, and bread crumbs and nutmeg if desired.

6. Bake for 10–12 minutes, or until cheese is melted.

What Is Quinoa?

Pronounced "keen-wa," this is actually a seed disguised as a whole grain. Quinoa has been a staple food in South America since ancient times, as it's one of the few crops that thrives in the high altitudes of the Andes. Look for these tiny round seeds in the bulk food bin or baking aisle of natural foods stores, or in the natural foods section of a well-stocked supermarket.

QUINOA "TAPIOCA" PUDDING

Instead of tapioca pudding or baked rice pudding, try this whole-grain version made with quinoa. Healthy enough to eat for breakfast, but sweet enough for dessert too.

INGREDIENTS

Serves 4

1 cup quinoa

2 cups water

2 cups soymilk or soy cream

2 tablespoons maple syrup or brown rice syrup

1 teaspoon cornstarch

2 bananas, sliced thin

½ teaspoon vanilla

⅓ cup raisins

Dash cinnamon or nutmeg (optional)

1. In a medium saucepan, cook quinoa in water over medium heat, stirring frequently, for 10–15 minutes, until done and water is absorbed.

2. Reduce heat to medium-low and stir in soymilk, maple syrup or brown rice syrup, cornstarch, and bananas, combining well. Heat, stirring constantly, for 6–8 minutes, until bananas are soft and pudding has thickened.

3. Stir in vanilla and raisins while still hot and sprinkle with a dash of cinnamon or nutmeg if desired, to taste.

MEDITERRANEAN QUINOA PILAF

Inspired by the flavors of the Mediterranean, bring this vibrant whole-grain entrée to a vegan potluck and watch it magically disappear.

INGREDIENTS

Serves 4

1½ cups quinoa

3 cups Vegetable Broth (Chapter 6)

3 tablespoons balsamic vinegar

2 tablespoons olive oil

1 tablespoon lemon juice

⅓ teaspoon salt

½ cup sun-dried tomatoes, chopped

½ cup artichoke hearts, chopped

½ cup black or kalamata olives, sliced

1. In a large skillet or saucepan, bring the quinoa and Vegetable Broth to a boil, then reduce to a simmer. Cover, and allow quinoa to cook until liquid is absorbed, about 15 minutes. Remove from heat, fluff quinoa with a fork, and allow to stand another 5 minutes.

2. Stir in the balsamic vinegar, olive oil, lemon juice, and salt, then add remaining ingredients, gently tossing to combine. Serve hot.

CHAPTER 9

CLASSIC PASTAS

ARTICHOKE AND SPINACH PESTO PASTA

Spinach, artichoke, and avocado combined with pesto is an impossibly delicious combination. Kermit would love this super-green dish!

INGREDIENTS

Serves 4

1 cup basil

1 cup spinach leaves

3 cloves garlic

½ cup pine nuts or walnuts

1 tablespoon lemon juice

2 tablespoons nutritional yeast

½ teaspoon sea salt

¼ teaspoon pepper

2 tablespoons olive oil

1 cup chopped artichoke hearts

2 tablespoons vegan margarine

1 tablespoon flour

¾ cup soymilk

2 cups cooked pasta

1 avocado, diced (optional)

1. Process together the basil, spinach leaves, garlic, nuts, lemon juice, nutritional yeast, sea salt, and pepper until almost smooth. Add olive oil, then artichoke hearts, and process until artichokes are finely diced.

2. In a small saucepan, melt the vegan margarine and stir in the flour to form a roux. Add soymilk and heat until thickened.

3. Remove from heat and stir in basil and spinach pesto mixture.

4. Toss with prepared pasta and avocado if desired.

WHITE SPINACH LASAGNA

Feel free to dream of Italian opera houses or old Tuscany while savoring this chic cashew butter lasagna by candlelight and listening to Pavarotti.

INGREDIENTS

Serves 6

½ onion, diced

4 cloves garlic, minced

2 tablespoons olive oil

1 (10-ounce) box frozen spinach, thawed and pressed to remove moisture

½ teaspoon salt

1 block firm tofu, crumbled

¾ cup Tropical Cashew Nut Butter (Chapter 3)

2 cups soymilk

1 tablespoon miso

2 tablespoons soy sauce

2 tablespoons lemon juice

3 tablespoons nutritional yeast

2 teaspoons onion powder

1 (12-ounce) package lasagna noodles

1. Sauté onion and garlic in olive oil until soft, about 4–5 minutes, and add spinach and salt, stirring to combine well and cooking just until spinach is heated through. Add crumbled tofu and mix well. Allow to cool completely.

2. In a small saucepan over low heat, combine the Tropical Cashew Nut Butter, soymilk, miso, soy sauce, lemon juice, nutritional yeast, and onion powder until smooth and creamy.

3. Prepare lasagna noodles according to package instructions and preheat oven to 350°F.

4. In a lightly greased lasagna pan, place a thin layer of cashew sauce and then a layer of noodles. Next add spinach mixture and more sauce, then a layer of noodles, continuing until all ingredients are used up. The top layer should be the spinach mixture and then sauce.

5. Bake for 40 minutes, or until done. Allow to cool for at least 10 minutes before serving to allow lasagna to set.

Like the Mona Lisa

Although you might not be the next Michelangelo, lasagna, vegan or not, is a bit of an art form, with so many variants affecting the outcome: moisture, temperature, assembly, the thickness of the noodles. If you're worried about presenting a crumbly lasagna, prepare it in advance and allow to cool completely. Then, reheat just before slicing and serving.

ZUCCHINI AND FRESH BASIL POMODORO

Pick out the finest fresh zucchinis and tomatoes for this one, as pomodoro is a simple pasta dish with little added flavor.

INGREDIENTS

Serves 4

2 zucchinis, sliced

4 cloves garlic, minced

2 tablespoons olive oil

4 large tomatoes, diced

1/3 cup chopped fresh basil

2 cups prepared angel hair or spaghetti pasta

Salt and pepper to taste

Vegan Parmesan cheese or nutritional yeast (optional)

1. Heat zucchinis and garlic over low heat in olive oil for just 1–2 minutes until zucchinis are just lightly softened. Add tomatoes and cook for another 4–5 minutes.

2. Toss zucchinis and tomatoes with basil and pasta and season with salt and pepper, to taste. Serve topped with a sprinkle of vegan Parmesan cheese or nutritional yeast if desired.

EASY PAD THAI NOODLES

Volumes could be written about Thailand's national dish. It's sweet, sour, spicy, and salty all at once, and filled with as much texture and flavor as the streets of Bangkok themselves.

INGREDIENTS

Serves 4

1 pound thin rice noodles

Hot water for soaking

¼ cup tahini

¼ cup ketchup

¼ cup soy sauce

2 tablespoons white, rice, or cider vinegar

3 tablespoons lime juice

2 tablespoons sugar

¾ teaspoon crushed red pepper flakes or cayenne

1 block firm or extra-firm tofu, diced small

3 cloves garlic

¼ cup vegetable or safflower oil

4 scallions, chopped

½ teaspoon salt

Optional toppings: bean sprouts, crushed toasted peanuts, extra scallions, sliced lime

1. Cover the noodles in hot water and set aside to soak until soft, about 5 minutes.

2. Whisk together the tahini, ketchup, soy sauce, vinegar, lime juice, sugar, and red pepper flakes.

3. In a large skillet, fry the tofu and garlic in oil until tofu is lightly golden browned. Add noodles, stirring to combine well, and fry for 2–3 minutes.

4. Reduce heat to medium and add tahini and ketchup sauce mixture, stirring well to combine. Allow to cook for 3–4 minutes until well combined and heated through. Add scallions and salt and heat 1 more minute, stirring well.

5. If desired, serve with extra chopped scallions, bean sprouts, crushed and toasted peanuts, and a lime wedge or two.

Truly Thai

Pad thai is supposed to be a bit greasy—which is why the noodles are fried in the oil. If you're not worried about fat and have quick-cooking thin rice noodles, you can omit the presoaking in water and just toss the noodles in with the tofu and garlic and add extra oil. For an authentic pad thai, however, you'll need tamarind juice or pulp, which you can often find at Mexican as well as Asian grocers.

EGGPLANT PUTTANESCA

Salty and garlicky puttanesca is a thick sauce traditionally served over pasta, but try it over a more wholesome grain, such as quinoa or even brown rice.

INGREDIENTS

Serves 4

3 cloves garlic, minced

1 red bell pepper, chopped

1 eggplant, chopped

2 tablespoons olive oil

2 tablespoons capers, rinsed

⅓ cup sliced kalamata or black olives

½ teaspoon red pepper flakes

1 (14-ounce) can diced tomatoes

1 tablespoon balsamic vinegar

½ teaspoon parsley

1. In a large skillet or saucepan, sauté the garlic, bell pepper, and eggplant in olive oil for 4–5 minutes until eggplant is almost soft. Add capers, olives, and red pepper flakes, and stir to combine.

2. Reduce heat to low and add remaining ingredients. Cover, and allow to simmer for 10–12 minutes until juice from tomatoes has reduced.

3. Serve over cooked pasta or rice.

CLASSIC FETTUCCINE ALFREDO

Most vegan Alfredo recipes start with a roux of margarine and soymilk, but this one uses cashew cream instead for a sensually decadent white sauce. Go ahead and lick the spoons; nobody's watching.

INGREDIENTS
Serves 6

½ cup raw cashews

1¼ cups water

1 tablespoon miso

2 tablespoons lemon juice

2 tablespoons tahini

¼ cup diced onion

1 teaspoon garlic

½ teaspoon salt

¼ cup nutritional yeast

2 tablespoons olive or safflower oil

1 (12-ounce) package fettuccine, cooked

1. Blend together the cashews and water until completely smooth and creamy, about 90 seconds.

2. Add remaining ingredients except oil and fettucine, and purée until smooth. Slowly add oil until thick and oil is emulsified.

3. Heat in a saucepan over low heat for 4–5 minutes, stirring frequently. Serve over cooked fettuccine noodles.

Alfredo Sauce Lasagna

Make a double batch and use this cheesy sauce to create a layered White Spinach Lasagna (this chapter). It's also great in macaroni and cheese for kids, or as a dip for veggies.

GNOCCHI WITH WALNUT PARSLEY SAUCE

A simple and savory pasta sauce that pairs perfectly with earthy potato gnocchi.

INGREDIENTS
Serves 4

1 cup chopped walnuts

2½ cups unsweetened soymilk

2 tablespoons vegan margarine

2 tablespoons all-purpose flour

¾ teaspoon parsley

2 teaspoons nutritional yeast (optional)

½ teaspoon salt

¼ teaspoon black pepper

Prepared Homemade Garlic and Herb Gnocchi (this chapter)

1. Heat walnuts and soymilk over low heat for 3–4 minutes, to soften the walnuts. Set aside.

2. In a small saucepan, heat vegan margarine over low heat until melted and whisk in flour, stirring continuously to prevent from burning.

3. Slowly stir in soymilk and walnuts, again stirring continuously. Heat until soymilk thickens into a sauce, about 4–5 minutes.

4. Remove from heat, stir in parsley, nutritional yeast if desired, salt, and pepper, and pour over cooked gnocchi. Serve immediately.

HOMEMADE GARLIC AND HERB GNOCCHI

Homemade gnocchi is well worth the effort if you have the time! Use a simple Walnut Parsley Sauce (this chapter) or minimal seasonings to make sure that the flavor from the gnocchi shines through.

INGREDIENTS
Serves 4

2 large potatoes

¾ teaspoon garlic powder

½ teaspoon dried basil

½ teaspoon dried parsley

¾ teaspoon salt

1½ cups all-purpose flour

Water for boiling

1. Bake potatoes until done, about 50 minutes at 400°F. Allow to cool, then peel skins.

2. Using a fork, mash potatoes with garlic powder, basil, parsley, and salt until potatoes are completely smooth, with no lumps.

3. On a floured work surface, place half of the flour, and the potatoes on top. Use your hands to work the flour into the potatoes to form a dough. Continue to add only as much flour as is needed to form a dough. Knead smooth.

4. Working in batches, roll out a rope of dough about 1" thick. Slice into 1"-long pieces, and gently roll against a fork to make grooves in the dough. This helps the sauce stick to the gnocchi.

5. Cook gnocchi in boiling water for 2–3 minutes until they rise to the surface. Serve immediately.

Top It With . . .
When making the effort to create fresh gnocchi (pronounced the Italian way—nyee-OH-kee), you want to taste the fresh doughy flavors, not a complex overpowering topping, so carefully choose your sauce. Melt a bit of vegan margarine with the gnocchi, or perhaps a flavored oil, and sprinkle with fresh herbs, salt, and pepper. Try a combination of garlic and nutritional yeast, or olive oil with a few crumbled sage or rosemary leaves.

BALSAMIC DIJON ORZO

Defying logic, this simple dish flavored with balsamic and Dijon is somehow exponentially greater than the sum of its parts. Add a dash of sugar or agave if you find the tangy Dijon overpowering.

INGREDIENTS

Serves 4

3 tablespoons balsamic vinegar

1½ tablespoons Dijon mustard

1½ tablespoons olive oil

1 teaspoon basil

1 teaspoon parsley

½ teaspoon oregano

1½ cups orzo, cooked

2 medium tomatoes, chopped

½ cup sliced black olives

1 (15-ounce) can great northern or cannellini beans, drained

½ teaspoon salt

¼ teaspoon pepper

1. In a small bowl or container, whisk together the vinegar, mustard, olive oil, basil, parsley, and oregano until well mixed.

2. Over low heat, combine the orzo with the balsamic dressing and add tomatoes, olives, and beans. Cook for 3–4 minutes, stirring to combine.

3. Season with salt and pepper.

LAZY AND HUNGRY GARLIC PASTA

It's not fancy, but that's the beauty of this recipe, which is, aptly, for those times when you're too hungry to cook and just want to fill your stomach.

INGREDIENTS
Serves 6

2 cloves garlic, minced

2 tablespoons olive oil

3 cups pasta, cooked

2 tablespoons nutritional yeast

½ teaspoon parsley

Dash red pepper flakes (optional)

Salt and pepper to taste

1. Heat the garlic in olive oil for just 1–2 minutes until almost browned.

2. Toss garlic and olive oil with remaining ingredients. Adjust seasonings to taste.

Really Hungry? Really Lazy?
Garlic powder, nutritional yeast, and salt is a delicious seasoning combination, and will give you a bit of a B12 perk-up. Use it over toast, veggies, popcorn, bagels, baked potatoes, and, of course, cooked pasta if you're feeling, well, lazy and hungry!

CALIFORNIA PICNIC PASTA SALAD

Lightly flavored with plenty of texture, this is a colorful salad that makes a meal on its own.

INGREDIENTS

Serves 6

3 cups corkscrew or bow tie pasta, cooked

2 large tomatoes, diced

½ cup jarred banana peppers, sliced thin

½ red onion, diced

½ cup sliced black olives

2 tablespoons olive oil

1 tablespoon lemon juice

2 teaspoons Dijon mustard

1 tablespoon red wine vinegar

½ teaspoon basil

½ teaspoon oregano

Salt and pepper to taste

2 avocadoes, diced

1. Combine the pasta, tomatoes, peppers, onion, and olives in a large bowl.

2. In a separate small bowl, whisk together the remaining ingredients except avocado, until well mixed.

3. Chill for at least 1 hour.

4. Add diced avocado and toss gently. Serve immediately.

BASIC VEGETABLE MARINARA

No Parmesan is needed to top off this chunky vegetable marinara. Toss in a handful of TVP or browned store-bought mock meat crumbles for a "meaty" sauce.

INGREDIENTS
Serves 4

4 cloves garlic, minced

1 carrot, sliced thin

2 ribs celery, chopped

2 tablespoons olive oil

1 (28-ounce) can diced or stewed tomatoes

1 (6-ounce) can tomato paste

1 teaspoon oregano

1 teaspoon parsley

2 tablespoons chopped fresh basil

2 bay leaves

½ cup corn (optional)

½ cup sliced black olives

1 tablespoon balsamic vinegar

½ teaspoon crushed red pepper flakes

½ teaspoon salt

1. Heat garlic, carrot, and celery in olive oil over medium heat, stirring frequently, for 4–5 minutes.

2. Reduce heat to medium-low, then add tomatoes, tomato paste, oregano, parsley, basil, and bay leaves, stirring well to combine.

3. Cover, and heat for at least 30 minutes, stirring frequently.

4. Add corn if desired, olives, balsamic vinegar, red pepper, and salt, and simmer for another 5 minutes uncovered.

5. Remove bay leaves before serving and adjust seasonings to taste.

In a Pinch
Don't have time to make marinara from scratch? Take 5 minutes to heat a store-bought jar on the stove and add in frozen veggies, Italian seasonings, and a bit of wine or balsamic vinegar for a fresh taste.

ARTICHOKE AND OLIVE PUTTANESCA

Use fresh basil and parsley if you have it on hand, but otherwise, dried is fine.

INGREDIENTS

Serves 6

3 cloves garlic, minced

2 tablespoons olive oil

1 (14-ounce) can diced or crushed tomatoes

¼ cup sliced black olives

¼ cup sliced green olives

1 cup chopped artichoke hearts

2 tablespoons capers

½ teaspoon red pepper flakes

½ teaspoon basil

¾ teaspoon parsley

¼ teaspoon salt

1 (12-ounce) package pasta, cooked

1. Heat garlic in olive oil for 2–3 minutes. Reduce heat and add remaining ingredients except pasta.

2. Cook over low heat uncovered for 10–12 minutes until most of the liquid from tomatoes is absorbed.

3. Toss with cooked pasta.

CREAMY SUN-DRIED TOMATO PASTA

Silken tofu makes a creamy low-fat sauce base. If using dried tomatoes rather than oil-packed, be sure to rehydrate them well first.

INGREDIENTS

Serves 6

1 block silken tofu, drained

¼ cup soymilk

2 tablespoons red wine vinegar

½ teaspoon garlic powder

½ teaspoon salt

1¼ cups sun-dried tomatoes, rehydrated

1 teaspoon parsley

1 (12-ounce) package pasta, cooked

2 tablespoons chopped fresh basil

1. Blend together the tofu, soymilk, vinegar, garlic powder, and salt in a blender or food processor until smooth and creamy. Add tomatoes and parsley and pulse until tomatoes are finely diced.

2. Transfer sauce to a small pot and heat over medium-low heat just until hot.

3. Pour sauce over pasta and sprinkle with chopped fresh basil.

Two in One

For another elegant twist on this dish, prepare this recipe with 1¼ cups chopped roasted red peppers instead of sun-dried tomatoes, or try a combination of the two.

PUMPKIN CREAM PASTA SAUCE

A simple recipe, but with such an unusual mix of flavors and ingredients, it's bound to impress. This sauce would also go well with Homemade Garlic and Herb Gnocchi (this chapter) or over stuffed Tofu "Ricotta" Manicotti (Chapter 11).

INGREDIENTS

Serves 4

1 onion, chopped

2 cloves garlic, minced

2 tablespoons vegan margarine

1 (15-ounce) can puréed pumpkin

1½ cups soy cream

¼ cup nutritional yeast

½ teaspoon parsley

Salt and pepper, to taste

1 (12-ounce) package pasta, cooked

1. Heat onion and garlic in margarine until soft, about 3–4 minutes.

2. Reduce heat to medium-low and add pumpkin and soy cream. Bring to a low simmer and cook for about 10 minutes, stirring frequently, until creamy.

3. Stir in nutritional yeast and parsley and season generously with salt and pepper, heating for just another 1–2 minutes.

4. Serve over cooked pasta.

EASY CREAMY PASTA AND PEAS

Great for the kids, but use artichoke hearts or broccoli to make it for adults, or any frozen mixed veggies you like.

INGREDIENTS
Serves 4

1½ cups soymilk

1 teaspoon garlic powder

2 tablespoons vegan margarine

1 tablespoon flour

1½ cups green peas

⅓ cup nutritional yeast

1 (12-ounce) package pasta, cooked

Salt and pepper, to taste

1. In a medium pot, whisk together the soymilk, garlic powder, and margarine over low heat. Add flour and stir well to combine, heating just until thickened.

2. Add peas and nutritional yeast until heated and well mixed, then pour over pasta.

3. Season generously with salt and pepper, to taste.

Basic Vegan White Sauce
Seeing a pattern? Melted vegan margarine, along with soymilk, is the base for many vegan cream sauces, roux, and cheese sauces. Flour is the simplest thickener, but cornstarch or arrowroot also work. Nutritional yeast is added for a cheesy flavor, and garlic powder, onion powder, and salt enhance the general flavor. Use an unsweetened soymilk for a more savory taste.

LEMON, BASIL, AND ARTICHOKE PASTA

The earthy rosemary, basil, and lemon flavor would complement gnocchi well, otherwise use a grooved pasta, such as corkscrews, to catch the sauce.

INGREDIENTS
Serves 6

12 ounces pasta, cooked

1 (6-ounce) jar artichoke hearts, drained and chopped

2 large tomatoes, chopped

½ cup fresh basil, chopped fine

½ cup sliced black olives

2 tablespoons olive oil

1 tablespoon lemon juice

½ teaspoon rosemary

2 tablespoons nutritional yeast

Salt and pepper, to taste

Over low heat, combine the cooked pasta with the remaining ingredients, combining well and heating just until well mixed and heated through, about 3–4 minutes.

FIVE-MINUTE VEGAN PASTA SALAD

Once you've got the pasta cooked and cooled, this takes just 5 minutes to assemble, as it's made with store-bought dressing. A balsamic vinaigrette or tomato dressing would also work well.

INGREDIENTS
Serves 4

4 cups pasta, cooked

¾ cup vegan Italian salad dressing

3 scallions, chopped

½ cup sliced black olives

1 tomato, chopped

1 avocado, diced (optional)

Salt and pepper to taste

Toss together all ingredients. Allow to chill for at least 1½ hours before serving if time allows, to allow flavors to combine.

Instant Add-Ons

Open up a jar and instantly add color, flavor, and texture to a basic pasta salad. What's in your cupboard? Try capers, roasted red peppers, canned veggies, jarred pimentos, sun-dried tomatoes, or even mandarin oranges or sliced beets. Snip in any leftover fresh herbs you have on hand.

SWEET AND SPICY PEANUT NOODLES

Like the song of the siren, these noodles entice you with their sweet pineapple flavor, then scorch your tongue with fiery chilies. Very sneaky, indeed.

INGREDIENTS

Serves 4

1 (12-ounce) package Asian-style noodles

⅓ cup peanut butter

2 tablespoons soy sauce

⅔ cup pineapple juice

2 cloves garlic, minced

1 teaspoon fresh ginger, grated

½ teaspoon salt

1 tablespoon olive oil

1 teaspoon sesame oil

2–3 small chilies, minced

¾ cup diced pineapple

1. Prepare noodles according to package instructions and set aside.

2. In a small saucepan, stir together the peanut butter, soy sauce, pineapple juice, garlic, ginger, and salt over low heat, just until well combined.

3. Place the olive oil and sesame oil in a large skillet and fry minced chilies and pineapple for 2–3 minutes, stirring frequently, until pineapple is lightly browned. Add noodles and fry for another minute, stirring well.

4. Reduce heat to low and add peanut butter sauce mixture, stirring to combine well. Heat for 1 more minute until well combined.

ORZO WITH WHITE WINE AND MUSHROOMS

Try using two different varieties of mushrooms for some extra color and depth of flavor.

INGREDIENTS

Serves 4

1 cup sliced mushrooms

1 yellow onion, chopped

3 cloves garlic, minced

2 tablespoons olive oil

1½ cups Vegetable Broth (Chapter 6)

½ cup white wine

1½ cups orzo

2 tablespoons vegan margarine

2 tablespoons nutritional yeast or vegan Parmesan (optional)

2 tablespoons chopped fresh basil or parsley

Salt and pepper, to taste

1. Heat mushrooms, onion, and garlic in olive oil until just soft, about 3–4 minutes.

2. Reduce heat and add Vegetable Broth, white wine, and orzo. Cover, and simmer for 8–10 minutes until orzo is cooked and liquid is absorbed.

3. While still hot, stir in margarine, nutritional yeast or Parmesan if desired, and fresh basil or parsley, and season generously with salt and pepper, to taste.

What Is Orzo?

Despite its abundant use at gourmet eateries, there's really nothing fancy about "orzo": It's just a funny-sounding word for "small, rice-shaped pasta." In other words, it's just pasta. Because of its small size, it can be used more like couscous and rice than other pastas, and it works well with lighter and thinner sauces and in pilaf-like salads.

BASIC TOFU LASAGNA

Seasoned tofu takes the place of ricotta cheese, and really does look and taste like the real thing. Fresh parsley adds flavor, and with store-bought sauce, it's quick to get in the oven.

INGREDIENTS

Serves 6

1 block firm tofu

1 (12-ounce) block silken tofu

¼ cup nutritional yeast

1 tablespoon lemon juice

1 tablespoon soy sauce

1 teaspoon garlic powder

2 teaspoons basil

3 tablespoons chopped fresh parsley

1 teaspoon salt

4 cups spaghetti sauce

1 (16-ounce) package lasagna noodles, cooked

1. Preheat oven to 350°F.

2. In a large bowl, mash together the firm tofu, silken tofu, nutritional yeast, lemon juice, soy sauce, garlic powder, basil, parsley, and salt until combined and crumbly like ricotta cheese.

3. To assemble the lasagna, spread about ⅔ cup spaghetti sauce on the bottom of a lasagna pan, then add a layer of noodles.

4. Spread about ½ the tofu mixture on top of the noodles, followed by another layer of sauce. Place a second layer of noodles on top, followed by the remaining tofu and more sauce. Finish it off with a third layer of noodles and the rest of the sauce.

5. Cover, and bake for 25 minutes.

STOVETOP CHEATER'S MAC 'N' CHEESE

Yes, it's cheating just a little to make vegan macaroni and cheese starting with store-bought "cheese," but who cares? The secret to getting this recipe super creamy and cheesy is using cream cheese as well as vegan Cheddar. It's not particularly healthy, but at least it's still cholesterol-free!

INGREDIENTS

Serves 6

1 (12-ounce) package macaroni

1 cup soymilk

2 tablespoons vegan margarine

½ teaspoon onion powder

1 teaspoon garlic powder

½ cup vegan cream cheese

½ cup vegan Cheddar cheese

⅓ cup nutritional yeast

½ teaspoon salt

Black pepper, to taste

1. Prepare macaroni according to package instructions. Drain well and return to pot.

2. Over low heat, stir in soymilk and vegan margarine until melted.

3. Add remaining ingredients, stirring to combine over low heat until cheese is melted and ingredients are well mixed.

Just Because It's Vegan . . .

. . . Doesn't mean it's healthy! If health is your main concern for going vegan, you may do well to avoid recipes such as this one. Vegan cream cheese usually contains hydrogenated oils, which are admittedly nearly as bad for your system as red meat. Nonhydrogenated vegan cream cheese is available, but unfortunately, it just doesn't taste as good!

LEMON THYME ORZO WITH ASPARAGUS

The combination of lemon and thyme is understated and rustic; it smells and tastes good enough to bathe in. If asparagus isn't in season, use green peas or lightly steamed broccoli.

INGREDIENTS

Serves 4

1½ cups orzo

1 bunch asparagus, chopped

2 tablespoons olive oil

Zest from 1 lemon

2 tablespoons lemon juice

½ teaspoon salt

¼ teaspoon pepper

2 teaspoons chopped fresh thyme

1. Cook orzo according to package instructions.

2. In a large skillet, heat asparagus in olive oil until just tender. Do not overcook.

3. Reduce heat to low and add in orzo and remaining ingredients, stirring to combine well. Cook for just 1–2 minutes until heated through, and adjust seasonings to taste.

PEANUT BUTTER NOODLES FOR KIDS

Drown your noodles in this mildly flavored peanut butter noodle recipe for kids. What kid doesn't love peanut butter?

INGREDIENTS

Serves 4

1 pound Asian-style noodles (or use regular pasta)

⅓ cup peanut butter

⅓ cup water

3 tablespoons soy sauce

2 tablespoons lime juice

2 tablespoons rice vinegar

1 tablespoon sesame oil

½ teaspoon ginger powder

1 teaspoon sugar

½ teaspoon crushed red pepper flakes (optional)

1. Prepare noodles or pasta according to package instructions and set aside.

2. Whisk together remaining ingredients over low heat just until combined, about 3 minutes. Toss with noodles.

Perfect Peanut Sauce

Experiment with the portions to get a ratio that works for you. Add fresh diced chilies for a perked-up version for adults, or for a satay-style sauce, add a couple of tablespoons of coconut milk. Use the sauce alone to dress steamed veggies or fried tofu—or to disguise anything the kids are reluctant to eat.

ASIAN SESAME TAHINI NOODLES

A creamy and nutty Chinese-inspired noodle dish. If you don't have Asian-style noodles on hand, spaghetti will do.

INGREDIENTS

Serves 4

1 pound Asian noodles

½ cup tahini

⅓ cup water

2 tablespoons soy sauce

1 clove garlic

2 teaspoons fresh ginger, minced

2 tablespoons rice vinegar

2 teaspoons sesame oil

1 red bell pepper, sliced thin

3 scallions, chopped

¾ cup snow peas, chopped

¼ teaspoon crushed red pepper flakes

1. Cook noodles according to package instructions; drain well.

2. Whisk or blend together the tahini, water, soy sauce, garlic, ginger, and rice vinegar.

3. In a large skillet, heat the sesame oil, bell pepper, scallions, and snow peas for 2–3 minutes. Add tahini sauce and noodles, stirring well to combine.

4. Cook over low heat just until heated, about 2–3 minutes.

5. Garnish with crushed red pepper flakes to taste.

SPAGHETTI WITH ITALIAN "MEATBALLS"

These little TVP nuggets are so chewy and addicting, you just might want to make a double batch.
If you can't find beef-flavored bouillon, just use what you've got. Don't be tempted to add extra water to
the TVP, as it needs to be a little dry for this recipe.

INGREDIENTS
Serves 6

½ vegetarian beef-flavored bouillon cube (optional)

⅔ cup hot water

⅔ cup TVP

Egg replacer for 2 eggs

½ onion, minced

2 tablespoons ketchup or barbecue sauce

½ teaspoon garlic powder

1 teaspoon basil

1 teaspoon parsley

½ teaspoon sage

½ teaspoon salt

½ cup bread crumbs

⅔–¾ cup flour

Oil for pan-frying

3 cups prepared spaghetti sauce

1 (12-ounce) package spaghetti noodles, cooked

1. Dissolve bouillon cube (if using) in hot water, and pour hot water over TVP to reconstitute. Allow to sit for 6–7 minutes. Gently press to remove any excess moisture.

2. In a large bowl, combine the TVP, egg replacer, onion, ketchup or barbecue sauce, and seasonings until well mixed.

3. Add bread crumbs and combine well, then add flour, a few tablespoons at a time, mixing well to combine until mixture is sticky and thick. You may need to adjust the amount of flour.

4. Using lightly floured hands, shape into balls 1½"–2" thick.

5. Pan-fry "meatballs" in a bit of oil over medium heat, rolling them around in the pan to maintain the shape, until golden brown on all sides.

6. Reduce heat to medium-low and add spaghetti sauce, heating thoroughly. Serve over cooked spaghetti noodles.

TVP Veggie Burgers

This recipe makes excellently chewy veggie burger patties. Cut down on the basil, sage, and parsley, and add some "beefier" seasonings: paprika, chili powder, seasoning salt, or pepper. Shape into patties instead of balls and pan-fry in oil on both sides. Delish!

BAKED MACARONI AND CHEESE

Vegan chefs all take pride in seeing who can create the best dairy-free macaroni and cheese ever. Join in the friendly rivalry with this recipe. Don't tell anyone that the silken tofu is the secret ingredient for super creaminess.

INGREDIENTS

Serves 6

1 (12-ounce) package macaroni

1 block silken tofu

1 cup soymilk

2 tablespoons tahini

2 tablespoons lemon juice

1 tablespoon miso

1 teaspoon garlic powder

1 teaspoon onion powder

¼ cup nutritional yeast

2 tablespoons vegan margarine

1 cup bread crumbs

⅓ teaspoon nutmeg (optional)

½ teaspoon salt

½ teaspoon pepper

1. Prepare macaroni according to package instructions. Drain well and place in a large casserole or baking dish.

2. In a blender or food processor, purée together the tofu, soymilk, tahini, lemon juice, miso, garlic and onion powders, and nutritional yeast until smooth and creamy, scraping the sides to blend well.

3. Heat oven to 350°F.

4. Combine tofu mixture with macaroni in the casserole dish.

5. In a small skillet, melt the vegan margarine and add bread crumbs, stirring to coat. Spread bread crumbs on top of macaroni and sprinkle with nutmeg if desired, and salt and pepper.

6. Bake for 20–25 minutes or until slightly crispy.

CHAPTER 10

MISCELLANEOUS MAINS

CARAMELIZED ONION AND BARBECUE SAUCE PIZZA

Sweet onions and barbecue sauce are the perfect pair in this tofu-topped pizza.

INGREDIENTS

Serves 4

1 vegan pizza crust

⅔ cup barbecue sauce

2 red onions, chopped

3 tablespoons olive oil

1 block tofu, diced small

½ cup diced pineapple

⅓ teaspoon garlic powder

Salt and pepper, to taste

1. Preheat oven to 450°F. Spread barbecue sauce on pizza crust.

2. Heat onions in olive oil for 2–3 minutes, stirring occasionally. Add tofu and sauté until tofu is lightly crisped and onions are soft and caramelized.

3. Top pizza with tofu, onions, and pineapple. Sprinkle with garlic powder and a generous amount of salt and pepper.

4. Bake for 12–14 minutes, or according to instructions on pizza dough.

Vegan Pizza

More and more pizzerias are offering vegan cheese, but cheeseless pizza is more delicious than you might think. When ordering out, fill your pizza with tons of extra toppings, and sprinkle it with nutritional yeast if you want that cheesy flavor, or make some Dairy-Free Ranch Dressing (Chapter 5) to dip it in.

BREADED EGGPLANT "PARMESAN"

Slowly baking these breaded eggplant cutlets brings out the best flavor, but they can also be pan-fried in a bit of oil.

INGREDIENTS

Serves 4

1 medium eggplant

½ teaspoon salt

¾ cup flour

1 teaspoon garlic powder

⅔ cup soymilk

Egg replacer for 2 eggs

1½ cups bread crumbs

2 tablespoons Italian seasoning

¼ cup nutritional yeast

1½ cups marinara sauce

1. Slice eggplant into ¾"-thick slices and sprinkle with salt. Allow to sit for 10 minutes. Gently pat dry to remove extra moisture.

2. In a shallow bowl or pie tin, combine flour and garlic. In a separate bowl, whisk together the soymilk and egg replacer. In a third bowl, combine the bread crumbs, Italian seasoning, and nutritional yeast.

3. Coat each eggplant slice with flour/garlic, then carefully dip in the soymilk mixture, then coat with the bread-crumb mixture and place in a lightly greased casserole dish.

4. Bake for 20–25 minutes, then top with marinara sauce and return to oven until sauce is hot, about 5 minutes.

BASIC CREAMY POLENTA

Whether for breakfast, lunch, or dinner, as an entrée or side, polenta is versatile, simple, and great for families on a budget. This is a basic recipe, so add spices if you prefer, or a bit of soymilk for a creamier texture.

INGREDIENTS

Serves 4

6½ cups water

2 cups cornmeal

3 tablespoons vegan margarine

1½ teaspoons garlic powder

¼ cup nutritional yeast

½ teaspoon salt

1. Bring the water to a boil, then slowly add the cornmeal to make the polenta, stirring to combine.

2. Reduce heat to low, and cook for 20 minutes, stirring frequently and scraping the bottom of the pot to prevent sticking and burning. Polenta is done when it is thick and sticky.

3. Stir in margarine, garlic powder, nutritional yeast, and salt.

Properties of Polenta

Homemade polenta can be eaten as it is, all soft and creamy, or transfer it to a loaf pan, smoothing the top with the back of a spoon. Chill it in the refrigerator and it will firm up into a loaf in about an hour or two. You can then slice it and pan-fry it in a bit of oil, or just reheat the loaf in your oven. The stuff you buy in a tube at the store is already cooked, so all you need to do is fry it up or heat it in the oven.

ITALIAN VEGGIE AND PASTA CASSEROLE

Veggies and pasta are baked into an Italian-spiced casserole with a crumbly topping. Add in a handful of TVP crumbles or some kidney beans if you want a protein boost.

INGREDIENTS

Serves 6

1 (16-ounce) package pasta (use a medium pasta like bow ties, corkscrews, or small shells)

1 onion, chopped

3 zucchinis, sliced

1 red bell pepper, chopped

4 cloves garlic, minced

2 tablespoons olive oil

1 (28-ounce) can diced tomatoes

¾ cup corn kernels

1 teaspoon parsley

1 teaspoon basil

½ teaspoon oregano

½ teaspoon crushed red pepper flakes

¼ teaspoon pepper

1 cup bread crumbs

½ cup grated vegan cheese

1. Cook pasta according to package instructions, drain well, and layer in a baking dish.

2. Preheat oven to 425°F.

3. Sauté onion, zucchinis, bell pepper, and garlic in olive oil just until soft, about 3–4 minutes. Add tomatoes, corn, parsley, basil, oregano, and crushed red pepper. Simmer for 8–10 minutes and season with black pepper.

4. Cover pasta with zucchini and tomato mixture. Sprinkle with bread crumbs and vegan cheese.

5. Bake for 10–12 minutes.

TOFU AND PORTOBELLO ENCHILADAS

Turn up the heat by adding some fresh minced or canned chilies. If you're addicted to vegan cheese, add a handful of grated cheese to the filling as well as on top.

INGREDIENTS

Serves 4

1 block firm tofu, diced small

5 portobello mushrooms, chopped

1 onion, diced

3 cloves garlic, minced

2 tablespoons oil

2 teaspoons chili powder

½ cup sliced black olives

1 (15-ounce) can enchilada sauce

8–10 flour tortillas

½ cup vegan cheese (optional)

1. Preheat oven to 350°F.

2. In a large skillet, heat the tofu, mushrooms, onion, and garlic in oil until tofu is just lightly sautéed, about 4–5 minutes. Add chili powder and heat for 1 more minute, stirring to coat well.

3. Remove from heat and add black olives and ⅓ cup enchilada sauce, and combine well.

4. Spread a thin layer of enchilada sauce in the bottom of a baking pan or casserole dish.

5. Place about ¼ cup of the tofu and mushrooms in each flour tortilla and roll, placing snugly in the baking dish. Top with remaining enchilada sauce, coating the tops of each tortilla well.

6. Sprinkle with vegan cheese if desired, and bake for 25–30 minutes.

Vegetable Enchiladas

Omit the mushrooms and grate a couple of carrots and zucchinis to use in the filling instead. They'll bake quickly when grated, so no need to precook.

PUMPKIN AND LENTIL CURRY

Red lentils complement the pumpkin and coconut best in this salty-sweet curry, but any kind you have on hand will do. Look for frozen chopped squash to cut the preparation time.

INGREDIENTS

Serves 3

1 yellow onion, chopped

2 cups chopped pumpkin or butternut squash

2 tablespoons olive oil

1 tablespoon curry powder

1 teaspoon cumin

2 small red chilies, minced, or ½ teaspoon red pepper flakes

2 whole cloves

3 cups water or Vegetable Broth (Chapter 6)

1 cup lentils

2 tomatoes, chopped

8–10 fresh green beans, trimmed and chopped

¾ cup coconut milk

1. Sauté onion and pumpkin or squash in olive oil until onion is soft, about 4 minutes. Add curry powder, cumin, chilies, and cloves, and toast for 1 minute, stirring frequently.

2. Reduce heat slightly and add water or Vegetable Broth and lentils. Cover, and cook for about 10–12 minutes, stirring occasionally.

3. Uncover, and add tomatoes, green beans, and coconut milk, stirring well to combine. Heat uncovered for 4–5 more minutes, just until tomatoes and beans are cooked.

4. Serve over rice or whole grains.

BLACK AND GREEN VEGGIE BURRITOS

These black bean burritos are filled with zucchini or yellow summer squash. Just add in the fixings—salsa, avocado slices, some nondairy sour cream . . . the works!

INGREDIENTS

Serves 4

1 onion, chopped

2 zucchinis or yellow squash, cut into thin strips

1 bell pepper, any color, chopped

2 tablespoons olive oil

½ teaspoon oregano

½ teaspoon cumin

1 (15-ounce) can black beans, drained

1 (4-ounce) can green chilies

1 cup cooked rice

4 large flour tortillas, warmed

1. Heat onion, zucchinis or yellow squash, and bell pepper in olive oil until vegetables are soft, about 4–5 minutes.

2. Reduce heat to low and add oregano, cumin, black beans, and green chilies, combining well. Cook, stirring, until well combined and heated through.

3. Place ¼ cup rice in the center of each flour tortilla and top with the bean mixture. Fold the bottom of the tortilla up, then snugly wrap one side, then the other.

4. Serve as is, or bake in a 350°F oven for 15 minutes for a crispy burrito.

Gluten-Free Bean Burritos

If you're gluten-free or just want an extra protein and nutrition boost, use a cooked grain other than rice in these burritos and shop for a gluten-free flatbread to wrap it up in. Quinoa in particular works well in burritos, as it is lighter than other grains.

POLENTA AND CHILI CASSEROLE

Using canned chili and thawed frozen veggies, you can get this quick one-pot casserole meal in the oven in just about 10 minutes.

INGREDIENTS

Serves 4

3 cans vegetarian chili (or about 6 cups homemade)

2 cups diced veggie mixture, any kind

1 cup cornmeal

2½ cups water

2 tablespoons vegan margarine

1 tablespoon chili powder

1. Combine vegetarian chili and vegetables and spread in the bottom of a lightly greased casserole dish.

2. Preheat oven to 375°F.

3. Over low heat, combine cornmeal and water. Simmer, stirring frequently, for 10 minutes. Stir in vegan margarine.

4. Spread cornmeal mixture over chili and sprinkle the top with chili powder.

5. Bake uncovered for 20–25 minutes.

THE EASIEST BLACK BEAN BURGER RECIPE IN THE WORLD

Veggie burgers are notorious for falling apart. If you're sick of crumbly burgers, try this simple method for making black bean patties. It's 100 percent guaranteed to stick together.

INGREDIENTS
Yields 6 patties

1 (15-ounce) can black beans, drained

3 tablespoons minced onions

1 teaspoon salt

1½ teaspoons garlic powder

2 teaspoons parsley

1 teaspoon chili powder

⅔ cup flour

Oil for pan-frying

1. Process the black beans in a blender or food processor until halfway mashed, or mash with a fork.

2. Add minced onions, salt, garlic powder, parsley, and chili powder and mash to combine.

3. Add flour, a bit at a time, again mashing together to combine. You may need a little bit more or less than ⅔ cup. Beans should stick together completely.

4. Form into patties and pan-fry in a bit of oil for 2–3 minutes on each side. Patties will appear to be done on the outside while still a bit mushy on the inside, so fry them a few minutes longer than you think they need.

Veggie Burger Tips

Although this recipe is foolproof, if you have trouble with your veggie burgers crumbling, try adding egg replacer to bind the ingredients, then chill the mixture before forming into patties. Veggie burger patties can be grilled, baked, or pan-fried, but they do tend to dry out a bit in the oven. Not a problem; just smother with extra ketchup!

CILANTRO POTATO AND PEA CURRY

A simple curried potato recipe with peas. Turn up the heat by adding in some fresh chilies or cayenne pepper, or sweeten it for kids by adding some pineapple.

INGREDIENTS

Serves 4

3 cloves garlic

¼ cup water

¼ cup tomato paste

1 teaspoon fresh ginger, minced

2 tablespoons curry powder

1 teaspoon sugar (optional)

2 tablespoons soy sauce

½ onion, chopped

1 tablespoon sesame oil

4 medium potatoes, chopped

2 tablespoons olive oil

1½ cups frozen green peas, thawed

1 (14-ounce) can coconut milk

3 tablespoons chopped fresh cilantro

1. Combine garlic, water, tomato paste, ginger, curry powder, sugar if desired, soy sauce, onion, and sesame oil in a blender or food processor and process until smooth.

2. In a large skillet, sauté potatoes in olive oil for 3–4 minutes, then add spice mix and peas and simmer, covered, for 10–12 minutes, stirring occasionally.

3. Add coconut milk and simmer for another 5–6 minutes, stirring well to combine.

4. Remove from heat and add fresh cilantro.

SWEET STUFFED BUTTERNUT SQUASH

For a Thanksgiving side dish or even an entrée that everyone will "ooh" and "ahh" over, try this stuffed squash. It has a beautiful presentation, but is super-easy to prepare. Use raisins if you don't like cranberries.

INGREDIENTS

Serves 4

2 small butternut squash

½ cup apple juice or orange juice (optional)

2 apples, diced

½ cup chopped pecans or walnuts

⅓ cup frozen or rehydrated dried cranberries

¼ cup maple syrup

2 tablespoons vegan margarine, melted

½ teaspoon cinnamon

¼ teaspoon nutmeg

1. Preheat oven to 350°F. Chop the squash in half and scrape out any stringy bits and seeds.

2. Pour apple or orange juice if desired into a rimmed baking sheet, and place squash cut side down. Roast in the oven for 20 minutes. Alternatively, you can microwave squash for 10 minutes. Remove from oven.

3. In a large bowl, combine the apples, nuts, and cranberries. Stir in maple syrup, melted vegan margarine, cinnamon, and nutmeg, tossing to coat well.

4. Stuff each half of squash with apple filling, piling any extra filling on top, and roast another 20–25 minutes.

How to Chop Squash

Even the finest chef armed with the sharpest knife may have a bit of trouble chopping squash. To make the task easier, pierce the squash several times with a fork and microwave for 3–4 minutes, just to soften it up a bit. Your knife will run through much easier afterward.

BLACK BEAN POLENTA CAKES WITH SALSA

All the flavors of the Southwest combine in this colorful confetti polenta loaf. Pan-fry individual slices if you like, or just enjoy it as it is.

INGREDIENTS
Serves 4

1 (15-ounce) can black beans, drained

6 cups water

2 cups cornmeal

½ red or yellow bell pepper, diced small

¾ teaspoon cumin

1 teaspoon chili powder

1 teaspoon garlic powder

¾ teaspoon oregano

½ teaspoon salt

½ teaspoon black pepper

2 tablespoons vegan margarine

Salsa

1. Place black beans in a bowl and mash with a fork until halfway mashed. Set aside.

2. Bring the water to a boil, then slowly add cornmeal, stirring to combine.

3. Reduce heat to low and cook for 10 minutes, stirring frequently and scraping the bottom of the pot to prevent sticking and burning.

4. Add bell pepper, cumin, chili powder, garlic powder, oregano, salt, and pepper and stir well to combine. Continue to heat, stirring frequently for 8–10 more minutes.

5. Add vegan margarine and stir well to combine, then add black beans, combining well.

6. Gently press into a lightly greased loaf pan, smoothing the top with the back of a spoon. Chill until firm, at least 1 hour. Reheat, slice, and serve topped with prepared salsa.

PORTOBELLO AND PEPPER FAJITAS

Chopped seitan could take the place of the portobellos if you prefer, or look for vegetarian "steak" or "chicken" strips.

INGREDIENTS

Serves 4

2 tablespoons olive oil

2 large portobello mushrooms, cut into strips

1 green bell pepper, cut into strips

1 red bell pepper, cut into strips

1 onion, cut into strips

¾ teaspoon chili powder

¼ teaspoon cumin

Dash hot sauce (optional)

1 tablespoon chopped fresh cilantro (optional)

4 flour tortillas, warmed

Toppings: salsa, sliced avocadoes, vegan sour cream, etc.

1. Heat olive oil in a large skillet and add mushrooms, bell peppers, and onion. Allow to cook for 3–5 minutes until vegetable are almost done.

2. Add chili powder, cumin, and hot sauce if desired, and stir to combine. Cook for 2–3 more minutes until mushrooms and peppers are soft. Remove from heat and stir in fresh cilantro if desired.

3. Layer the mushrooms and peppers in flour tortillas and top with salsa, fresh sliced avocados, and/or vegan sour cream.

Time-Saving Tips

Fresh is always best, but you can usually find frozen bell pepper strips ready to go in your grocery freezer, and a taco seasoning blend can take the place of the individual spices.

SAVORY STUFFED ACORN SQUASH

All the flavors of fall baked into one nutritious dish. Use fresh herbs if you have them, and breathe deep to savor the impossibly magical aromas coming from your kitchen.

INGREDIENTS

Serves 4

2 acorn squash

1 teaspoon garlic powder

½ teaspoon salt

2 ribs celery, chopped

1 onion, diced

½ cup sliced mushrooms

2 tablespoons vegan margarine or oil

¼ cup chopped walnuts

1 tablespoon soy sauce

1 teaspoon parsley

½ teaspoon thyme

½ teaspoon sage

Salt and pepper, to taste

½ cup grated vegan cheese (optional)

1. Preheat oven to 350°F. Chop the squash in half and scrape out any stringy bits and seeds.

2. Drizzle squash with garlic and salt, then place cut side down on a baking sheet and bake for 30 minutes or until almost soft; remove from oven.

3. In a large skillet, heat celery, onion, and mushrooms in vegan margarine until soft, about 4–5 minutes.

4. Add walnuts, soy sauce, parsley, thyme, and sage, stirring to combine well, and season generously with salt and pepper. Heat for another 1–2 minutes until fragrant.

5. Fill squash with mushroom mixture and sprinkle with vegan cheese if desired. Bake another 5–10 minutes until squash is soft.

EASY VEGAN PIZZA BAGELS

Need a quick lunch or afterschool snack for the kids? Pizza bagels to the rescue! For a real treat, shop for vegetarian "pepperoni" slices to top it off!

INGREDIENTS

Serves 4

⅓ cup pizza sauce or tomato sauce

½ teaspoon garlic powder

¼ teaspoon salt

½ teaspoon basil

½ teaspoon oregano

4 bagels, sliced in half

8 slices vegan cheese, or 1 cup grated vegan cheese

¼ cup sliced mushrooms (optional)

¼ cup sliced black olives

1. Preheat oven to 325°F.

2. Combine pizza sauce, garlic powder, salt, basil, and oregano.

3. Spread sauce over each bagel half and top with cheese, mushrooms if desired, olives, or any other toppings.

4. Heat in oven for 8–10 minutes or until cheese is melted.

Individual Pizzas

Flour tortillas (use two stacked together) and pita bread also make an easy base for individual pizza servings.

CHICKPEA SOFT TACOS

For an easy and healthy taco filling wrapped up in flour tortillas, try using chickpeas! Short on time? Pick up taco seasoning packets to use instead of the spice blend—but watch out for added MSG.

INGREDIENTS

Serves 6

2 (15-ounce) cans chickpeas, drained

½ cup water

1 (6-ounce) can tomato paste

1 tablespoon chili powder

1 teaspoon garlic powder

½ teaspoon onion powder

½ teaspoon cumin

¼ cup chopped fresh cilantro (optional)

4 flour tortillas

Optional taco fillings: shredded lettuce, black olives, vegan cheese, nondairy sour cream

1. Combine chickpeas, water, tomato paste, chili powder, garlic powder, onion powder, and cumin in a large skillet. Cover, and simmer for 10 minutes, stirring occasionally. Uncover, and simmer another 1–2 minutes until most of the liquid is absorbed.

2. Uncover, and use a fork or potato masher to mash the chickpeas until half mashed. Stir in fresh cilantro if desired.

3. Spoon mixture into flour tortillas, add toppings, and wrap.

CARAMELIZED ONION AND MUSHROOM CHEESELESS QUESADILLAS

Sure, you can easily make vegan quesadillas using vegan cheese, but try this more nutritious version filled with a cheesy bean spread.

INGREDIENTS

Serves 6

½ onion, chopped

1 cup sliced mushrooms

2 cloves garlic

2 tablespoons olive oil

Dash salt and pepper

1 (15-ounce) can white beans, any kind, drained

1 medium tomato

3 tablespoons nutritional yeast

3 tablespoons lemon juice

½ teaspoon cumin

6 flour tortillas

Oil for frying

1. Sauté onion, mushrooms, and garlic in olive oil in a large skillet and add a dash of salt and pepper. Cook, stirring occasionally, until onion and mushrooms are browned and caramelized, about 8 minutes.

2. In a food processor or blender, purée together the white beans, tomato, nutritional yeast, lemon juice, and cumin until smooth.

3. Spread ⅓ of the bean mixture on each of 3 tortillas, then top with a portion of the mushrooms and onions. Top with additional tortillas.

4. Lightly fry in oil for 2–3 minutes on each side, just until tortillas are lightly crispy.

"Chicken" Quesadillas

Pick up some store-bought vegan chicken strips and make cheesy chicken quesadillas, omitting the onion and mushrooms. A great lunch for kids, or add some canned jalapeño slices for an easy game-day snack for adults!

CHEESY MACARONI AND "HAMBURGER" CASSEROLE

Reminiscent of the boxed version, this is guilt-free vegan comfort food at its finest.

INGREDIENTS
Serves 6

1 (12-ounce) bag macaroni noodles

4 veggie burgers, thawed and crumbled, or 1 (12-ounce) package vegetarian beef crumbles

1 tomato, diced

1 tablespoon olive oil

1 teaspoon chili powder

1 cup soymilk

2 tablespoons vegan margarine

2 tablespoons flour

1 teaspoon garlic powder

1 teaspoon onion powder

¼ cup nutritional yeast

Salt and pepper, to taste

1. Prepare macaroni noodles according to package instructions.

2. Sauté the veggie burgers and tomato in oil until burgers are lightly browned and season with chili powder.

3. In a separate small skillet, melt together the soymilk and margarine over low heat until well mixed. Stir in flour and heat until thickened, then stir in garlic and onion powder and nutritional yeast and remove from heat.

4. Combine macaroni, veggie burgers, tomatoes, and sauce, gently tossing to coat.

5. Season generously with salt and pepper and allow to cool slightly before serving to allow ingredients to combine.

LENTIL AND RICE LOAF

Made from two of the cheapest ingredients on the planet, this one is a great filler for families on a budget. Serve with mashed potatoes and Mushroom Gravy (Chapter 3) for an all-American meal. Use poultry seasoning in place of the individual herbs if you prefer.

INGREDIENTS

Serves 6

1 large onion, diced

3 cloves garlic

2 tablespoons oil

3½ cups cooked lentils

2¼ cups rice, cooked

⅓ cup ketchup, plus 3 tablespoons

2 tablespoons flour

Egg replacer for 1 egg

½ teaspoon parsley

½ teaspoon thyme

½ teaspoon oregano

¼ teaspoon sage

¾ teaspoon salt

½ teaspoon black pepper

1. Preheat oven to 350°F.

2. Sauté onion and garlic in oil until onion is soft and clear, about 3–4 minutes.

3. In a large bowl, use a fork or a potato masher to mash the lentils until about ⅔ mashed.

4. Add garlic and onion, rice, ⅓ cup ketchup, and flour and combine well, then add egg replacer and remaining ingredients, mashing to combine.

5. Gently press the mixture into a lightly greased loaf pan. Drizzle the remaining 3 tablespoons ketchup on top.

6. Bake for 60 minutes. Allow to cool at least 10 minutes before serving, as loaf will firm slightly as it cools.

Perfect Loaf Tips

Cook the rice and lentils in vegetable broth and add a bay leaf for maximum flavor. Overcook the lentils a bit so they'll be soft and mash easily, but let them cool before mashing. To avoid a mushy loaf, allow both the rice and lentils to cool completely before making your loaf, as they'll be drier that way. Finally, smother the top with loads of ketchup—that's the best part!

EASY FALAFEL PATTIES

Health foods stores sell a vegan instant falafel mix, but it's not very much work at all to make your own from scratch.

INGREDIENTS
Serves 4

1 (15-ounce) can chickpeas, well drained

½ onion, minced

1 tablespoon flour

1 teaspoon cumin

¾ teaspoon garlic powder

¾ teaspoon salt

Egg replacer for 1 egg

¼ cup chopped fresh parsley

2 tablespoons chopped fresh cilantro (optional)

1. Preheat oven to 375°F.

2. Place chickpeas in a large bowl and mash with a fork until coarsely mashed or pulse in a food processor until chopped.

3. Combine chickpeas with onion, flour, cumin, garlic, salt, and egg replacer, mashing together to combine. Add parsley and cilantro if desired.

4. Shape mixture into 2" balls or 1"-thick patties and bake in oven for 15 minutes or until crisp. Falafel can also be fried in oil for about 5–6 minutes on each side.

Falafel Sandwiches

Stuff falafel into a pita bread with some sliced tomatoes and lettuce and top it off with a bit of Homemade Tahini (Chapter 3), Vegan Tzatziki (Chapter 3), or hummus for a Middle Eastern sandwich.

GREEN OLIVE AND ARTICHOKE FOCACCIA PIZZA

This is a gourmet vegan pizza with plenty of Italian seasonings; no cheese needed.

INGREDIENTS

Serves 3

1 loaf vegan focaccia bread

1 tablespoon olive oil

½ teaspoon salt

½ teaspoon rosemary

½ teaspoon basil

⅓ cup tomato paste

½ cup sliced green olives

¾ cup chopped artichoke hearts

½ cup sliced mushrooms

3 cloves garlic, minced

½ teaspoon parsley

¼ teaspoon oregano

½ teaspoon red pepper flakes (optional)

1. Preheat oven to 400°F.

2. Drizzle focaccia with olive oil and sprinkle with salt, rosemary, and basil.

3. Spread a thin layer of tomato paste on the focaccia, then top with olives, artichoke hearts, mushrooms, and garlic.

4. Sprinkle with parsley, oregano, and red pepper flakes if desired, then bake for 20 minutes, or until done.

Focaccia Pizza

Sure, you could use this recipe and a regular pizza crust, but vegan food is all about maximum flavor, and focaccia has much more than a regular crust. If you do prefer a store-bought pizza crust, drizzle it with olive oil and herbs, as in this recipe, on both sides.

MAPLE BAKED BEANS

Tailor these saucy, Boston-style baked beans to your liking by adding extra molasses, a bit of cayenne, or some TVP crumbles for a meaty texture.

INGREDIENTS

Serves 6

3 cups navy or pinto beans

9 cups water

1 onion, chopped

2/3 cup maple syrup

1/4 cup barbecue sauce

2 tablespoons molasses

1 tablespoon Dijon mustard

1 tablespoon chili powder

1 teaspoon paprika

1½ teaspoons salt

¾ teaspoon pepper

1. Cover beans in water and allow to soak at least 8 hours or overnight.

2. Preheat oven to 350°F.

3. In a large Dutch oven or sturdy pot, combine beans and remaining ingredients. Bring to a rolling boil on the stove.

4. Cover, and bake beans for 1½ hours, stirring once or twice. Uncover, and cook 1 more hour.

5. Alternatively, beans can be simmered over low heat for 1½–2 hours on the stovetop.

POTATO AND VEGGIE FRITTERS

These easy potato fritters are similar to an Indian snack, called "bajji" or "pakoras." To get the idea, add a few shakes of some Indian spices: cumin, curry, turmeric, or garam masala and cayenne.

INGREDIENTS

Serves 3

3 medium potatoes

Water for boiling

¼ cup soymilk

¼–⅓ cup flour

½ teaspoon garlic powder

½ teaspoon onion powder

½ teaspoon chili powder (optional)

½ cup frozen peas, corn, or diced carrots mix

Salt and pepper, to taste

Oil for frying

1. Boil potatoes until cooked, about 20 minutes. Drain and allow to cool.

2. Mash potatoes together with soymilk, flour, garlic powder, onion powder, chili powder if desired, veggies, salt, and pepper until mixture is thick and potatoes are well mashed, adding a little less soymilk and more flour as needed. Mixture should be dry but sticky.

3. Form into patties and pan-fry in oil over medium heat for 3–4 minutes on each side or until browned and crispy.

Leftover Baked Potatoes

This recipe is a great way to use up leftover baked potatoes. Looking for more ideas for leftover potatoes? Make Potato and Leek Soup (Chapter 6) or No Shepherd, No Sheep Pie (Chapter 12).

BAKED POLENTA WITH ITALIAN HERBS

If you don't feel like stirring your polenta over the stove, it can also be baked; here's how. Use fresh herbs if you have them on hand.

INGREDIENTS

Serves 2

1 cup cornmeal

4 cups Vegetable Broth (Chapter 6)

1 teaspoon parsley

¼ teaspoon sage

¼ teaspoon oregano

½ teaspoon salt

¼ teaspoon black pepper

1 tablespoon chopped fresh basil

3 tablespoons vegan margarine, melted

2 tablespoons nutritional yeast (optional)

1. Preheat oven to 450°F.

2. Combine cornmeal and Vegetable Broth in a casserole dish. Add parsley, sage, oregano, salt, and pepper.

3. Cover, and bake for 25 minutes. Uncover, and bake another 5–10 minutes until liquid is mostly absorbed.

4. Stir in fresh basil, vegan margarine, and nutritional yeast if desired.

5. Serve as is or transfer to a loaf pan and chill until firm, then slice and pan-fry in a bit of oil.

SOUTHWEST SWEET POTATO ENCHILADAS

Enchiladas freeze well, so make a double batch and thaw and reheat when you're hungry!

INGREDIENTS

Serves 4

2 medium sweet potatoes, baked and diced

½ onion, minced

3 cloves garlic, minced

1 (15-ounce) can black beans, drained

2 teaspoons lime juice

2 tablespoons sliced green chilies (optional)

2 teaspoons chili powder

1 teaspoon cumin

1 (15-ounce) can green chili enchilada sauce

½ cup water

10–12 corn tortillas, warmed

1. Preheat oven to 350°F.

2. In a large bowl, combine the sweet potatoes, onion, garlic, beans, lime juice, chilies if desired, chili powder, and cumin until well mixed.

3. In a separate bowl, combine the enchilada sauce and water. Add ¼ cup of this mixture to the beans and sweet potatoes and combine well.

4. Spread about ⅓ cup sauce in the bottom of a casserole or baking dish.

5. Place about ⅓ cup bean and potato mixture in each tortilla and wrap, then place in the casserole dish. Repeat until filling is used.

6. Spread a generous layer of the remaining enchilada sauce over the top of the rolled tortillas, being sure to coat all the edges and corners well. You may have a little sauce left over.

7. Bake for 25–30 minutes. If enchiladas dry out while baking, top with more sauce.

Sweet Potato Burritos

Sweet potatoes and black beans make lovely vegan burritos as well as enchiladas. Omit the enchilada sauce and wrap the mixture in flour tortillas along with the usual taco fixings.

EASY THREE-BEAN CASSEROLE

If you like baked beans, you'll like this easy bean casserole. It's an entrée you can get in the oven in just a few minutes.

INGREDIENTS

Serves 8

1 (15-ounce) can vegetarian baked beans

1 (15-ounce) can black beans, drained

1 (15-ounce) can kidney beans, drained

1 onion, chopped

⅓ cup ketchup

3 tablespoons apple cider vinegar

⅓ cup brown sugar

2 teaspoons mustard powder

2 teaspoons garlic powder

4 vegan hot dogs, cooked and chopped (optional)

1. Preheat oven to 350°F.

2. Combine all ingredients except vegan hot dogs in a large casserole dish.

3. Bake for 55 minutes, uncovered. Add precooked vegan hot dogs just before serving if desired.

CHAPTER 11

TOFU

EASY FRIED TOFU

This is a simple fried tofu that you can serve with just about any dipping sauce for a snack, or add to salads or stir-fries instead of plain tofu.

INGREDIENTS
Serves 3

1 block firm or extra-firm tofu, cubed

¼ cup soy sauce (optional)

2 tablespoons flour

2 tablespoons nutritional yeast

1 teaspoon garlic powder

¼ teaspoon salt

Dash pepper

Oil for frying

1. Marinate sliced tofu in soy sauce for at least 1 hour if desired.

2. In a small bowl, combine flour, nutritional yeast, garlic powder, salt, and pepper.

3. Coat tofu well with flour mixture on all sides, then fry in hot oil until crispy and lightly golden brown on all sides, about 4–5 minutes.

AGAVE MUSTARD GLAZED TOFU

Miss honey mustard glazed ham? Try this vegan version with agave and tofu.

INGREDIENTS
Serves 3

2 tablespoons lemon juice

2 tablespoons water

1 teaspoon soy sauce

¼ cup agave nectar

2 tablespoons prepared mustard

½ teaspoon garlic powder

½ teaspoon sugar

¾ teaspoon curry powder (optional)

1 block firm or extra-firm tofu

1. Whisk together all other ingredients in a shallow pan and add tofu. Allow to marinate for at least 1 hour, flipping tofu and basting with sauce.

2. Preheat oven to 400°F.

3. Transfer tofu to a baking sheet or casserole dish, basting with extra sauce. Bake tofu for 20–25 minutes, turning over once and spooning extra marinade over the top.

Honey: To Bee or Not to Bee?

Many vegans assume honey is cruelty-free and gently collected from bees that are producing it naturally. This is simply not true. According to the manifesto set forth by the British Vegan Society in 1944, honey is an animal by-product and therefore not vegan.

BARBECUE TOFU

Serve this barbecue tofu with a side of baked beans and coleslaw, or use it as the filling for a delicious sandwich served on a hoagie.

INGREDIENTS
Serves 4

4 cups ketchup

½ cup apple cider vinegar

1 cup water

½ cup vegan Worcestershire sauce

½ cup light brown sugar, firmly packed

¼ cup molasses

¼ cup prepared mustard

2 tablespoons barbecue seasoning

1 teaspoon freshly ground black pepper

1 tablespoon liquid smoke

1 (14-ounce) package extra-firm tofu, pressed and quartered

1. In a large bowl, combine all the ingredients except the tofu. Pour the mixture into the slow cooker and add the tofu, making sure that it is fully covered with sauce.

2. Set the slow cooker to high and cook for 1–2 hours, flipping the tofu at the halfway point.

Types of Barbecue

Barbecue sauce recipes vary greatly by region in the United States and most fall into one of two categories. They are either vinegar-based and have very little sugar, resulting in a thin and somewhat sour taste, or they are tomato-based.

BEER-BATTERED TOFU FILLET

Who needs eggs for a tangy and light batter when beer works just as well? Add some fries for a British pub-style "fish 'n' chips" meal.

INGREDIENTS
Serves 8

2 teaspoons garlic powder

2 teaspoons onion powder

2 teaspoons paprika

1 teaspoon salt

½ teaspoon black pepper

3 blocks extra-firm tofu, chopped into chunks

1 (12-ounce) bottle of beer

1⅓ cups flour

Oil for frying

1. Combine the garlic powder, onion powder, paprika, salt, and pepper. Sprinkle the mixture over the tofu, gently pressing to stick.

2. Pour the beer into a large bowl and add flour, stirring to combine.

3. Dip the tofu in the beer batter, then fry in plenty of oil on both sides until crispy.

Bourbon Street Treats

Venture south to New Orleans and into the heart of the city and you might be lucky enough to find an old jazz restaurant humbly serving battered fried pickles, a New Orleans cult favorite. Sound odd? Try this recipe using dill pickle slices instead of tofu (or okra if you're less adventurous but still want a taste of the Big Easy) and taste for yourself.

BLACKENED TOFU

Preparing blackened tofu on the grill is a delicious alternative to using a slow cooker on a warm summer day.

INGREDIENTS
Serves 4

2 (14-ounce) packages extra-firm tofu, pressed and quartered

⅓ cup soy sauce

1 tablespoon apple cider vinegar

1 tablespoon garlic, minced

1 tablespoon paprika

2 teaspoons black pepper

1½ teaspoons salt

1 teaspoon garlic powder

1 teaspoon cayenne pepper

½ teaspoon dried oregano

½ teaspoon dried thyme

2 tablespoons vegetable oil

1. Place the tofu, soy sauce, vinegar, and garlic in a small bowl and allow to marinate for 10 minutes.

2. To make the blackened seasoning mixture, combine the paprika, black pepper, salt, garlic powder, cayenne, oregano, and thyme in a small bowl. Remove the tofu from the soy marinade and dip each side into the blackened seasoning.

3. Add the oil and blackened tofu to the 2-quart slow cooker. Cover, and cook on low heat for 4 hours.

Types of Tofu
Most major grocery stores carry two different types of tofu—regular or silken. Regular tofu is what you should always use unless the recipe specifically calls for silken, which is most commonly used in desserts or recipes where the tofu needs a creamy consistency.

BRAISED TOFU AND VEGGIE CACCIATORE

If you'd like a more "grown-up" Italian dish, use ½ cup white cooking wine in place of ½ cup broth. Serve over pasta or try it with rice, whole grains, or even baked potatoes or polenta.

INGREDIENTS

Serves 4

½ yellow onion, chopped

½ cup mushrooms, sliced

1 carrot, chopped

3 cloves garlic, minced

2 blocks firm or extra-firm tofu, chopped into cubes

2 tablespoons olive oil

1½ cups Vegetable Broth (Chapter 6)

1 (14-ounce) can diced tomatoes or 3 large fresh tomatoes, diced

1 (6-ounce) can tomato paste

1 bay leaf (optional)

½ teaspoon salt

1 teaspoon parsley

1 teaspoon basil

1 teaspoon oregano

1. Sauté the onion, mushrooms, carrot, garlic, and tofu in olive oil for 4–5 minutes, stirring frequently.

2. Reduce heat to medium-low and add Vegetable Broth, diced or fresh tomatoes, tomato paste, bay leaf if desired, salt, and spices.

3. Cover, and allow to simmer for 20 minutes, stirring occasionally. Remove bay leaf before serving.

CAJUN-SPICED CORNMEAL-BREADED TOFU

Reminiscent of oven-fried breaded catfish, this is a Southern-inspired breaded tofu that can be baked or fried.

INGREDIENTS

Serves 3

⅔ cup soymilk

2 tablespoons lime juice

¼ cup flour

⅓ cup cornmeal

1 tablespoon Cajun seasoning

1 teaspoon onion powder

½ teaspoon cayenne pepper, or to taste

½ teaspoon salt

½ teaspoon black pepper

1 block firm or extra-firm tofu, well pressed

1. Preheat oven to 375°F and lightly grease a baking pan.

2. Combine soymilk and lime juice in a wide shallow bowl. In a separate bowl, combine flour, cornmeal, Cajun seasoning, onion powder, cayenne, salt, and pepper.

3. Slice tofu into triangles or rectangular strips and dip in soymilk and lime juice mixture. Next, coat well with cornmeal and flour mixture

4. Transfer to baking pan and bake for 8–10 minutes on each side. Serve with hot sauce or barbecue sauce.

5. Alternatively, you can pan-fry in a bit of oil for 2–3 minutes on each side.

CHILI AND CURRY BAKED TOFU

If you like tofu and you like Indian- or Thai-style curries, you'll love this spicy baked tofu, which tastes like a slowly simmered curry in each bite. Use the extra marinade to dress a bowl of plain steamed rice.

INGREDIENTS

Serves 3

⅓ cup coconut milk

½ teaspoon garlic powder

1 teaspoon cumin

1 teaspoon curry

½ teaspoon turmeric

2–3 small chilies, minced

2 tablespoons maple syrup

1 block firm or extra-firm tofu, sliced into thin strips

1. Whisk together coconut milk, garlic, cumin, curry, turmeric, chilies, and maple syrup in a shallow bowl. Add tofu and marinate for at least 1 hour, flipping once or twice to coat well.

2. Preheat oven to 425°F.

3. Transfer tofu to a casserole dish in a single layer, reserving marinade.

4. Bake for 8–10 minutes. Turn tofu over and spoon 1–2 tablespoons of marinade over the tofu. Bake 10–12 more minutes.

CRACKED PEPPER TOFU

Before serving, you can top these tofu fillets with thin slices of fresh lemon, which will perfectly complement the pepper and herbs.

INGREDIENTS

Serves 4

6 cloves garlic

¼ cup parsley, chopped

¼ cup rosemary, chopped

¼ cup rice vinegar

½ cup olive oil

¼ cup water

1 teaspoon black pepper

1 (14-ounce) package extra-firm tofu, pressed and quartered

1. In a large bowl, combine all the ingredients except the tofu. Pour the mixture into the slow cooker and add the tofu.

2. Set the slow cooker to high and cook for 1–2 hours, flipping the tofu at the halfway point.

EASY LEMON THYME MARINATED TOFU

The leftover marinade can be whisked with some extra olive oil for a lemony salad dressing.

INGREDIENTS

Serves 3

3 tablespoons lemon juice

3 tablespoons soy sauce

1 tablespoon olive oil

3 tablespoons water

1 tablespoon chopped fresh or
   2 teaspoons dried thyme

1 block firm or extra-firm tofu, pressed

Dash salt and pepper

1. In a shallow pan, whisk together the lemon juice, soy sauce, olive oil, water, and thyme.

2. Slice pressed tofu into desired shape, about ½" thick, and cover with marinade. Allow to marinate for at least 1 hour, preferably longer.

3. Heat oven to 400°F and transfer tofu to a lightly greased baking sheet or casserole dish. Sprinkle with a bit of salt and pepper.

4. Bake tofu for 10–12 minutes or until lightly crispy.

EGGLESS EGG SALAD

Vegan egg salad looks just like the real thing and is much quicker to make. Use this recipe to make egg salad sandwiches, or serve it on a bed of lettuce with tomato slices and enjoy it just as it is.

INGREDIENTS

Serves 4

1 block firm tofu

1 block silken tofu

½ cup vegan mayonnaise

⅓ cup sweet pickle relish

¾ teaspoon apple cider vinegar

½ stalk celery, diced

2 tablespoons minced onion

1½ tablespoons Dijon mustard

1 teaspoon paprika

2 tablespoons chopped chives (optional)

2 tablespoons vegetarian bacon bits (optional)

1. In a medium-size bowl, use a fork to mash the tofu together with the rest of the ingredients except the paprika, chives, and bacon bits.

2. Chill for at least 15 minutes before serving to allow flavors to mingle.

3. Garnish with paprika, as well as chives and vegetarian bacon bits if desired, just before serving.

GENERAL TSO'S TOFU

The combination of sweet and spicy is what makes this dish a hit at Chinese restaurants across the country.

INGREDIENTS

Serves 2

1 (14-ounce) package of extra-firm tofu, pressed and cubed

1 cup water

2 tablespoons cornstarch

2 cloves garlic, minced

1 teaspoon ginger, minced

⅛ cup sugar

2 tablespoons soy sauce

⅛ cup white wine vinegar

⅛ cup sherry

2 teaspoons cayenne pepper

2 tablespoons vegetable oil

2 cups broccoli, chopped

Add all ingredients to a 4-quart slow cooker. Cover, and cook on medium heat for 4 hours.

GINGER-LIME TOFU

The slow cooker does all the work in this recipe, creating a healthy yet impressive dish that requires virtually no hands-on time.

INGREDIENTS

Serves 8

2 (14-ounce) packages extra-firm tofu, pressed and sliced into quarters

¼ cup minced fresh ginger

¼ cup lime juice

1 lime, thinly sliced

1 onion, thinly sliced

1. Place the tofu fillets in an oval 6- to 7-quart slow cooker. Pour the ginger and lime juice over the tofu, then arrange the lime and then the onion in a single layer over the top.

2. Cook on low for 3–4 hours.

Cracked!

Before each use, check your slow cooker for cracks. Even small cracks in the glaze can allow bacteria to grow in the ceramic insert. If there are cracks, replace the insert or the whole slow cooker.

INDIAN TOFU PALAK

Palak paneer is a popular Indian dish of creamed spinach and soft cheese. This version uses tofu for a similar dish.

INGREDIENTS

Serves 4

1 block firm or extra-firm tofu, cut into small cubes

3 cloves garlic, minced

2 tablespoons olive oil

2 tablespoons nutritional yeast

½ teaspoon onion powder

4 bunches fresh spinach

3 tablespoons water

1 tablespoon curry powder

2 teaspoons cumin

½ teaspoon salt

½ cup plain soy yogurt

1. Heat tofu and garlic in olive oil over low heat and add nutritional yeast and onion powder, stirring to coat tofu. Heat for 2–3 minutes until tofu is lightly browned.

2. Add spinach, water, curry, cumin, and salt, stirring well to combine. Once spinach starts to wilt, add soy yogurt and heat just until spinach is fully wilted and soft.

Types of Tofu

Made from cooked, coagulated soybeans and little else, tofu is a minimally processed, low-fat source of calcium and protein. Plain tofu comes in either firm, extra-firm, or silken (also called silk or soft tofu), and many grocers stock a variety of prebaked or flavored tofu. Firm or extra-firm tofu is used in stir-fries and baked dishes when you want the tofu to hold shape. For creamy sauces, use silken tofu.

INDIAN SPINACH AND TOFU

Traditional Indian dishes often call for cooking the spices over dry heat before using them in a recipe. If you have time, add this step to the recipe.

INGREDIENTS

Serves 4

2 tablespoons olive oil

4 cloves garlic, minced

1 teaspoon ginger, minced

1 cup frozen spinach, thawed and drained

1 tablespoon cumin

1 tablespoon coriander

1 teaspoon turmeric

½ teaspoon red pepper flakes

¼ teaspoon mustard seed

1 (15-ounce) can coconut milk

¼ cup soy sauce

1 (14-ounce) package extra-firm tofu, pressed and quartered

1. Add the olive oil to the slow cooker and sauté the garlic and ginger on medium-high heat for 1 minute. Mix in the spinach, cumin, coriander, turmeric, red pepper flakes, mustard seeds, coconut milk, and soy sauce.

2. Add the tofu, set the slow cooker to high, and cook for 1–2 hours, flipping the tofu at the halfway point.

ITALIAN BALSAMIC BAKED TOFU

This is a sweet and crunchy Italian-inspired baked tofu delicious on its own or in salads or pastas. The extra marinade makes a great salad dressing!

INGREDIENTS

Serves 3

1 tablespoon soy sauce

½ teaspoon sugar

¼ cup balsamic vinegar

½ teaspoon garlic powder

2 tablespoons olive oil

½ teaspoon parsley

½ teaspoon basil

¼ teaspoon thyme or oregano

¼ teaspoon salt

¼ teaspoon black pepper

2 blocks firm or extra-firm tofu, well pressed

1. Whisk together all ingredients except tofu and transfer to a wide, shallow pan or zip-top bag.

2. Slice the tofu into ½"-thick strips or triangles.

3. Place the tofu in the marinade and coat well. Allow to marinate for at least 1 hour or overnight, being sure tofu is well coated in marinade.

4. Preheat oven to 400°F. Coat a baking sheet well with nonstick spray or olive oil, or line with foil. Place tofu on sheet.

5. Bake for 15–20 minutes, turn over, then bake for another 5–10 minutes or until done.

Press, Marinate, Bake!

Now that you know how to make baked tofu, try creating your own marinades with your favorite spices and flavors. For quick and easy baked tofu dishes, try a store-bought salad dressing, teriyaki sauce, barbecue sauce, or steak marinades. Thicker dressings may need to be thinned with a bit of water first, and to get the best glazing action make sure there's a bit of sugar added.

LEMON BASIL TOFU

Moist and chewy, this zesty baked tofu is reminiscent of lemon chicken. Serve over steamed rice with extra marinade.

INGREDIENTS

Serves 6

3 tablespoons lemon juice

1 tablespoon soy sauce

2 teaspoons apple cider vinegar

1 tablespoon Dijon mustard

¾ teaspoon sugar

3 tablespoons olive oil

2 tablespoons chopped basil, plus extra for garnish

2 blocks firm or extra-firm tofu, well pressed

1. Whisk together all ingredients except tofu and transfer to a baking dish or casserole pan.

2. Slice the tofu into ½"-thick strips or triangles.

3. Place the tofu in the marinade and coat well. Allow to marinate for at least 1 hour or overnight, being sure tofu is well coated in marinade.

4. Preheat oven to 350°F.

5. Bake for 15 minutes, turn over, then bake for another 10–12 minutes or until done. Garnish with a few extra bits of chopped fresh basil.

MAPLE GLAZED TOFU

Simple and sweet, like this recipe, is sometimes all you need for a delicious dish!

INGREDIENTS

Serves 4

4 cloves garlic, minced

1 tablespoon ginger, minced

½ cup maple syrup

¼ cup soy sauce

½ cup water

⅛ cup brown sugar

1 lemon, juiced

¼ teaspoon black pepper

1 (14-ounce) package extra-firm tofu, pressed and quartered

1. In a large bowl, combine all the ingredients except the tofu. Pour the mixture into the slow cooker and add the tofu.

2. Set the slow cooker to high and cook for 1–2 hours, flipping the tofu at the halfway point.

MEXICAN SPICE–CRUSTED TOFU

These little bites are packed with spices, so no dipping sauce is needed. Use them to top off Mexican Rice with Corn and Peppers (Chapter 8) or Confetti "Rice" with TVP (Chapter 8), or just eat plain.

INGREDIENTS

Serves 3

3 tablespoons soy sauce

3 tablespoons hot chili sauce

1 teaspoon sugar

1 block firm or extra-firm tofu, sliced into strips

1 teaspoon garlic powder

1 teaspoon onion powder

1 tablespoon chili powder

¾ teaspoon cumin

¾ teaspoon oregano

2 tablespoons flour

1. Whisk together the soy sauce, chili sauce, and sugar in a shallow pan and add tofu. Marinate tofu for at least 1 hour.

2. In a separate dish, combine the garlic powder, onion powder, chili powder, cumin, oregano, and flour to form a spice rub. Carefully dip each piece of tofu in the spices on each side, then transfer to a lightly greased baking sheet.

3. Bake at 350°F for 7–9 minutes, turning once.

Pressing and Freezing Tofu

Tofu doesn't taste like much on its own, but soaks up spices and marinades wonderfully. It's like a sponge: The drier it is, the more flavor it absorbs. Wrap firm tofu in a couple of layers of paper towels and place a can of beans or another light weight on top. After 10 minutes, flip the tofu over and let it sit weighted down for another 10 minutes. "Pressing" firm and extra-firm tofu will substantially enhance just about every recipe.

MEXICO CITY PROTEIN BOWL

A quick meal for one in a bowl, reminiscent of Mexico City street food stalls, but healthier and with less pollution.

INGREDIENTS

Serves 1

½ block firm tofu, diced small

1 scallion, chopped

1 tablespoon olive oil

½ cup peas

½ cup corn kernels

½ teaspoon chili powder

1 can black beans, drained

2 corn tortillas

Hot sauce, to taste

1. Heat tofu and scallion in olive oil for 2–3 minutes, then add peas, corn, and chili powder. Cook another 1–2 minutes, stirring frequently.

2. Reduce heat to medium-low and add black beans. Heat for 4–5 minutes until well combined and heated through.

3. Place 2 corn tortillas in the bottom of a bowl and spoon beans and tofu over the top. Season with hot sauce to taste.

MOCK MEATLOAF

Crumbled tofu, veggie beef crumbles, or TVP will work as the base for this recipe.

INGREDIENTS

Serves 4

2 (14-ounce) packages extra-firm tofu, pressed and crumbled

¼ cup oats

¼ cup panko bread crumbs

½ cup ketchup, divided

1 teaspoon garlic powder

2 teaspoons vegan Worcestershire sauce, divided

½ onion, diced

3 cloves garlic, minced

½ jalapeño, minced

½ teaspoon black pepper

1 tablespoon brown sugar

2 teaspoons mustard

1. In a large bowl, combine the tofu, oats, bread crumbs, 3 tablespoons ketchup, garlic powder, 1 teaspoon Worcestershire sauce, onion, garlic, jalapeño, and black pepper.

2. Press the mixture into the base of 2-quart slow cooker that has been prepped with cooking spray. Cover, and cook on low heat for 4–6 hours.

3. In a small bowl, combine the remaining ketchup, Worcestershire sauce, brown sugar, and mustard. Pour the sauce on top of the meatloaf and continue cooking for 20 more minutes.

NUTTY PESTO-CRUSTED TOFU

Make sure your basil leaves are completely dry before trying these nutty, crispy herbed tofu cutlets.

INGREDIENTS

Serves 3

½ cup roasted cashews

½ cup basil, packed

3 cloves garlic

½ cup nutritional yeast

⅔ cup bread crumbs

½ teaspoon salt

¼ teaspoon pepper

⅔ cup flour

⅔ cup soymilk

2 blocks firm or extra-firm tofu, pressed

Oil for pan-frying (optional)

1. In a blender or food processor, process the nuts until coarse and fine but not powdery. Separately, process the basil and garlic until finely minced.

2. Combine the cashews, basil, garlic, nutritional yeast, bread crumbs, salt, and pepper in a bowl. Place the flour in a separate shallow bowl and the soymilk in a third bowl.

3. Slice each block of tofu into triangular cutlets, about ¾" thick. Using tongs, dip in flour and coat well, then dip in soymilk. Next, coat well with the basil and bread crumb mixture and transfer to a lightly greased baking sheet.

4. Pan-fry in oil over medium heat a few minutes on each side until lightly crispy. Alternatively, tofu can be baked for 10–12 minutes at 350°F, or until lightly crispy.

Why Do Vegans Love Tofu So Much?

Aside from low cost and ease of preparation, tofu is beloved by vegans as an excellent source of protein, calcium, and iron. Plain sautéed tofu with a dash of salt is a quick addition to just about any meal, and many grocery stores offer premarinated and even prebaked tofu that is ready to go out of the package. What's not to love?

ORANGE-GLAZED "CHICKEN" TOFU

If you're missing Chinese restaurant–style orange-glazed chicken, try this easy tofu version. It's slightly sweet, slightly salty, and if you add some crushed red pepper, it'll have a bit of spice as well! Double the sauce and add some veggies for a full meal over rice.

INGREDIENTS

Serves 3

⅔ cup orange juice

2 tablespoons soy sauce

2 tablespoons rice vinegar

1 tablespoon maple syrup

½ teaspoon red pepper flakes (optional)

2 tablespoons olive oil

1 block firm or extra-firm tofu, well pressed

3 cloves garlic, minced

1½ teaspoons cornstarch

2 tablespoons water

1. Whisk together the orange juice, soy sauce, vinegar, maple syrup, and red pepper flakes if desired, and set aside.

2. In a large skillet, heat the oil and add tofu and garlic. Lightly fry just a few minutes over medium heat.

3. Reduce heat to medium-low and add in orange juice mixture. Bring to a very low simmer and allow to cook for 7–8 minutes over low heat.

4. Whisk together the cornstarch and water in a small bowl until cornstarch is dissolved. Add to tofu mixture, stirring well to combine.

5. Bring to a simmer and heat for 3–4 minutes until sauce thickens. Serve over rice or another whole grain if desired.

SAAG TOFU ALOO

Saag Tofu Aloo is a fresh-tasting, protein-rich Indian dish that is only slightly spicy. "Saag" means "spinach" and "aloo" means "potato."

INGREDIENTS

Serves 4

1 (14-ounce) package extra-firm tofu

1 tablespoon canola oil

1 teaspoon cumin seeds

2 cloves garlic, minced

2 jalapeños, minced

¾ pound red potatoes, diced

½ teaspoon ground ginger

¾ teaspoon garam masala

1 pound frozen cut-leaf spinach

¼ cup fresh cilantro

1. Cut the tofu into ½" cubes. Set aside.

2. Heat the oil in a nonstick skillet. Add the cumin seeds and sauté for 1 minute.

3. Add the garlic and jalapeños. Sauté until fragrant, about 1 minute.

4. Add the tofu and potatoes. Sauté for 3 minutes.

5. Add the ginger, garam masala, frozen spinach, and cilantro. Sauté 1 minute.

6. Pour the mixture into a 4-quart slow cooker and cook for 4 hours on low.

Serving Suggestions

There are many different ways to enjoy Indian dishes such as this one. Try it over a bed of Jasmine Rice (Chapter 8), scoop it up with naan (flatbread), or roll it up in chapati (another type of flatbread).

PANANG TOFU

Panang is a red curry that is often milder than other curries, but if you'd like to spice it up, you can add extra peppers.

INGREDIENTS

Serves 2

1 (14-ounce) package extra-firm tofu, pressed and cubed

1 (13-ounce) can coconut milk

1 tablespoon panang curry paste

2 tablespoons soy sauce

1 tablespoon lime juice

2 tablespoons sugar

2 tablespoons olive oil

¼ onion, sliced

½ carrot, sliced diagonally

½ red bell pepper, chopped

½ cup fresh basil, chopped

1. Add all ingredients except the basil to a 4-quart slow cooker.

2. Cover, and cook on low heat for 4–6 hours.

3. Add the basil before serving.

PEANUT AND SESAME SAUCE TOFU

If you are having a hard time combining the ingredients, use a hand mixer or toss them into a blender for about 15 seconds.

INGREDIENTS

Serves 6

4 cloves garlic, minced

1 tablespoon ginger, minced

1 cup creamy peanut butter

1 cup coconut milk

¼ cup unsweetened soymilk

⅛ cup soy sauce

Juice of 1 lime

1 (14-ounce) package extra-firm tofu, pressed and cut into 1" cubes

1. In a large bowl, combine all the ingredients except the tofu. Pour the mixture into the slow cooker and add the tofu.

2. Set the slow cooker to high and cook for 1–2 hours, flipping the tofu at the halfway point.

Serving Suggestions

There are endless options for serving Asian-style tofu. Try this tofu as the filling for lettuce wraps, over rice noodles, as the protein on a tasty kabob, or you can play it safe and serve over a bed of steamed rice.

PINEAPPLE GLAZED TOFU

If you like orange chicken or sweet-and-sour dishes, try this saucy, sweet, Pineapple Glazed Tofu; it's excellent for kids. Toss with some noodles or add some diced veggies to make it an entrée.

INGREDIENTS

Serves 3

½ cup pineapple preserves

2 tablespoons balsamic vinegar

2 tablespoons soy sauce

⅔ cup pineapple juice

1 block firm or extra-firm tofu, cubed

3 tablespoons flour

2 tablespoons oil

1 teaspoon cornstarch

1. Whisk together the pineapple preserves, vinegar, soy sauce, and pineapple juice.

2. Coat tofu in flour, then sauté in oil for a few minutes, just until lightly golden. Reduce heat to medium-low and add pineapple sauce, stirring well to combine and coat tofu.

3. Heat for 3–4 minutes, stirring frequently, then add cornstarch, whisking to combine and avoid lumps. Heat for a few more minutes, stirring, until sauce has thickened.

SAUCY KUNG PAO TOFU

Try adding in a few more Asian ingredients to stretch this recipe—bok choy, water chestnut, or bamboo shoots, perhaps—and spoon on top of cooked noodles or plain rice.

INGREDIENTS

Serves 6

3 tablespoons soy sauce

2 tablespoons rice vinegar or cooking sherry

1 tablespoon sesame oil

2 blocks firm or extra-firm tofu

1 red bell pepper, chopped

1 green bell pepper, chopped

⅔ cup sliced mushrooms

3 cloves garlic

3 small red or green chili peppers, diced small

1 teaspoon red pepper flakes

2 tablespoons oil

1 teaspoon ginger powder

½ cup water or Vegetable Broth (Chapter 6)

½ teaspoon sugar

1½ teaspoons cornstarch

2 green onions, chopped

½ cup peanuts

1. Whisk together the soy sauce, rice vinegar or sherry, and sesame oil in a shallow pan or zip-top bag. Add tofu and marinate for at least 1 hour—the longer, the better. Drain tofu, reserving marinade.

2. Sauté bell pepper, mushrooms, garlic, chili peppers, and red pepper flakes in oil for 2–3 minutes, then add tofu and heat for another 1–2 minutes until veggies are almost soft.

3. Reduce heat to medium-low and add marinade, ginger powder, water or Vegetable Broth, sugar, and cornstarch, whisking in the cornstarch to avoid lumps.

4. Heat a few more minutes, stirring constantly, until sauce has almost thickened.

5. Add green onions and peanuts and heat for 1 more minute.

SESAME BAKED TOFU

Baking tofu makes it meaty and chewy, and this is a quick and basic marinade to try if you're new to baking tofu. Serve these marinated tofu strips as an entrée or use as a salad topper or as a meat substitute in a sandwich.

INGREDIENTS

Serves 6

¼ cup soy sauce

2 tablespoons sesame oil

¾ teaspoon garlic powder

½ teaspoon ginger powder

2 blocks firm or extra-firm tofu, well pressed

1. Whisk together the soy sauce, sesame oil, garlic powder, and ginger powder and transfer to a wide, shallow pan.

2. Slice the tofu into ½"-thick strips or triangles.

3. Place the tofu in the marinade and coat well. Allow to marinate for at least 1 hour or overnight.

4. Preheat oven to 400°F. Coat a baking sheet well with nonstick spray or olive oil, or line with foil. Place tofu on sheet.

5. Bake for 20–25 minutes, turn over, then bake for another 10–15 minutes or until done.

Marinating Tofu

For marinated baked tofu dishes, a zip-top bag can be helpful in getting the tofu well covered with marinade. Place the tofu in the bag, pour the marinade in, seal, and set in the fridge, turning and lightly shaking occasionally to coat all sides of the tofu.

SIMMERED COCONUT CURRIED TOFU

Serve on top of Coconut Rice (Chapter 8) or Pineapple Lime Rice (Chapter 8).

INGREDIENTS

Serves 3

1 block firm or extra-firm tofu, cubed

1 tablespoon olive oil

2 teaspoons sesame oil

3 tablespoons peanut butter

2 tablespoons soy sauce

2 tablespoons water

1 teaspoon curry powder

¼ cup coconut flakes

2 tablespoons fresh cilantro, minced

1. Sauté tofu in olive oil for just a few minutes until lightly golden brown.

2. Reduce heat to medium-low and add sesame oil, peanut butter, soy sauce, water, and curry powder, stirring well to combine. Heat, gently stirring, for 4–5 minutes.

3. Add coconut flakes and cilantro and heat just until well combined, about 1 more minute.

SPICY CHILI BASIL TOFU

This saucy stir-fry is a favorite in Thailand when made with chicken and fish sauce, but many restaurants offer a vegetarian version with soy sauce and tofu instead. Serve with rice or rice noodles to sop up all the sauce.

INGREDIENTS

Serves 3

4 cloves garlic, minced

5 small red or green chilies, diced

3 shallots, diced

2 tablespoons oil

1 block firm tofu, diced

¼ cup soy sauce

1 tablespoon vegetarian oyster mushroom sauce

1 teaspoon sugar

1 bunch Thai or holy basil leaves, whole

1. In a large skillet, sauté garlic, chilies, and shallots in oil until fragrant and browned, about 3–4 minutes.

2. Add tofu and heat for another 2–3 minutes until tofu is just lightly golden brown.

3. Reduce heat to medium-low and add soy sauce, mushroom sauce, and sugar, whisking to combine and dissolve sugar. Heat 2–3 more minutes, stirring frequently, then add basil and heat, stirring 1 more minute, just until basil is wilted.

Make It Last

If tofu and chilies aren't enough for you, add in some onions, mushrooms, or green bell peppers to fill it out. Or, for a bit of variety, try it with half basil and half fresh mint leaves.

STICKY TERIYAKI TOFU CUBES

Cut tofu into wide slabs or triangular cutlets for a main dish or smaller cubes to add to a salad, or just for an appetizer or snack.

INGREDIENTS

Serves 3

⅓ cup soy sauce

3 tablespoons barbecue sauce

2 teaspoons hot chili sauce

¼ cup maple syrup

¾ teaspoon garlic powder

1 block firm or extra-firm tofu, cut into thin chunks

1. Preheat oven to 375°F.

2. In a casserole or baking dish, whisk together the soy sauce, barbecue sauce, chili sauce, maple syrup, and garlic powder.

3. Add tofu and cover with sauce.

4. Bake for 35–40 minutes, tossing once.

Storing and Freezing Tofu

Freezing firm or extra-firm tofu creates an even meatier and chewier texture, which some people prefer, and makes it even more absorbent. After pressing your tofu, stick it in the freezer until solid and thaw just before using. If you don't use the whole block, cover any leftover bits of uncooked tofu with water in a sealed container and stick it in the fridge.

THAI TOFU COCONUT CURRY

Try this easy curry tossed with rice noodles or over brown rice.

INGREDIENTS

Serves 6

12 ounces extra-firm tofu

¼ cup unsweetened shredded coconut

¼ cup water

4 cloves garlic, minced

1 tablespoon minced fresh ginger

1 tablespoon minced galangal root

½ cup chopped onion

1 cup peeled and diced sweet potato

1 cup broccoli florets

1 cup snow peas

3 tablespoons tamari

1 tablespoon vegetarian fish sauce

1 tablespoon chili-garlic sauce

½ cup minced fresh cilantro

½ cup light coconut milk

1. Slice the tofu into ½" thick triangles.

2. Place the tofu into a 4-quart slow cooker. Top with coconut, water, garlic, ginger, galangal, onion, sweet potato, broccoli, snow peas, tamari, vegetarian fish sauce, and chili-garlic sauce.

3. Stir to distribute all ingredients evenly. Cook on low for 5 hours.

4. Stir in the cilantro and coconut milk. Cook on low for an additional 20 minutes. Stir prior to serving.

Vegetarian Fish Sauce

Vegetarian fish sauce can be found in some Asian markets or online stores such as VeryAsia.com. Ingredients vary, but it usually contains soybeans, salt, sugar, water, and chili with citric acid for a preservative since it's not fermented.

TOFU BARBECUE SAUCE "STEAKS"

These chewy tofu "steaks" have a hearty texture and a meaty flavor. Delicious as is, or add it to a sandwich. If you've never cooked tofu before, this is a super-easy foolproof recipe to start with.

INGREDIENTS

Serves 3

⅓ cup barbecue sauce

¼ cup water

2 teaspoons balsamic vinegar

2 tablespoons soy sauce

1–2 tablespoons hot sauce (or to taste)

2 teaspoons sugar

2 blocks firm or extra-firm tofu, well pressed

½ onion, chopped

2 tablespoons olive oil

1. In a small bowl, whisk together the barbecue sauce, water, vinegar, soy sauce, hot sauce, and sugar until well combined. Set aside.

2. Slice pressed tofu into ¼"-thick strips.

3. Sauté onion in oil, and carefully add tofu. Fry tofu on both sides until lightly golden brown, about 2 minutes on each side.

4. Reduce heat and add barbecue sauce mixture, stirring to coat tofu well. Cook over medium-low heat until sauce absorbs and thickens, about 5–6 minutes.

Tofu Versus Seitan

This recipe, like many pan-fried or stir-fried tofu recipes, will also work well with seitan, though seitan needs a bit longer to cook all the way through—otherwise it ends up tough and chewy.

TOFU "CHICKEN" NUGGETS

If the kids like chicken nuggets, try this tofu version with poultry seasoning instead.

INGREDIENTS

Serves 4

¼ cup soymilk

2 tablespoons mustard

3 tablespoons nutritional yeast

½ cup bread crumbs

½ cup flour

1 teaspoon poultry seasoning

1 teaspoon garlic powder

1 teaspoon onion powder

½ teaspoon salt

¼ teaspoon pepper

1 block firm or extra-firm tofu, sliced into thin strips

Oil for frying (optional)

1. In a large shallow pan, whisk together the soymilk, mustard, and nutritional yeast. In a separate bowl, combine the bread crumbs with the flour, poultry seasoning, garlic and onion powders, salt, and pepper.

2. Coat each piece of tofu with the soymilk mixture, then coat well in bread crumbs and flour mixture.

3. Fry in hot oil if desired until lightly golden brown, about 3–4 minutes on each side, or bake in 375°F oven for 20 minutes, turning over once.

TOFU "FISH" STICKS

Adding seaweed and lemon juice to baked and breaded tofu gives it a "fishy" taste. Crumbled nori sushi sheets would work well too if you can't find kelp or dulse flakes. You could also pan-fry these fish sticks in a bit of oil instead of baking if you prefer.

INGREDIENTS

Serves 3

½ cup flour

⅓ cup soymilk

2 tablespoons lemon juice

1½ cups fine ground bread crumbs

2 tablespoons kelp or dulse
   seaweed flakes

1 tablespoon Old Bay Seasoning

1 teaspoon onion powder

1 block extra-firm tofu,
   well pressed

1. Preheat oven to 350°F.

2. Place flour in a shallow bowl or pie tin and set aside. Combine the soymilk and lemon juice in a separate shallow bowl or pie tin. In a third bowl or pie tin, combine the bread crumbs, kelp or dulse, Old Bay Seasoning, and onion powder.

3. Slice tofu into twelve ½"-thick strips. Place each strip into the flour mixture to coat well, then dip into the soymilk. Next, place each strip into the bread crumbs, gently patting to coat well.

4. Bake for 15–20 minutes, turn once, then bake for another 10–15 minutes or until crispy.

5. Serve with ketchup or a vegan tartar sauce.

Tartar Sauce

To make a simple vegan tartar sauce, combine Vegan Mayonnaise (Chapter 3) with sweet pickle relish and a generous squeeze of lemon juice. Or dip your fishy tofu sticks in ketchup or barbecue sauce.

TOFU "RICOTTA" MANICOTTI

Check the label on your manicotti package, as some need to be precooked and some can be placed straight into the oven.

INGREDIENTS

Serves 4

12 large manicotti

2 blocks firm tofu, crumbled

2 tablespoons lemon juice

2 tablespoons olive oil

2 tablespoons soymilk

¼ cup nutritional yeast

½ teaspoon garlic powder

½ teaspoon onion powder

¼ teaspoon salt

1 teaspoon basil

2 tablespoons fresh chopped parsley

3 cups prepared marinara sauce

⅓ cup grated vegan cheese (optional)

1. Precook the manicotti shells according to package instructions if needed. Preheat oven to 350°F.

2. In a large bowl, mash together the tofu, lemon juice, olive oil, soymilk, nutritional yeast, garlic powder, onion powder, salt, basil, and parsley until well mixed, crumbly, and almost smooth.

3. Stuff each manicotti noodle with the tofu mixture.

4. Spread half of the marinara sauce in the bottom of a casserole or baking dish, then place the manicotti on top. Sprinkle with grated vegan cheese if desired, and cover with the remaining sauce.

5. Cover, and bake for 30 minutes.

Mani—Canne—What?

If you can't find manicotti noodles (sometimes called cannelloni), use a large shell pasta. Or cook some lasagna noodles al dente, then place the filling on top of a noodle and roll it up. Place seam side down in your casserole dish, and stuff them in tight to get them to stick together.

TOFU WITH LEMON, CAPERS, AND ROSEMARY

For an even bolder flavor, try marinating the tofu overnight before cooking.

INGREDIENTS

Serves 4

1 (14-ounce) package extra-firm tofu, pressed and sliced into 4 fillets

⅓ cup water

2 tablespoons lemon juice

½ teaspoon salt

3 thin slices fresh lemon

1 tablespoon nonpareil capers

½ teaspoon minced fresh rosemary

1. Place the tofu fillets on the bottom of a 2-quart slow cooker. Pour the water, lemon juice, and salt over the tofu.

2. Arrange the lemon slices in a single layer on top of the tofu. Sprinkle with capers and rosemary.

3. Cover, and cook on low for 2 hours. Discard lemon slices prior to serving.

CHAPTER 12

SEITAN AND TVP

ADOBO SEITAN

Serve this dish over steamed white rice, which will help balance out the strong acidic flavor from the vinegar.

INGREDIENTS

Serves 6

½ cup soy sauce

1 cup white vinegar

1 cup water

4 cloves garlic, minced

1 teaspoon ginger, minced

4 bay leaves

1 teaspoon paprika

10 black peppercorns

1 (16-ounce) package seitan, cut into bite-size pieces

Add all ingredients to a 4-quart slow cooker, cover, and cook on high for 2 hours.

Spanish Versus Filipino

There are Spanish and Filipino dishes that share the name adobo but the two are slightly different. Both share the ingredients of vinegar and garlic but the Spanish version mostly refers to a marinade that is used before cooking and the Filipino version is a cooking method.

APPLES AND ONIONS SEITAN

Try Sonya apples in this sweet and savory dish; they are crisp and sweet.

INGREDIENTS

Serves 4

4 crisp sweet apples, cut into wedges

2 large onions, sliced

1 cup water

4 equal-size seitan cutlets (about 1 pound)

½ teaspoon ground cayenne

½ teaspoon ground cinnamon

¼ teaspoon allspice

¼ teaspoon ground fennel

1. Place half of the apple wedges and half of the sliced onions in the bottom of a 4-quart slow cooker, then add water. Top with a single layer of seitan.

2. Sprinkle with spices and top with the remaining apples and onions.

3. Cover, and cook on low for 8 hours.

In Season

Apples are in peak season only once a year, so grab your basket and head to the orchard during the fall. However, you can find good apples during other seasons too. Just check your local supermarket.

BASIC HOMEMADE SEITAN

Homemade seitan may seem like a lot of work at first, but it's quite simple once you get the hang of it, and at just a fraction of the cost of store-bought.

INGREDIENTS
Serves 8

1 cup vital wheat gluten flour

1 teaspoon onion powder

1 teaspoon garlic powder

2 tablespoons soy sauce

¾ cup strong Vegetable Broth (Chapter 6), plus 6 cups

1. Combine the vital wheat gluten with the onion powder and garlic powder. In a separate bowl, combine the soy sauce and ¾ cup Vegetable Broth.

2. Slowly add the soy sauce and ¾ cup Vegetable Broth to the wheat gluten mixture, mixing with your hands until all of the flour is combined. You'll have one big rubbery ball of dough, and you may need a bit more or less than ¾ cup broth.

3. Knead the dough a few times to get an even texture. Let dough rest for a few minutes, then knead again for 1–2 minutes.

4. Divide dough into 3 (or more) pieces and stretch and press to about 1" thickness.

5. Slowly simmer in 6 cups Vegetable Broth for 45 minutes to 1 hour over low heat.

Seitan Tips

Shop for vital wheat gluten, also called wheat gluten flour, at your natural foods store in the bulk section or baking aisle. Note that this recipe is for a basic, raw seitan. It won't be too tasty if you eat it plain, as it still needs to be cooked, even after all that boiling! Make a batch, then use it in any of the recipes in this book calling for seitan. Seitan expands when it cooks, so use more broth and a larger pot than you think you might need, and add an extra bouillon cube for maximum flavor if you like.

BRAISED SEITAN WITH MUSHROOMS

The best gravies are usually made with the "drippings," or leftover liquid from a cooked dish. They are packed with flavor and guaranteed to complement the meal.

INGREDIENTS

Serves 6

1 cup mushrooms, sliced

4 cups water

2 tablespoons Better Than Bouillon No Beef Base

½ cup red wine

1 teaspoon dried tarragon or thyme

1 teaspoon salt

¼ teaspoon black pepper

1 (16-ounce) package seitan, cut into bite-size pieces

2 tablespoons cornstarch, dissolved in ⅛ cup water

1. Add all of the ingredients except the cornstarch to a 4-quart slow cooker, cover, and cook on low heat for 6 hours.

2. Use a slotted spoon to remove the seitan from the slow cooker and set aside. Whisk in the cornstarch until it creates a gravy consistency and then serve the mushroom gravy over the braised seitan.

CASHEW SEITAN

Hoisin is a soy-based, sweet and spicy sauce that is often used as a glaze for meats in Chinese dishes.

INGREDIENTS

Serves 6

¼ cup rice wine

½ cup hoisin sauce

¼ cup soy sauce

½ cup water

1 tablespoon sugar

1 (16-ounce) package seitan, cut into bite-size pieces

2 tablespoons olive oil

1 red bell pepper, chopped

1 green bell pepper, chopped

4 cloves garlic, minced

½ cup cashew pieces

1. Combine the rice wine, hoisin, soy sauce, water, and sugar in a 4-quart slow cooker, stir well, and then add all remaining ingredients except the cashews.

2. Cover, and cook on low for 6 hours. Garnish with cashew pieces before serving.

CHICKENY SEITAN

Use a vegetarian chicken-flavored broth instead of regular vegetable broth, or add vegetarian chicken-flavored bouillon to the broth if you can find it.

INGREDIENTS
Serves 8

1 cup vital wheat gluten flour

1 tablespoon nutritional yeast

½ teaspoon sage

¼ teaspoon thyme

½ teaspoon garlic powder

½ teaspoon onion powder

¾ cup Vegetable Broth (Chapter 6),
    plus 6 cups

1. Combine the vital wheat gluten with the nutritional yeast, sage, thyme, and garlic and onion powder.

2. Slowly add ¾ cup Vegetable Broth to the wheat gluten, mixing with your hands until all of the flour is combined. You'll have one big rubbery ball of dough, and you may need a bit more or less than ¾ cup broth.

3. Knead the dough a few times to get an even texture. Let dough rest for a few minutes, then knead again for 1–2 minutes.

4. Divide dough into 3 (or more) pieces and stretch and press to about 1" thickness.

5. Slowly simmer in 6 cups Vegetable Broth for 45 minutes to 1 hour over low heat.

Seitan Stylings

When making homemade seitan, experiment with different seasonings to determine what you like best; no two batches ever seem to turn out the same anyway. Try adding lemon juice and minced seaweed for a fishy taste, and try out different vegetable broths and bouillon flavorings.

GARLIC SEITAN

Garlic has many health benefits and is said to protect against certain types of cancer and heart disease.

INGREDIENTS

Serves 6

½ cup olive oil

4 cloves garlic, crushed

1 (16-ounce) package seitan, cut into 4 fillets

1 cup panko bread crumbs

1 teaspoon salt

¼ teaspoon black pepper

1. Add the olive oil, garlic, and seitan to a medium bowl and allow the seitan to marinate for 5 minutes.

2. In a separate bowl, mix the bread crumbs, salt, and pepper. Dip the seitan into the bread crumbs and place in a 4-quart slow cooker.

3. Pour the remaining oil and garlic into the slow cooker, cover, and cook on high for 2 hours. Flip the seitan halfway through cooking.

GREEK SEITAN GYROS

Wander the streets of Manhattan or Cairo and you'll find that these messy sandwiches have a huge cult following among street food lovers. If raw onion isn't your thing, just leave it out.

INGREDIENTS

Serves 6

1 (16-ounce) package seitan, thinly sliced

2 tablespoons oil

¾ teaspoon paprika

½ teaspoon parsley

¼ teaspoon garlic powder

¼ teaspoon oregano

Salt and pepper, to taste

6 pitas

2 tomatoes, sliced thin

1 onion, chopped (optional)

½ head iceberg lettuce shredded

1 cup Vegan Tzatziki (Chapter 3) or nondairy sour cream

1. Sauté seitan in oil and coat well with seasonings. Heat until seitan is lightly browned and spices are fragrant, about 5–7 minutes.

2. Top each pita with a portion of seitan, tomatoes, onion if desired, lettuce, and about 2 tablespoons Vegan Tzatziki or sour cream, and fold in half to eat.

HOMEMADE BAKED SEITAN

Homemade seitan can be baked instead of boiled, for a similar result. This version is deliciously chewy straight out of the oven, and makes an excellent deli-style lunch "meat" when sliced thin.

INGREDIENTS

Serves 8

1 (12-ounce) block silken tofu

2/3 cup water

1/3 cup olive oil

1/3 cup barbecue sauce

2 teaspoons hot chili sauce (optional)

1 teaspoon onion powder

1 teaspoon garlic powder

1 teaspoon seasoning salt

2¼ cups vital wheat gluten flour

1. Preheat oven to 350°F and grease a loaf pan well.

2. Purée the tofu, water, and olive oil until smooth and creamy, at least 1 minute. Stir in barbecue sauce, hot chili sauce if desired, onion and garlic powders, and seasoning salt.

3. Combine vital wheat gluten and mix in with your hands to form a dough. Knead the dough a few times to get an even texture. Let dough rest for a few minutes, then knead again for 1–2 minutes.

4. Firmly press down into a small loaf pan, forming a compacted loaf.

5. Bake for 35–40 minutes or until just starting to brown. Cool completely before using.

ITALIAN HERB SEITAN

Serve this simple Italian dish over a bed of angel hair pasta and use the remaining liquid as a sauce to dress your pasta.

INGREDIENTS

Serves 6

1 (16-ounce) package seitan, cut into bite-size pieces

6 cloves garlic, minced

¼ cup rice wine vinegar

½ cup Vegetable Broth (Chapter 6)

½ cup rosemary, chopped

½ cup parsley, chopped

1 teaspoon salt

¼ teaspoon black pepper

Add all of the ingredients to a 4-quart slow cooker, cover, and cook on low heat for 6 hours.

The Power of Seitan

Seitan, otherwise known as wheat gluten, is a powerful source of protein and a great alternative to meat. One serving has a whopping 18 grams of protein and the benefits don't stop there—it's also a great source of iron.

JERK SEITAN

Many jerk recipes call for rubbing the spice mixture into the protein before cooking, but in a slow cooker that step isn't necessary.

INGREDIENTS
Serves 4

1 pound shredded seitan

½ cup Vegetable Broth (Chapter 6)

½ teaspoon allspice

¼ teaspoon cinnamon

½ teaspoon dried thyme

¼ teaspoon ground nutmeg

1 teaspoon salt

¼ cup red onion, diced

2 cloves garlic, minced

2 tablespoons fresh jalapeño, seeded and minced

1. Prepare a 4-quart slow cooker with nonstick cooking spray, then add the shredded seitan.

2. In a medium bowl, combine all remaining ingredients, then pour over the seitan.

3. Cover, and cook on low for 6 hours.

MANDARIN SEITAN

Surprisingly, this vegan take on Mandarin chicken doesn't call for mandarin oranges at all!

INGREDIENTS
Serves 6

4 cloves garlic, minced

1 teaspoon ginger, minced

1 (16-ounce) package seitan, cut into bite-size pieces

½ cup soy sauce

⅓ cup sugar

1 lemon, juiced

1 cup water

2 tablespoons cornstarch, dissolved in ⅛ cup water

1. Add all of the ingredients except the cornstarch to a 4-quart slow cooker, cover, and cook on high for 2 hours.

2. Remove the seitan with a slotted spoon. Whisk in the cornstarch until the liquid has the consistency of a sauce.

MASSAMAN CURRIED SEITAN

With Indian influences and being popular among Muslim communities in Southern Thailand, Massaman curry is a truly global dish. This version is simplified but still has a distinct kick. Diced tomatoes, baby corn, or green peas would go well in this recipe if you want to add veggies.

INGREDIENTS

Serves 4

1 tablespoon Chinese five-spice powder

½ teaspoon fresh ginger, grated

½ teaspoon turmeric

¼ teaspoon cayenne pepper, or to taste

1 tablespoon oil

1½ cups coconut milk

1 cup Vegetable Broth (Chapter 6)

2 potatoes, chopped

1½ cups seitan, chopped small

2 whole cloves

1 tablespoon peanut butter

¼ teaspoon cinnamon

1 teaspoon salt

2 teaspoons brown sugar

⅓ cup peanuts or cashews (optional)

1 tablespoon cornstarch plus 3 tablespoons water (optional)

1. In a large skillet or stockpot, heat five-spice powder, ginger, turmeric, and cayenne in oil for just 1 minute, stirring constantly, until fragrant.

2. Reduce heat to medium-low and add coconut milk and Vegetable Broth, stirring to combine. Add potatoes, seitan, and cloves; cover, and cook for 15–20 minutes, stirring occasionally.

3. Uncover, add peanut butter, cinnamon, salt, sugar, and peanuts or cashews if desired, and heat for 1 more minute. Serve over rice.

4. If you prefer a thicker curry, dissolve 1 tablespoon cornstarch in 3 tablespoons water and add to curry, simmering for 2–3 minutes, until thick.

MIDDLE EASTERN LEMON SEITAN

In Middle Eastern cuisine, chickpeas are most commonly used in hummus but they are also delicious when left whole and slow-cooked in a rich sauce.

INGREDIENTS
Serves 6

Juice of 1 lemon

1 (15-ounce) can diced tomatoes

1 (15-ounce) can chickpeas, drained

½ cup water

1 teaspoon cumin

1 teaspoon coriander

4 garlic cloves, minced

½ teaspoon cinnamon

½ teaspoon salt

1 (16-ounce) package seitan, cut into bite-size pieces

Add all of the ingredients to a 4-quart slow cooker, cover, and cook on low heat for 6 hours.

Being Vegan in the Middle East

The concept of veganism is still very far from being widely accepted in the Middle East but that doesn't mean there isn't plenty for vegans to eat when sampling the cuisine. Several dishes are naturally vegan, such as baba ganoush and tabbouleh.

MOROCCAN "CHICKEN"

This dish was inspired by traditional North African tagines and adapted for the slow cooker.

INGREDIENTS
Serves 8

½ teaspoon coriander

½ teaspoon cinnamon

¼ teaspoon salt

1 teaspoon cumin

2 pounds seitan, cubed

½ cup water

4 cloves garlic, minced

1 onion, thinly sliced

1 knob ginger, minced

1 (15-ounce) can chickpeas, drained and rinsed

4 ounces dried apricots, halved

1. Place all of the spices, seitan, water, garlic, onion, and ginger into a 4-quart slow cooker. Cook on low for 5 hours.

2. Stir in the chickpeas and apricots and cook on high for 40 minutes.

Moroccan Cuisine

Moroccan cuisine uses many different spices. Some of the most common are cumin, cinnamon, turmeric, saffron, and paprika. Traditional Moroccan food is served in a communal bowl at a low, round table. Diners take food from the bowl using pieces of bread or their hands.

NO SHEPHERD, NO SHEEP PIE

Sheep- and shepherd-less pie is a hearty vegetarian entrée for big appetites!

INGREDIENTS
Serves 6

1½ cups TVP

1½ cups hot water or Vegetable Broth (Chapter 6)

½ onion, chopped

2 cloves garlic, minced

1 large carrot, sliced thin

¾ cup sliced mushrooms

½ cup green peas

½ cup Vegetable Broth

½ cup soymilk, plus 3 tablespoons

1 tablespoon flour

5 medium potatoes, cooked

2 tablespoons vegan margarine

¼ teaspoon rosemary

¼ teaspoon sage

½ teaspoon paprika (optional)

½ teaspoon salt

¼ teaspoon black pepper

1. Preheat oven to 350°F.

2. Combine TVP and hot water or Vegetable Broth and allow to sit for 6–7 minutes. Gently drain any excess moisture.

3. In a large skillet, sauté onion, garlic, and carrot in oil until onion is soft, about 5 minutes. Add mushrooms, green peas, Vegetable Broth, and ½ cup soymilk. Whisk in flour just until sauce thickens, then transfer to a casserole dish.

4. Mash together the potatoes, margarine, and 3 tablespoons soymilk with the rosemary, sage, and paprika if desired, and spread over the vegetables.

PINEAPPLE TVP BAKED BEANS

Add a kick to these saucy homemade vegetarian baked beans with a bit of cayenne pepper if you'd like.

INGREDIENTS
Serves 4

2 (15-ounce) cans pinto or navy beans, partially drained

1 onion, diced

⅔ cup barbecue sauce

2 tablespoons prepared mustard

2 tablespoons brown sugar

1 cup TVP

1 cup hot water

1 (8-ounce) can diced pineapple, drained

¾ teaspoon salt

½ teaspoon pepper

1. In a large stockpot, combine beans and about half the liquid, onion, barbecue sauce, mustard, and brown sugar and bring to a slow simmer. Cover, and allow to cook for at least 10 minutes, stirring occasionally.

2. Combine TVP and hot water and allow to sit for 6–8 minutes, to rehydrate TVP.

3. Add TVP, pineapple, salt, and pepper to beans; cover, and slowly simmer another 10–12 minutes.

Canadian Baked Beans
Why not omit the brown sugar and use pure maple syrup for sweetened Canadian-style baked beans, eh?

SEITAN BARBECUE "MEAT"

Sooner or later, all vegans discover the magically delicious combination of seitan and barbecue sauce in some variation of this classic favorite.

INGREDIENTS
Serves 6

1 package prepared seitan, chopped into thin strips (about 2 cups)

1 large onion, chopped

3 cloves garlic, minced

2 tablespoons oil

1 cup barbecue sauce

2 tablespoons water

1. Heat seitan, onion, and garlic in oil, stirring frequently, until onion is just soft and seitan is lightly browned.

2. Reduce heat to medium-low and stir in barbecue sauce and water. Allow to simmer, stirring to coat seitan, until most of the liquid has been absorbed, about 10 minutes.

Seitan Sandwiches
Piled on top of sourdough along with some vegan mayonnaise, lettuce, and tomato, this makes a perfect sandwich. Melt some vegan cheese for a simple Philly "cheesesteak"-style sandwich, or pile on the vegan Thousand Island and sauerkraut for a seitan Reuben.

RED WINE "POT ROAST"

A little bit of wine goes a long way in flavoring this simple one-crock meal.

INGREDIENTS

Serves 6

⅓ cup red wine

½ cup water

4 red potatoes, quartered

3 carrots, cut into thirds

2 bulbs fennel, quartered

2 rutabagas, quartered

1 onion, sliced

4 cloves garlic, sliced

1½ pounds seitan, cubed

½ teaspoon salt

½ teaspoon freshly ground black pepper

1. Pour the wine and water into a 4-quart slow cooker. Add the potatoes, carrots, fennel, rutabagas, onion, and garlic. Stir.

2. Add the seitan. Sprinkle with salt and pepper. Cover, and cook on low for 8 hours.

SEITAN BUFFALO WINGS

To tame these spicy wings, dip in cooling Dairy-Free Ranch Dressing (Chapter 5), or serve with chilled cucumber slices.

INGREDIENTS

Serves 4

⅓ cup vegan margarine

⅓ cup Louisiana Hot Sauce

1 cup flour

1 teaspoon garlic powder

1 teaspoon onion powder

¼ teaspoon pepper

½ cup soymilk

Oil for frying

1 (16-ounce) package seitan or mock chicken, chopped

1. Over low heat, combine the margarine and Louisiana Hot Sauce just until margarine is melted. Set aside.

2. In a small bowl, combine the flour, garlic powder, onion powder, and pepper. Place soymilk in a separate bowl and heat oil.

3. Dip each piece of seitan in the soymilk, then dredge in flour mixture. Carefully place in hot oil and deep-fry in oil until lightly golden browned on all sides, about 4–5 minutes.

4. Coat fried seitan with margarine and Louisiana Hot Sauce mixture.

Baked, Not Fried

This is, admittedly, not the healthiest of vegan recipes, but you can cut some of the fat out by skipping the breading and deep-frying. Instead, lightly brown the seitan in a bit of oil, then coat with the sauce. Alternatively, bake the seitan with the sauce for 25 minutes at 325°F.

SEITAN CACCIATORE

"Cacciatore-style" typically means a piece of meat that is seared and then slow-cooked with tomatoes, herbs, and wine but you can veganize it by opting for tempeh, tofu, or seitan as the protein.

INGREDIENTS

Serves 6

2 tablespoons olive oil

1 (16-ounce) package seitan, cut into bite-size pieces

1 onion, chopped

1 red bell pepper, chopped

1 green bell pepper, chopped

4 cloves garlic, minced

1 (28-ounce) can diced tomatoes

1 cup Vegetable Broth (Chapter 6)

2 tablespoons soy sauce

½ cup white wine

¼ teaspoon black pepper

2 tablespoons cornstarch, dissolved in ⅛ cup water

¼ cup basil, chopped

1. Add the olive oil to a large sauté pan on medium heat and sauté the seitan on high heat for 3–5 minutes. Add the onion, bell peppers, and garlic and sauté for an additional 3 minutes, then transfer to a 4-quart slow cooker.

2. Add the tomatoes, Vegetable Broth, soy sauce, white wine, and black pepper, cover, and cook on low heat for 6 hours.

3. With a slotted spoon, remove the seitan from the slow cooker and set aside. Whisk in the cornstarch until it creates a sauce consistency. Garnish with the chopped basil before serving.

Skip the Alcohol

If you'd like to leave the alcohol out of this dish, it's easy to substitute it with another liquid. Simply replace it with an additional half cup of Vegetable Broth.

SEITAN CUBAN SANDWICH

Cuban sandwiches are often pressed after assembly. No need for a panini press or grill pan though—just use your hand!

INGREDIENTS

Serves 4

1 (16-ounce) package seitan, thinly sliced

6 oranges, juiced

6 limes, juiced

½ teaspoon cumin

1 teaspoon dried oregano

½ teaspoon lemon pepper

⅛ cup soy sauce

¼ cup olive oil

1 loaf Cuban bread, sliced in half

4 slices vegan pepper jack cheese

12 dill pickle slices

Mustard

1. Add all of the ingredients except the bread, cheese, pickles, and mustard to a 4-quart slow cooker. Cover, and cook on high heat for 1–2 hours.

2. Remove the slices of seitan with tongs and assemble the sandwiches on the bread by layering the seitan, cheese, pickles, and mustard.

SEITAN FRICASSEE

A fricassee is a versatile dish that is easily adapted for personal taste. Fennel, mushrooms, or parsnips can be used with great success.

INGREDIENTS
Serves 6

2 cups sliced red cabbage

2 carrots, cut into coin-size pieces

2 stalks celery, diced

1 onion, sliced

1 pound seitan, cut into large cubes

¾ cup faux chicken stock

2 teaspoons paprika

2 teaspoons dried thyme

2 teaspoons dried parsley

1. Place the cabbage, carrots, celery, and onion on the bottom of a 4-quart slow cooker. Place the seitan on top of the vegetables.

2. Pour the stock over the seitan and sprinkle it evenly with the spices. Pat the spices onto the seitan.

3. Cook on low 6 hours or until the seitan is cooked through.

SEITAN POT PIE

Gardein Chick'n Strips are a good alternative to seitan in this recipe and can be found in many major grocery stores.

INGREDIENTS
Serves 8

1 (16-ounce) package seitan, cut into bite-size pieces

4 red potatoes, quartered

2 carrots, peeled and chopped

½ cup celery, chopped

½ cup onions, sliced

2 (15-ounce) cans vegan cream of mushroom soup

2 teaspoons soy sauce

¼ teaspoon black pepper

2 sheets frozen puff pastry, cut into 4 squares each

1. Add all the ingredients except puff pastry to a 4-quart slow cooker. Cover, and cook on low heat for 6 hours.

2. Meanwhile, cook the puff pastry according to package directions or until it is golden brown. Serve the pot pie in a bowl and top each bowl with one piece of the puff pastry.

Homemade Vegan Cream of Mushroom
Make vegan cream of mushroom soup by adding 2 tablespoons of a light roux to 2 cups unsweetened soymilk and then add sautéed mushrooms and onions.

SEITAN PROVENÇAL

"Provençal" means food from the southern region of France and it is full of Mediterranean ingredients, such as olives, garlic, and herbs.

INGREDIENTS

Serves 6

1 (16-ounce) package seitan, cut into bite-size pieces

1 (28-ounce) can diced tomatoes

½ cup white wine

1 cup Vegetable Broth (Chapter 6)

4 cloves garlic, minced

¼ cup kalamata olives, pitted and chopped

1 teaspoon salt

¼ teaspoon black pepper

¼ cup fresh basil, chopped

1. Add all ingredients except the basil to a 4-quart slow cooker, cover, and cook on low heat for 6 hours.

2. Sprinkle with basil just before serving.

SEITAN "SCALOPPINE"

Scaloppine traditionally calls for coating the protein in bread crumbs before cooking but in this slow cooker version, you sprinkle them on top after cooking.

INGREDIENTS

Serves 6

1 (16-ounce) package seitan, cut into 6 thin fillets

Juice of 1 lemon

1 cup water

1 tablespoon Better Than Bouillon No Chicken Base

¼ cup white wine

¼ cup capers

¼ teaspoon black pepper

1 cup toasted panko bread crumbs

¼ cup parsley, chopped

1. Add the seitan, lemon juice, water, Better Than Bouillon No Chicken Base, white wine, capers, and black pepper to a 4-quart slow cooker, cover, and cook on low heat for 4–6 hours.

2. Remove the seitan from the slow cooker and garnish with toasted bread crumbs and chopped parsley before serving.

SINLESS CHILI CHEESE FRIES

Chili cheese fries sin carne (without meat) are almost healthy enough to eat as an entrée. Almost. But go ahead and eat them for dinner—you deserve it, and no one will ever know.

INGREDIENTS

Serves 4

1 (20-ounce) bag frozen french fries

½ onion, chopped

1 tablespoon oil

1 (15-ounce) can kidney beans

1½ cups TVP, rehydrated in water

1⅓ cups tomato paste

2 tablespoons chili powder

½ teaspoon cumin

½ teaspoon cayenne pepper, or to taste

2 tablespoons vegan margarine

2 tablespoons flour

1½ cups soymilk

2 tablespoons prepared mustard

½ teaspoon garlic powder

½ teaspoon salt

½ cup grated vegan cheese

1. Prepare french fries according to package instructions.

2. Sauté onion in oil until soft. Reduce heat and add beans, TVP, tomato paste, chili powder, cumin, and cayenne pepper. Cover, and simmer for 8–10 minutes.

3. In a separate pot, melt the vegan margarine and flour together until thick and pasty, then stir in soymilk, mustard, garlic, and salt. Add vegan cheese and heat just until melted and mixture has thickened.

4. Smother french fries with TVP chili, and top with cheese sauce.

"SLOPPY JOLINDAS" WITH TVP

TVP "Sloppy Jolindas" are reminiscent of those goopy sloppy joes served up in primary school cafeterias, with all of the nostalgic comfort and none of the gristle or mystery meat. The TVP is only partially rehydrated—the better to absorb all the flavors.

INGREDIENTS

Serves 8

1¾ cups TVP

1 cup hot water or Vegetable Broth (Chapter 6)

1 onion, chopped

1 green bell pepper, chopped small

2 tablespoons oil

1 (16-ounce) can tomato sauce

¼ cup barbecue sauce

2 tablespoons chili powder

1 tablespoon mustard powder

1 tablespoon soy sauce

2 tablespoons molasses

2 tablespoons apple cider vinegar

1 teaspoon hot sauce, or to taste

1 teaspoon garlic powder

½ teaspoon salt

1. Combine the TVP and water or Vegetable Broth and allow to sit at least 5 minutes.

2. In a large soup pot or stockpot, sauté onion and bell pepper in oil until soft.

3. Reduce heat to medium-low and add TVP and remaining ingredients. Simmer, covered, for at least 15 minutes, stirring occasionally.

4. For thicker and less sloppy "Sloppy Jolindas," simmer a bit longer, uncovered, to reduce the liquid.

SOUTHERN FRIED SEITAN

Deep-fried seitan is one the best things about eating vegan. Feel free to gloat when eating this amazing dish—those omnivores don't know what they're missing!

INGREDIENTS

Serves 4

2 tablespoons soy sauce

¼ cup soymilk

3 tablespoons mustard

⅔ cup flour

¼ cup nutritional yeast

1 tablespoon baking powder

1 teaspoon garlic powder

1 teaspoon onion powder

½ teaspoon paprika

½ teaspoon salt

½ teaspoon black pepper

1 (16-ounce) package prepared seitan

Oil for frying

1. In a small bowl, combine the soy sauce, soymilk, and mustard. In a separate medium bowl, combine the flour, nutritional yeast, and remaining ingredients except the seitan and the oil.

2. Coat the seitan pieces well with the soymilk and mustard mixture, then coat well with the flour and nutritional yeast mixture.

3. Fry in oil, turning as needed, for 4–5 minutes or until golden brown, and drain on paper towels.

Any Way You Slice It . . .

For an appetizer or snack, chop your seitan into 2" chunks and dip in ketchup or barbecue sauce. Or flatten your seitan into patties for Southern "chicken-fried steak" and top with Mushroom Gravy (Chapter 3) and a side of Roasted Garlic Mashed Potatoes (Chapter 7).

SPICED APPLE CIDER SEITAN

This recipe makes candied sweet potatoes while it cooks the seitan in the sweetened cider sauce.

INGREDIENTS

Serves 8

3 pounds seitan, cubed

Salt and freshly ground black pepper, to taste

2 apples, peeled, cored, and sliced

4 large sweet potatoes, peeled and cut in half

½ cup apple cider or apple juice

½ teaspoon ground cinnamon

¼ teaspoon ground cloves

¼ teaspoon ground allspice

2 tablespoons brown sugar

1. Treat the crock of a 4-quart slow cooker with nonstick spray.

2. Add seitan and season it with salt and pepper.

3. Arrange apple slices over and around the seitan. Add the sweet potatoes.

4. In a bowl or measuring cup, stir together the cider or juice, cinnamon, cloves, allspice, and brown sugar. Pour over the ingredients in the slow cooker.

5. Cover, and cook on low for 8 hours.

SPICY SEITAN TACO "MEAT"

Finely dice the seitan, or pulse it in the food processor until diced small, for maximum surface area and spice in this recipe, and pile up the taco fixings!

INGREDIENTS

Serves 6

½ onion, diced

½ green or red bell pepper, chopped small

1 large tomato, chopped

1 package prepared seitan, chopped small (about 2½ cups)

2 tablespoons oil

1 tablespoon soy sauce

1 teaspoon hot sauce, or to taste

2 teaspoons chili powder

½ teaspoon cumin

1. In a large skillet, sauté onion, bell pepper, tomato, and seitan in oil, stirring frequently, until seitan is browned and tomatoes and pepper are soft.

2. Reduce heat and add soy sauce, hot sauce, chili powder, and cumin, coating well. Heat for 1 more minute.

STROGANOFF

The beef commonly used in stroganoff can be replaced with mushrooms, tempeh, or seitan to create a vegan dish.

INGREDIENTS

Serves 8

1 tablespoon extra-virgin olive oil

1 yellow onion, diced

2 cloves garlic, minced

1 pound seitan, chopped

1 teaspoon salt

4 cups Vegetable Broth (Chapter 6)

½ cup vegan sour cream

1 tablespoon ground mustard

¼ cup chopped parsley

1 pound cooked linguine or fettuccine pasta

1. Heat the olive oil in a sauté pan over medium heat. Add the onion and garlic and cook for 2 minutes.

2. Place the sautéed onion and garlic, seitan, salt, and Vegetable Broth in a 4-quart slow cooker. Cover, and cook on low for 7 hours.

3. In a small bowl, combine the sour cream, mustard, and parsley, then add to the slow cooker, stirring well.

4. Cover, and cook on low for an additional 15 minutes, then serve over cooked pasta.

SUPER-MEATY TVP MEATLOAF

With a pinkish hue and chewy texture, this meatloaf impersonates the real thing well. Top with gravy for a Thanksgiving entrée.

INGREDIENTS

Serves 6

2 cups TVP

1¾ cups hot Vegetable Broth (Chapter 6)

1 onion, chopped

1 tablespoon oil

¼ cup ketchup

⅓ cup barbecue sauce, plus 3 tablespoons

1 cup vital wheat gluten flour

1 cup bread crumbs

1 teaspoon parsley

½ teaspoon sage

½ teaspoon salt

¼ teaspoon pepper

1. Combine TVP in hot Vegetable Broth and allow to sit for 6–7 minutes until rehydrated. Gently squeeze out any excess moisture.

2. Heat onion in oil until translucent, about 3–4 minutes.

3. Preheat oven to 400°F.

4. In a large bowl, combine TVP, onions, ketchup, and ⅓ cup barbecue sauce. Add vital wheat gluten flour, bread crumbs, and spices.

5. Gently press mixture into a lightly greased loaf pan. Drizzle 3 tablespoons of barbecue sauce on top and bake for 45–50 minutes until lightly browned. Allow to cool for at least 10 minutes before serving, as loaf will set as it cools.

TANDOORI SEITAN

You can enjoy the flavors of traditional Indian tandoori without firing up your grill by simmering the seitan on the stovetop.

INGREDIENTS

Serves 6

⅔ cup soy yogurt

2 tablespoons lemon juice

1½ tablespoons tandoori spice blend

½ teaspoon cumin

½ teaspoon garlic powder

¼ teaspoon salt

1 (16-ounce) package prepared seitan, chopped

1 bell pepper, chopped

1 onion, chopped

1 tomato, chopped

2 tablespoons oil

1. Whisk together the yogurt, lemon juice, and all the spices in a shallow bowl or pan and add seitan. Allow to marinate for at least 1 hour. Reserve marinade.

2. Sauté pepper, onion, and tomato in oil until just barely soft. Reduce heat to low and add seitan. Cook, tossing seitan occasionally, for 8–10 minutes.

3. Serve topped with extra marinade.

TVP TACO "MEAT"

Whip up this meaty and economical taco filling in just a few minutes using prepared salsa and have diners fill their own tacos according to their taste. Nondairy sour cream, fresh tomatoes, shredded lettuce, and extra hot sauce are a must, and find some room on your table for sliced avocadoes or vegan cheese if you can.

INGREDIENTS

Serves 6

2 cups TVP flakes

2 cups hot water

1 yellow onion, diced

½ red or yellow bell pepper, diced

½ green bell pepper, diced

2 tablespoons olive oil

2 teaspoons chili powder

1 teaspoon cumin

½ cup salsa

½ teaspoon hot sauce, or to taste

5–6 flour tortillas or taco shells

1. Combine TVP with hot water and allow to sit for 5–10 minutes to reconstitute. Drain.

2. In a large skillet, heat onion and bell peppers in olive oil. Add TVP, chili powder, and cumin. Cook, stirring frequently, for 4–5 minutes or until pepper and onion are soft.

3. Add salsa and hot sauce, stirring to combine. Remove from heat.

4. Wrap TVP mixture in flour tortillas or spoon into taco shells and serve with taco fillings.

TVP: Cheap, Chewy, and Meaty

TVP is inexpensive and has such a meaty texture that many budget-conscious nonvegetarian cooks use it to stretch their dollar, adding it to homemade burgers and meatloaf. For the best deal, buy it in bulk. TVP is usually found in small crumbles, but some specialty shops also sell it in strips or chunks.

TVP, MUSHROOM, AND WHITE WINE STROGANOFF

Vegetable broth may be used in place of the white wine. Serve this stroganoff over noodles, rice, pasta, or baked potatoes.

INGREDIENTS

Serves 4

¾ cup TVP

¾ cup hot water or Vegetable Broth (Chapter 6)

1½ cups sliced mushrooms

1 onion, diced

2 tablespoons vegan margarine

½ cup white wine

½ teaspoon sage

½ teaspoon parsley

½ teaspoon garlic powder

1 tablespoon flour

2 cups soymilk

½ cup vegan sour cream

2 teaspoons Dijon mustard

Salt and pepper, to taste

1. Rehydrate TVP in hot water or Vegetable Broth and drain any excess moisture.

2. Heat the mushrooms and onion in vegan margarine for just 1–2 minutes, then add white wine, sage, parsley, and garlic powder and simmer until soft, about 3–4 more minutes, over medium-low heat.

3. Add flour and stir constantly until pasty and thick. Slowly add soymilk, whisking to combine. Heat until thick and creamy.

4. Stir in sour cream and Dijon mustard, and season generously with salt and pepper.

Mix and Match

Instead of plain TVP, make a batch of Italian "meatballs" from the recipe for Spaghetti with Italian "Meatballs" (Chapter 9) to smother in stroganoff sauce and top off a plate of noodles.

TVP STUFFED PEPPERS

This is a great way to use up any leftover rice. Top with a bit of grated vegan cheese if you'd like.

INGREDIENTS

Serves 6

6 bell peppers, any color

¾ cup TVP

¾ cup hot Vegetable Broth (Chapter 6)

1 onion, chopped

2 ribs celery, diced

⅔ cup mushrooms, chopped small

2 tablespoons olive oil

1½ cups rice, cooked

1 teaspoon parsley

½ teaspoon oregano

½ teaspoon salt

2 cups tomato or marinara sauce

1. Preheat oven to 325°F.

2. Slice tops off bell peppers and remove inner seeds.

3. Combine TVP and Vegetable Broth and allow to sit for 6–7 minutes to rehydrate.

4. In a large skillet, sauté onion, celery, and mushrooms in oil until onion is soft and mushrooms are browned, about 5 minutes. Reduce heat to medium-low and add cooked rice, TVP, parsley, oregano, salt, and tomato or marinara sauce, reserving about ½ cup. Heat just until combined.

5. Stuff mixture into bell peppers, place in a baking pan or casserole dish, and spoon a bit of the remaining sauce on top of each. Place "lids" back on bell peppers if desired.

6. Bake for 30 minutes, or until peppers are cooked.

VEGAN ROPA VIEJA

Serve this Cuban dish with yellow rice and black beans. It also makes a great filling for corn or flour tortillas.

INGREDIENTS
Serves 8

2 pounds seitan, cubed

1 cubanelle pepper, diced

1 large onion, diced

2 carrots, diced

2 (15-ounce) cans canned crushed tomatoes

2 cloves garlic

1 teaspoon dried oregano

½ teaspoon cumin

½ cup sliced green olives stuffed with pimientos

1. Place all ingredients into a 4-quart slow cooker. Cook on low for 7 hours.

2. Shred the seitan with a fork, knife, or grater, then mash it with a potato masher until very well mixed.

All about Cumin

Cumin is a spice made from the seed of a plant by the same name. It is dried and ground before use and gives a strong earthy and somewhat nutty flavor to dishes.

CHAPTER 13

TEMPEH

BAKED MEXICAN TEMPEH CAKES

Like tofu, tempeh can be baked in a flavorful sauce, but it does need to be simmered first, just to soften it up a bit.

INGREDIENTS

Serves 4

2 (8-ounce) packages tempeh

1 cup water or Vegetable Broth (Chapter 6)

⅓ cup tomato paste

3 cloves garlic, minced

2 tablespoons soy sauce

2 tablespoons apple cider vinegar

3 tablespoons water

1½ teaspoons chili powder

½ teaspoon oregano

¼ teaspoon cayenne, or to taste

Tomato salsa or hot sauce

1. If your tempeh is thicker than ¾", slice it in half through the middle to create 2 thinner halves. Then slice each block of tempeh into 4 fillets. Simmer in water or Vegetable Broth for 10 minutes, and drain well.

2. Whisk together the tomato paste, garlic, soy sauce, vinegar, water, chili powder, oregano, and cayenne. Add tempeh, and allow to marinate for at least 1 hour or overnight.

3. Preheat oven to 375°.

4. Transfer tempeh to a lightly greased baking sheet or casserole dish and baste with a bit of the marinade.

5. Bake for 15–17 minutes. Turn tempeh pieces over and baste with a bit more marinade. Bake another 15–17 minutes. Serve topped with tomato salsa or hot sauce.

BASIC BAKED TEMPEH PATTIES

Baked tempeh is a simple entrée, or use as a patty to make veggie burgers or sandwiches.
Slice your tempeh into cubes to add to fried rice, noodles, or stir-fries.

INGREDIENTS
Serves 2

1 (8-ounce) package tempeh

1 cup water or Vegetable Broth (Chapter 6), plus 2 tablespoons

3 tablespoons soy sauce

2 tablespoons apple cider vinegar

3 cloves garlic, minced

2 teaspoons sesame oil

1. If your tempeh is thicker than ¾", slice in half through the center to make 2 thinner pieces, then slice into desired shape.

2. Simmer tempeh in 1 cup water or Vegetable Broth for 10 minutes; drain well.

3. Whisk together remaining ingredients, including 2 tablespoons of water or Vegetable Broth, and marinate tempeh for at least 1 hour or overnight.

4. Preheat oven to 375°F and transfer tempeh to a lightly greased baking sheet.

5. Bake for 10–12 minutes on each side.

What Is Tempeh?

Long a staple food in the Indonesian islands, tempeh sounds a bit odd when described: It's made from cultured (that is, fermented) cooked soybeans. Don't let that turn you off though, as tempeh is chewy, textured, meaty, and super-tasty! Look for tempeh in the refrigerator section of natural foods stores. Several different kinds are usually available, but they're all interchangeable, so try them all!

BUFFALO TEMPEH

This recipe makes appetizer-size servings, not full entrée-size servings.

INGREDIENTS

Serves 8

1 (13-ounce) package tempeh, cut into strips

1 cup vegan margarine, melted

1 cup Tabasco sauce

3 stalks celery, cut into strips

1 cup vegan ranch dressing

1. Add the tempeh, vegan margarine, and Tabasco sauce to a 4-quart slow cooker. Cover, and cook on low heat for 6 hours.

2. Serve on a platter with the celery sticks and dressing.

Vegan Ranch Dressing

Vegan ranch dressing is sold in some grocery stores and can be ordered online. Try OrganicVille Non Dairy Organic Ranch Dressing as a delicious alternative to traditional ranch.

CAJUN TEMPEH PO'BOYS

This recipe makes two very large sandwiches so bring your appetite or you can save some for later.

INGREDIENTS
Serves 2

1 (13-ounce) package tempeh, cut into small, bite-size squares

½ cup olive oil

5 cloves garlic, minced

1 onion, chopped

2 teaspoons oregano

2 teaspoons thyme

2 teaspoons cayenne pepper

2 tablespoons paprika

1 teaspoon salt

¼ teaspoon black pepper

1 loaf French bread, sliced horizontally

2 cups lettuce, shredded

2 tomatoes, sliced

1. Add all ingredients except the bread, lettuce, and tomato to a 4-quart slow cooker, cover, and cook on high heat for 2 hours.

2. Assemble the sandwiches on the bread by layering the tempeh, lettuce, and tomatoes.

All "Dressed" Up
Traditional New Orleans po'boys are served either plain or dressed. Dressed means it's topped with lettuce, tomatoes, pickles, and mayo, but you can substitute Vegenaise to keep the sandwich vegan.

CRISPY TEMPEH FRIES

Frying these tempeh sticks twice makes them extra-crispy.

INGREDIENTS
Serves 2

1 (8-ounce) package tempeh

Water for boiling

½ teaspoon salt

½ teaspoon garlic powder

Oil for frying

Seasoning salt, to taste

1. Slice tempeh into thin strips. Simmer tempeh, covered, in 1" of water for 10 minutes. Drain.

2. While tempeh is still moist, sprinkle with salt and garlic powder.

3. Heat oil and fry tempeh for 5–6 minutes until crispy and browned. Place tempeh on paper towels and allow to cool for at least 30 minutes.

4. Reheat oil and fry again for another 4–5 minutes. Season lightly with seasoning salt while still warm.

Simmering Tempeh

Most tempeh recipes will turn out better if your tempeh is simmered in a bit of water or vegetable broth first. This improves the digestibility of the tempeh, softens it up, and decreases the cooking time. And if you add some seasonings such as soy sauce, garlic powder, or some herbs, it will increase the flavor as well.

CURRIED TEMPEH IN COCONUT CREAM

Try serving Curried Tempeh in Coconut Cream over rice or in cool, crisp lettuce leaves.

INGREDIENTS

Serves 4

2 cloves garlic, minced

1 teaspoon fresh ginger, minced

¼ cup soy sauce

1 tablespoon vegetable oil

1 tablespoon sriracha sauce

1 (13-ounce) can coconut milk

1 cup water

1 (13-ounce) package tempeh, cut into bite-size squares

¼ cup fresh basil, chopped

1. Add all ingredients except the basil to a 4-quart slow cooker. Cover, and cook on low heat for 6 hours.

2. About 10 minutes before the tempeh is done cooking, stir in the basil, cook for the remaining time, and serve.

GINGER-SOY TEMPEH CUBES

Tempeh is made from fermented soybeans, and is used as a meat replacement in many vegan dishes.

INGREDIENTS

Serves 4

3 cloves garlic, minced

1 tablespoon fresh ginger, minced

½ cup soy sauce

1 cup water

2 limes, juiced

¼ cup olive oil

2 tablespoons sugar

1 (13-ounce) package tempeh, cut into bite-size squares

3 green onions, sliced

1. In a small bowl, combine garlic, ginger, soy sauce, water, lime juice, olive oil, and sugar.

2. Add all ingredients except the green onions to a 4-quart slow cooker. Cover, and cook on medium heat for 4 hours. Garnish with the green onions.

LEMON-PEPPER TEMPEH

When fresh herbs are in season, add chopped curly or flat leaf parsley to this dish before serving.

INGREDIENTS

Serves 4

1 (13-ounce) package tempeh, cut into bite-size squares

6 cloves garlic, minced

1 teaspoon fresh ginger, minced

¾ cup water

¼ cup soy sauce

½ cup extra-virgin olive oil

¼ cup fresh lemon juice

1 teaspoon black pepper

Add all ingredients to a 4-quart slow cooker. Cover, and cook on low heat for 6 hours.

Serving Suggestions

Make this tempeh dish the star of the show and serve as a main course, with a vegetable and grain on the side. Or place the strips on a hoagie roll topped with vegan mayonnaise and lettuce to make a tasty sub sandwich.

ORANGE-POMEGRANATE TEMPEH BITES

Pomegranate juice is a good source of Vitamin C and while the debate still goes on, it may be a good source of antioxidants too.

INGREDIENTS
Serves 4

1 (13-ounce) package tempeh, cut into bite-size squares

1 tablespoon olive oil

¼ cup soy sauce

¼ teriyaki glaze

⅛ cup brown sugar

3 oranges, juiced

¼ cup pomegranate juice

Add all ingredients to a 4-quart slow cooker, cover, and cook on high heat for 2 hours.

PESTO MARINATED TEMPEH

What goes better with pesto than al dente pasta!

INGREDIENTS
Serves 4

¼ cup olive oil

2 cloves garlic

2 cups basil

¼ cup pine nuts, toasted

1 cup water

1 (13-ounce) package tempeh, cut into bite-size squares

1. Place the olive oil, garlic, basil, and toasted pine nuts into a food processor and purée to make the pesto.

2. Pour the pesto, water, and tempeh into a 4-quart slow cooker, cover, and cook on low heat for 6 hours.

How to Toast Pine Nuts
Toasting pine nuts is quite simple and all you need is a dry pan. Bring the pan to medium heat, add the nuts, and gently stir them so that the nuts toast evenly. Be careful not to burn the nuts; they should be removed from the heat as they begin to turn a light brown color.

ROSEMARY TEMPEH HASH

Diner-style breakfast hash with tempeh for protein and a little less grease on your spoon. Use a tablespoon of fresh rosemary if you have some in your herb garden instead of dried.

INGREDIENTS

Serves 4

2 potatoes, diced

Water for boiling

1 (8-ounce) package tempeh, cubed

2 tablespoons olive oil

2 green onions, chopped

1 teaspoon chili powder

1 teaspoon rosemary

Salt and pepper to taste

1. Cover the potatoes with water in a large pot and bring to a boil. Cook just until potatoes are almost soft, about 15 minutes. Drain.

2. In a large pan, sauté the potatoes and tempeh in olive oil for 3–4 minutes, lightly browning tempeh on all sides.

3. Add green onions, chili powder, and rosemary, stirring to combine, and heat for 3–4 more minutes. Season well with salt and pepper.

"SHORT RIB" TEMPEH

No pigs necessary for this mouthwatering "rib" recipe!

INGREDIENTS

Serves 4

1 (13-ounce) package tempeh, cut into strips

1 (28-ounce) can tomato sauce

½ cup water

⅛ cup vegan Worcestershire sauce

2 tablespoons brown sugar

2 tablespoons dried parsley

1 teaspoon Tabasco sauce

¼ teaspoon black pepper

1 lemon, juiced

1 tablespoon soy sauce

Add all ingredients to a 4-quart slow cooker. Cover, and cook on low heat for 6 hours.

SPICY TEMPEH FAJITAS

Add a dollop of soy sour cream and salsa to finish off each of your fajitas.

INGREDIENTS

Serves 4

1 (13-ounce) package tempeh, cut into bite-size pieces

2 cloves garlic, minced

1 teaspoon fresh ginger, minced

¼ cup soy sauce

1 cup water

1 tablespoon olive oil

½ teaspoon chili powder

¼ teaspoon chipotle powder

¼ teaspoon black pepper

½ onion, sliced

½ green bell pepper, sliced

1 jalapeño, minced

½ cup mushrooms, sliced

8–12 corn tortillas

1 tomato, diced

¼ cup cilantro, chopped

1 lime, cut into wedges

1. Add the tempeh, garlic, ginger, soy sauce, water, olive oil, chili powder, chipotle powder, black pepper, onion, green bell pepper, jalapeño, and mushrooms to a 4-quart slow cooker. Cover, and cook on low heat for 6 hours.

2. Serve the fajitas on the tortillas and garnish with tomato, cilantro, and lime.

SRIRACHA AND SOY TEMPEH

Sriracha is sometimes affectionately referred to as "rooster sauce" because of the drawing on the bottle of the most familiar brand, but don't let the cute name fool you because this sauce packs a spicy punch.

INGREDIENTS

Serves 4

1 (13-ounce) package tempeh, cut into bite-size squares

4 cloves garlic, minced

1 teaspoon ginger, minced

1 tablespoon olive oil

½ cup soy sauce

¼ cup water

2 tablespoons brown sugar

1 teaspoon sriracha sauce

Add all ingredients to a 4-quart slow cooker, cover, and cook on high heat for 2 hours.

SWEET AND SOUR TEMPEH

With maple syrup instead of white sugar, this is a sweet and sour dish that's slightly less sweet than other versions. There's plenty of sauce, so plan on serving with some plain white rice or another grain to mop it all up. A handful of broccoli or baby corn could go in along with the bell peppers if you have some on hand.

INGREDIENTS

Serves 4

1 cup Vegetable Broth (Chapter 6)

2 tablespoons soy sauce

1 (8-ounce) package tempeh, diced into cubes

2 tablespoons barbecue sauce

½ teaspoon ground ginger

2 tablespoons maple syrup

⅓ cup rice vinegar or apple cider vinegar

1 tablespoon cornstarch

1 (15-ounce) can pineapple chunks, drained, reserving juice

2 tablespoons olive oil

1 green bell pepper, chopped

1 red bell pepper, chopped

1 yellow onion, chopped

1. Whisk together the Vegetable Broth and soy sauce and bring to a simmer in a large skillet. Simmer the tempeh for 10 minutes. Remove tempeh from the pan and reserve ½ cup Vegetable Broth mix.

2. In a small bowl, whisk together the barbecue sauce, ginger, maple syrup, vinegar, cornstarch, and juice from pineapples until cornstarch is dissolved. Set aside.

3. Heat olive oil in skillet, and add tempeh, bell peppers, and onions. Sauté for just 1–2 minutes, then add sauce mixture and bring to a simmer.

4. Allow to cook until sauce thickens, about 6–8 minutes. Reduce heat and stir in pineapples. Serve over rice or another whole grain.

Like Sweet and Sour?

This sauce would go equally well with some sautéed tofu, lightly browned seitan, or any vegetables that you like.

TEMPEH AND GREENS

Collard greens are a Southern staple but if you prefer a more tender green, opt for kale instead.

INGREDIENTS

Serves 6

1 (13-ounce) package tempeh, cut into bite-size squares

4 cloves garlic

1 onion, chopped

8 cups collard greens, stemmed and chopped

1 teaspoon Better Than Bouillon No Chicken Base

4 cups water

⅛ cup soy sauce

1 teaspoon hot sauce

1 teaspoon salt

¼ teaspoon black pepper

Add all ingredients to a 4-quart slow cooker, cover, and cook on low heat for 6 hours. Use a slotted spoon to serve the tempeh and greens in a bowl.

TEMPEH BRAISED IN SAUERKRAUT

Sauerkraut is fermented cabbage that is often sold canned or in jars in grocery stores nationwide.

INGREDIENTS
Serves 6

3 cups sauerkraut

½ tablespoon caraway seeds

1 tablespoon yellow mustard seeds

1 small onion, thinly sliced

2 tablespoons apple cider vinegar

1 pound tempeh, cut into 1½" cubes

1. Place the sauerkraut, caraway seeds, mustard seeds, onion, and vinegar into a 4- or 6-quart slow cooker. Stir to distribute all ingredients evenly.

2. Add the tempeh; toss.

3. Cover, and cook for 3–4 hours on low.

TEMPEH CARNITAS

Serve up these delicious vegan carnitas in warm corn tortillas.

INGREDIENTS
Serves 4

1 (13-ounce) package tempeh, cut into thin strips

1 onion, chopped

4 cloves garlic, minced

1 teaspoon cumin

1 teaspoon dried oregano

¼ teaspoon cinnamon

2 cups Vegetable Broth (Chapter 6)

1 teaspoon salt

¼ teaspoon black pepper

Add all of the ingredients to a 4-quart slow cooker, cover, and cook on high heat for 2–3 hours.

TEMPEH JAMBALAYA

Unlike the famous New Orleans dish gumbo, jambalaya isn't meant to be brothy; instead you cook the rice dish until all of the liquid is absorbed.

INGREDIENTS

Serves 6

1 (13-ounce) package tempeh, cut into bite-size squares

1 onion, chopped

2 stalks celery, chopped

1 bell pepper, chopped

4 cloves garlic, minced

2 cups uncooked white rice

2 teaspoons Better Than Bouillon No Chicken Base

5 cups water

1 (15-ounce) can tomato sauce

2 bay leaves

⅛ cup Cajun seasoning

¼ teaspoon dried thyme

2 teaspoons hot sauce

1 teaspoon salt

¼ teaspoon black pepper

Add all ingredients to a 4-quart slow cooker, cover, and cook on low heat for 6 hours or until all of the liquid is absorbed. Remove bay leaves before serving.

Bay Leaves

Bay leaves are often used to flavor soups, stews, and other liquids during cooking. They are typically dried and used whole, but you can also crumble them into a dish and you won't need to remove before serving.

TEMPEH MOLE

Mole is a type of Mexican sauce that is used on a variety of proteins. Try serving this Tempeh Mole on a bed of rice or warm flour tortillas.

INGREDIENTS

Serves 4

2 tablespoons olive oil

1 onion, chopped

4 cloves garlic, minced

2 tablespoons flour

2 teaspoons Better Than Bouillon No Chicken Base

3 cups water

2 tablespoons chili powder

1 teaspoon cumin

1 teaspoon dried oregano

½ teaspoon cinnamon

⅓ cup vegan chocolate chips

½ teaspoon salt

⅛ teaspoon black pepper

1 (13-ounce) package tempeh, cut into bite-size squares

1. Place the olive oil in a sauté pan over medium heat. Add the onion and garlic, then sauté for 2–3 minutes. When done, add the flour and whisk to create a roux.

2. Transfer the roux mixture and all remaining ingredients to a 4-quart slow cooker, cover, and cook on high for 2 hours.

TEMPEH POT PIE

Some brands of frozen puff pastry are "accidentally vegan." Just be sure to read the ingredients before purchasing.

INGREDIENTS

Serves 4

½ cup vegan margarine

1 onion, chopped

2 carrots, peeled and chopped

1 cup mushrooms, chopped

½ cup flour

1 cup unsweetened soymilk

1 cup frozen peas

1 (13-ounce) package tempeh, cut into bite-size squares

½ cup water

2 teaspoons lemon pepper

1 teaspoon salt

¼ teaspoon black pepper

1 sheet frozen puff pastry, cut into 4 squares

1. Add the vegan margarine to a large sauté pan over medium heat. Once melted, add the onion, carrots, and mushrooms and sauté for 3–5 minutes.

2. Add the flour and whisk to create a roux, then slowly whisk in the soymilk and stir until all lumps have been removed.

3. Transfer the contents of the sauté pan to a 4-quart slow cooker and add all remaining ingredients except the puff pastry, cover, and cook on low heat for 6 hours.

4. Meanwhile, cook the puff pastry according to package directions or until it is golden brown. Serve the pot pie in a bowl and top each bowl with 1 piece of the puff pastry.

TEMPEH REUBEN SANDWICHES

Some grocery store–brand Thousand Island dressings are "accidentally vegan"; just be sure to read the label.

INGREDIENTS

Serves 6

1 (13-ounce) package tempeh, cut into strips

1 cup water

¼ cup apple cider vinegar

2 tablespoons paprika

1 tablespoon dried oregano

¼ cup Dijon mustard

¼ teaspoon liquid smoke

2 teaspoons allspice

3 cloves garlic, minced

1 teaspoon salt

¼ teaspoon black pepper

12 slices rye bread

1 cup sauerkraut

6 slices vegan Cheddar cheese

½ cup Thousand Island dressing

1. Add the tempeh, water, apple cider vinegar, paprika, oregano, Dijon mustard, liquid smoke, allspice, garlic, salt, and pepper to a 4-quart slow cooker. Cover, and cook on medium heat for 4 hours.

2. Serve on the rye bread with sauerkraut, cheese, and Thousand Island dressing.

TEMPEH SAUSAGE CRUMBLES

For a healthier alternative to store bought faux-sausage, you can make your own using crumbled tempeh.

INGREDIENTS

Serves 4

1 (13-ounce) package tempeh, crumbled

2 tablespoons olive oil

¼ cup water

4 cloves garlic, minced

1 tablespoon dried sage

¼ teaspoon dried marjoram

2 tablespoons brown sugar

¼ teaspoon crushed red pepper

1 teaspoon salt

¼ teaspoon black pepper

Add all ingredients to a 4-quart slow cooker, cover, and cook on high heat for 2 hours.

TEMPEH SLIDERS

Sliders are mini sandwiches, perfect as an appetizer or a snack.

INGREDIENTS

Serves 4

1 (13-ounce) package tempeh, cut into 8 squares

2 cloves garlic, minced

1 teaspoon fresh ginger, minced

¼ cup soy sauce

1 cup water

¼ teaspoon black pepper

½ teaspoon garlic powder

½ teaspoon onion powder

¼ teaspoon cumin

⅛ teaspoon cayenne pepper

2 teaspoons olive oil

½ onion, sliced

6–8 slices vegan Cheddar cheese

8 mini sandwich buns

1. Add the tempeh, garlic, ginger, soy sauce, water, and black pepper, garlic powder, onion powder, cumin, and cayenne pepper to a 4-quart slow cooker. Cover, and cook on low heat for 6 hours.

2. About 5 minutes before the sliders are done cooking, add the olive oil to a pan and sauté the onion over medium-high heat until it is soft, about 5 minutes.

3. Melt a slice of cheese on each piece of tempeh and top with onion. Serve on mini sandwich buns.

Finding Vegan Bread

Some bread recipes call for eggs, dairy, and honey, but there are also many that do not, and finding vegan sandwich buns shouldn't be a challenge. Some grocery stores such as Kroger even label Kroger-brand bread as vegan if it is.

TEMPEH TAMALE PIE

In a slight variation on the baked classic, this version of tamale pie features plump, moist cornmeal dumplings.

INGREDIENTS

Serves 4

2 tablespoons olive oil

1 large onion, minced

1 pound tempeh, crumbled

1 jalapeño, minced

2 cloves garlic, minced

1 (15-ounce) can diced tomatoes

1 (10-ounce) can diced tomatoes with green chilies

1 (15-ounce) can dark red kidney beans, drained and rinsed

4 chipotle peppers in adobo, minced

½ teaspoon hot Mexican chili powder

⅔ cup unsweetened soymilk

2 tablespoons canola oil

2 teaspoons baking powder

½ cup cornmeal

½ teaspoon salt

1. In a large sauté pan over medium heat, add the olive oil. Sauté the onion, tempeh, jalapeño, and garlic for 5 minutes.

2. Pour the tempeh mixture into a 4-quart slow cooker. Add the tomatoes, tomatoes with green chilies, beans, chipotles, and chili powder. Cover, and cook on low for 8 hours.

3. In a medium bowl, mix the soymilk, oil, baking powder, cornmeal, and salt. Drop in ¼-cup mounds in a single layer on top of the tempeh.

4. Cover, and cook on high for 20 minutes without lifting the lid. The dumplings will look fluffy and light when fully cooked.

Canned Versus Fresh Tomatoes

While fresh tomatoes are delicious, canned tomatoes are a better choice in some recipes because they have already been cooked. Skins and seeds have been removed from canned tomatoes, which is also a bonus when seeds and skin might detract from the dish. There is also reason to believe that canned tomatoes are better sources of cancer-preventing lycopene simply because they are cooked, and that one can of crushed tomatoes or sauce is the equivalent of dozens of fresh tomatoes.

CHAPTER 14

DELICIOUS DESSERTS

"BAKED" APPLES

Serve these lightly spiced apples as a simple dessert or a breakfast treat.

INGREDIENTS
Serves 6

6 baking apples, cored and halved

½ cup water

1 cinnamon stick

1 knob peeled fresh ginger

1 vanilla bean

1. Place the apples in a single layer on the bottom of a 4- or 6-quart slow cooker. Add the water, cinnamon stick, ginger, and vanilla bean.

2. Cover, and cook on low for 6–8 hours, or until the apples are tender and easily pierced with a fork.

3. Use a slotted spoon to remove the apples from the insert. Discard the cinnamon stick, ginger, vanilla bean, and water. Serve hot.

Baking with Apples

When baking or cooking, choose apples with firm flesh such as Granny Smith, Jonathan, McIntosh, Cortland, Pink Lady, Pippin, or Winesap. They will be able to hold up to low cooking times without turning to mush. Leaving the skin on adds fiber.

BANANAS FOSTER

Bananas Foster is usually made from flambéed bananas served over vanilla ice cream, but as this recipe proves, the bananas can be made in a slow cooker too.

INGREDIENTS
Serves 8

1 cup dark corn syrup

⅛ cup rum

½ teaspoon vanilla extract

1 teaspoon cinnamon

¾ cup vegan margarine

½ teaspoon salt

10 bananas, peeled and cut into bite-size pieces

4 cups vegan vanilla ice cream

1. In a medium bowl, stir in the corn syrup, rum, vanilla extract, cinnamon, vegan margarine, and salt.

2. Add mixture and bananas to a 4-quart slow cooker. Cover, and cook on low heat for 1–2 hours. Serve over a scoop of vegan ice cream.

BANANA BREAD

Oat bran adds extra fiber to this recipe, making it a heart-healthier bread.

INGREDIENTS

Serves 8

1½ cups all-purpose flour

½ cup oat bran

¾ cup sugar

¼ teaspoon baking soda

2 teaspoons baking powder

½ teaspoon salt

3 ripe bananas, mashed

6 tablespoons vegan margarine, softened

2 teaspoons cornstarch plus 2 tablespoons warm water

¼ cup plain vegan yogurt

1 teaspoon vanilla

1¼ cups walnuts

1. Add the flour, oat bran, sugar, baking soda, baking powder, and salt to a mixing bowl. Stir to mix.

2. In a food processor, add the bananas, vegan margarine, cornstarch mixture, yogurt, and vanilla. Pulse to cream together.

3. Add the walnuts and flour mixture to the food processor. Pulse to combine and chop the walnuts. Scrape down the sides of the container with a spatula and pulse until mixed.

4. Treat a 4-quart slow cooker with nonstick spray. Add the batter to the slow cooker, using a spatula to spread it evenly across the bottom of the crock.

5. Cover, and cook on high for 3 hours, or until a toothpick inserted in the center of the bread comes out clean.

6. Allow to cool uncovered before removing it from the slow cooker.

Spiced Banana Bread

For cinnamon-spiced banana bread, in Step 1 add 1 teaspoon of ground cinnamon and ¼ teaspoon each of ground cloves, ginger, allspice, and nutmeg to the flour.

CHUNKY CINNAMON PEAR SAUCE

Pears make this dessert an interesting twist on classic applesauce.

INGREDIENTS

Serves 6

10 pears, peeled, cored, and chopped

1 lemon, juiced

¼ cup water

2 teaspoons cinnamon

¼ cup sugar

1. Add all ingredients to a 4-quart slow cooker. Cover, and cook on low heat for 6 hours.

2. Mash the pears with a potato masher and allow to cool. Serve chilled.

GINGER POACHED PEARS

Fresh ginger best complements pear flavor, but if you only have ground, start by adding a smaller amount and then increase after tasting if desired.

INGREDIENTS

Serves 8

5 pears, peeled, cored, and cut into wedges

3 cups water

1 cup white sugar

2 tablespoons ginger, minced

1 teaspoon cinnamon

Add all ingredients to a 4-quart slow cooker. Cover, and cook on low heat for 4 hours.

MIXED BERRY COBBLER

Fresh berries are best for a delicious cobbler but frozen will work too. Just thaw and drain excess water before using them in a recipe.

INGREDIENTS
Serves 8

1 cup flour

¾ cup sugar

1 teaspoon baking powder

¼ teaspoon cinnamon

¼ teaspoon salt

Egg replacer for 2 eggs

¼ cup puréed silken tofu

1½ cups strawberries, chopped

1½ cups raspberries

1 cup blueberries

1 teaspoon lemon juice

1. In a large bowl, combine the flour, ½ cup sugar, baking powder, cinnamon, and salt, then add the egg replacer and tofu. Stir until well combined, then pour the mixture into a greased 4-quart slow cooker.

2. In a small bowl, combine the remaining ¼ cup sugar, strawberries, raspberries, blueberries, and lemon juice, then add the berry mixture to the slow cooker. Cover, and cook for 2½–3 hours.

POACHED FIGS AND ICE CREAM

Poach means to cook in a liquid over high heat, and it is a wonderful technique to use on delicate figs.

INGREDIENTS
Serves 8

15 Black Mission figs

2 cups port wine

1 cup sugar

1 strip orange zest

½ teaspoon vanilla

2 cinnamon sticks

6 cups vegan vanilla ice cream

1. Add all of the ingredients except the ice cream to a 4-quart slow cooker, cover, and cook on high heat for 3–4 hours.

2. Allow to cool slightly, then serve over a scoop of vanilla ice cream.

Vegan Ice Cream

These days there are many options for vegan ice cream in major grocery stores. The most popular types are made from one of three base ingredients—soy, rice milk, or coconut milk—and you should choose one based on your personal preference. Rice-based ice creams tend to have a lighter flavor because the milk is not as rich or fatty. Soy ice cream and coconut milk ice cream tend to be richer and smoother.

SPICED APPLES AND PEARS

This bold dessert is a great way to warm up on a cold winter night.

INGREDIENTS

Serves 6

4 apples, peeled, cored, and sliced

4 pears, peeled, cored, and sliced

½ cup vegan margarine

⅛ cup lemon juice

2 tablespoons vanilla extract

1 cup brown sugar

1 teaspoon cinnamon

Add all ingredients to a 4-quart slow cooker. Cover, and cook on low heat for 6 hours.

CHOCOLATE COCONUT BARS

Shredded coconut sometimes comes sweetened, but if you'd like to cut the sugar in this treat, use unsweetened instead.

INGREDIENTS

Serves 16

2 (14-ounce) packages semisweet vegan chocolate chips

1 cup shredded coconut

1. Add all ingredients to a 4-quart slow cooker. Cover, and cook on low heat for 1 hour, stirring every 15 minutes.

2. With a large spoon, scoop out the chocolate mixture and drop it onto wax paper. Allow to cool for 20–30 minutes.

CHOCOLATE GRAHAM CRACKER CANDY BARS

Have the kids help out by spreading the peanut butter while you do the dipping. Matzo, saltines, or any cracker will work, really, and because half of them will disappear before you're finished making them, you may want to make a double—or even triple—batch!

INGREDIENTS
Yields 16 bars

1 cup peanut butter or other nut butter

8 vegan graham crackers, quartered, or any vegan cracker

1 cup vegan chocolate chips

¼ cup vegan margarine

Toppings: vegan sprinkles, coconut flakes, chopped nuts (optional)

1. Line a baking pan with wax paper.

2. Spread about 1 tablespoon of peanut or other nut butter on a cracker, then top with another to make a "sandwich."

3. In a double boiler or over very low heat, melt together the chocolate chips and margarine until smooth and creamy.

4. Using tongs, dip each cracker sandwich into the chocolate and lightly coat. Pick up with the tongs and allow excess chocolate to drip off, then transfer to lined baking sheet.

5. Top with any additional toppings if desired and chill until firm.

Half and Half

For a fancier presentation, shop for vegan white chocolate. Dip only half the cracker into the chocolate, then chill, and dip the other half into melted white chocolate. Beautiful and delicious.

DATE AND NUT BARS

Once these bars are completely cooled, you can store them in an airtight container and enjoy as a snack later.

INGREDIENTS
Serves 15

1 cup dates, pitted and chopped

1 cup cranberries

½ cup almonds

½ cup pecans

1 cup flour

1 cup sugar

1 teaspoon baking powder

¼ cup puréed silken tofu

2 tablespoons vegan margarine

1 teaspoon vanilla

1. Combine all of the ingredients in a large mixing bowl, then pour into a 4-quart slow cooker that has been prepared with cooking spray. Cover, and cook over high heat for 2 hours.

2. Allow to cool slightly, then cut into small bars. Transfer to a wire rack and allow the bars to cool completely.

All about Dates
Dates, which are a fruit, come from a type of palm tree and can be eaten fresh or dried, which is more common. If you can only find dried dates, be sure to rehydrate them by soaking in water before use.

FOOLPROOF VEGAN FUDGE

Vegan fudge is much easier to make than nonvegan fudge, so don't worry about a thing when making this fudge. Regular soymilk will work just fine, but the soy cream has a richer taste.

INGREDIENTS
Yields 24 (1") pieces

⅓ cup vegan margarine

⅓ cup cocoa

⅓ cup soy cream

½ teaspoon vanilla

2 tablespoons peanut butter

3–3½ cups powdered sugar

¾ cup nuts, finely chopped

1. Lightly grease a small baking dish or square cake pan.

2. Using a double boiler, or over very low heat, melt the vegan margarine with the cocoa, soy cream, vanilla, and peanut butter.

3. Slowly incorporate powdered sugar until mixture is smooth, creamy, and thick. Stir in nuts.

4. Immediately transfer to pan and chill until completely firm, at least 2 hours.

Mint Fudge? Almond Fudge?
For a variation, halve the vanilla extract and add ¼ teaspoon of flavored extract: almond, mint, or whatever you enjoy.

SUGAR-FREE NO-BAKE COCOA BALLS

Craving a healthy chocolate snack? Try these fudgy little cocoa balls, similar to a soft no-bake cookie, but with no refined sugar. Much better than a pint of rocky road on chick-flick film night.

INGREDIENTS
Serves 4

1 cup chopped pitted dates

Water for soaking

1 cup walnuts or cashews

¼ cup cocoa powder

1 tablespoon peanut butter

¼ cup coconut flakes

1. Cover dates in water and soak for about 10 minutes until softened. Drain.

2. Process dates, nuts, cocoa powder, and peanut butter in a food processor until combined and sticky. Add coconut flakes and process until coarse.

3. Shape into balls and chill.

4. If mixture is too wet, add more nuts and coconut, or add just a touch of water if the mixture is dry and crumbly.

Variations
Roll these little balls in extra coconut flakes for a sweet presentation, or try it with carob powder instead of cocoa—they're just as satisfying. Don't have fresh dates on hand? Raisins may be substituted, but skip the soaking. Even with raisins, you really won't believe they're sugar-free.

CHOCOLATE "MUD" CAKE

Slow cooker "mud" cakes might not look pretty but the taste more than makes up for it.

INGREDIENTS

Serves 8

1 cup flour

½ cup sugar

2 teaspoons baking powder

¼ teaspoon salt

3 tablespoons cocoa powder

3 tablespoons vegan margarine, softened

1 teaspoon vanilla

⅓ cup soymilk

½ cup vegan chocolate chips

1 cup vegan chocolate icing

1. In a large mixing bowl, combine the flour, sugar, baking powder, salt, and cocoa powder. In a medium bowl, combine the vegan margarine, vanilla, and soymilk until well blended. Add the wet mixture and the chocolate chips to the large mixing bowl and stir until just combined.

2. Pour the batter into a greased 4-quart slow cooker, cover, and cook on high heat for 2½ hours.

3. Once done, allow the cake to cool slightly, then top with chocolate icing.

Vegan Chocolate Icing

There are many vegan icings available in your local grocery store and you might be surprised that they are made by brands such as Duncan Hines and Pillsbury. They are "accidentally vegan," though, which means they aren't advertised as such, as the recipes could change, so be sure to read the label before buying.

COOKIES AND CREAM CHEESECAKE

Vegan cheesecake is a great way to dispel those stereotypes about granola-munching, wheatgrass-sipping vegan hippies. Look for Trader Joe's brand chocolate sandwich cookies, Newman's Own Organics cookies, or use plain, mint, or chocolate Oreos, which may not be healthy, but are absolutely vegan!

INGREDIENTS
Serves 6

¼ cup soymilk

1 tablespoon cornstarch

1 (8-ounce) container vegan cream cheese

1 (12-ounce) block silken tofu

2 tablespoons lemon juice

2 teaspoons vanilla

¼ cup powdered sugar

¼ cup maple syrup

¼ cup oil

8–10 vegan chocolate sandwich cookies, crumbled

1 Vegan Cookie Pie Crust (this chapter)

1. Preheat oven to 350°F.

2. Whisk together the soymilk and cornstarch in a small bowl. Combine the soymilk with the cream cheese, tofu, lemon juice, vanilla, powdered sugar, and maple syrup and blend until completely smooth. Slowly add oil on high speed until combined.

3. Stir in crumbled cookies by hand and pour into prepared crust.

4. Bake 40–45 minutes. Allow to cool slightly, then chill. Cheesecake will firm up more as it cools, so avoid the temptation to overbake.

That Extra Finishing Touch
Drizzle the top of your vegan cheesecake with some chocolate sauce or vegan hot fudge sauce and some extra crumbled cookies.

CARROT CAKE

Ice this cake with vegan cream cheese frosting or glaze the cake while it's still warm.

INGREDIENTS
Serves 8

1½ cups all-purpose flour

½ teaspoon baking soda

1 teaspoon baking powder

¼ teaspoon salt

¾ teaspoon cinnamon

¼ teaspoon ground cloves

⅛ teaspoon freshly grated nutmeg

2 mashed bananas

¾ cup sugar

⅓ cup vegan margarine

¼ cup water

1 cup carrots, grated

½ cup chopped walnuts

1. In a mixing bowl, add the flour, baking soda, baking powder, salt, cinnamon, cloves, and nutmeg. Stir to combine.

2. In a food processor, add the bananas, sugar, and vegan margarine. Process to cream together. Scrape into the flour mixture.

3. Pour in the water and add the grated carrots to the mixing bowl. Stir and fold to combine all ingredients. Fold in the nuts.

4. Treat a 4-quart slow cooker with nonstick spray. Add the carrot cake batter and use a spatula to spread it evenly in the crock.

5. Cover, and cook on low for 2 hours, or until cake is firm in the center.

Carrot Cake Glaze

Repeatedly pierce the top of the cake with a fork. Add ½ cup lemon, orange, or unsweetened pineapple juice; 1 teaspoon freshly grated lemon or orange zest; and 1½ cups of sifted powdered sugar to a microwave-safe measuring cup and stir to combine. Microwave on high for 30 seconds. Stir and repeat until sugar is dissolved. Pour evenly over the cake.

MAPLE DATE CARROT CAKE

Free of refined sugar and with applesauce for moisture and just a touch of oil, this is a cake you can feel good about eating for breakfast. Leave out the dates if you want even less natural sugar.

INGREDIENTS
Serves 8

1½ cups raisins

1⅓ cups pineapple juice

6 dates, diced

Water for soaking

2¼ cups grated carrots

½ cup maple syrup

¼ cup applesauce

2 tablespoons oil

3 cups flour

1½ teaspoons baking soda

½ teaspoon salt

1 teaspoon cinnamon

½ teaspoon allspice or nutmeg

Egg replacer for 2 eggs

1. Preheat oven to 375°F and grease and flour a cake pan.

2. Combine the raisins with pineapple juice and allow to sit for 5–10 minutes to soften. In a separate small bowl, cover the dates with water until soft, about 10 minutes. Drain water from dates.

3. In a large mixing bowl, combine the raisins and pineapple juice, carrots, maple syrup, applesauce, oil, and dates. In a separate large bowl, combine the flour, baking soda, salt, cinnamon, and allspice or nutmeg.

4. Combine the dry ingredients with the wet ingredients, and add prepared egg replacer. Mix well.

5. Pour batter into prepared cake pan and bake for 30 minutes or until a toothpick inserted in the center comes out clean.

Egg Substitutes

Commercial egg replacers are convenient, but ground flax meal works just as well. Whisk together 1 tablespoon of flax meal with 2 tablespoons of water for each "egg." Let it sit for a few minutes and you'll see why it makes such a great binder, as it quickly becomes gooey and gelatinous. If you prefer a store-bought brand of egg replacer, Ener-G Egg Replacer is the most popular, but Bob's Red Mill brand works quite well too.

NO EGG REPLACER CHOCOLATE CAKE

Applesauce helps keep this chocolate cake moist without eggs or egg replacer and cuts down on the fat too, and the vinegar helps to lighten it up a bit.

INGREDIENTS

Serves 8

1½ cups flour

¾ cup sugar

⅓ cup cocoa powder

1 teaspoon baking soda

1 cup soymilk

1 teaspoon vanilla

¼ cup applesauce

2 tablespoons oil

1 tablespoon vinegar

1. Preheat oven to 350°F and lightly grease and flour a large cake pan.

2. In a large bowl, combine the flour, sugar, cocoa, and baking powder. In a separate small bowl, mix together the soymilk, vanilla, applesauce, oil, and vinegar.

3. Quickly mix together the dry ingredients with the wet ingredients, combining just until smooth.

4. Pour into prepared cake pan and bake for 26–28 minutes, or until toothpick or fork inserted comes out clean.

For the Perfect Vegan Cake . . .

Vegan cakes tend to be heavier and denser than regular cakes. Here are a few ways to compensate: Really beat the margarine and sugar together, and make sure all the sugar is incorporated, even those pesky little bits on the side of the bowl. A well-aerated margarine and sugar mix means a fluffier cake. To make sure your cake rises to perfection, get it in the oven right away to take advantage of the leavening ingredients. And of course, allow your cake to cool completely before frosting. Patience, patience!

PEANUT BUTTER CAKE

Serve this cake with a drizzling of chocolate sauce on top to make it a "peanut butter cup" cake.

INGREDIENTS
Serves 8

1 cup all-purpose flour

1 cup sugar

1 teaspoon baking powder

½ teaspoon baking soda

¾ cup water

½ cup peanut butter

⅛ cup vegetable oil

1 teaspoon vanilla extract

1. In a medium bowl, mix all the dry ingredients.

2. In another medium bowl, mix all the wet ingredients.

3. Spray slow cooker with nonstick cooking oil.

4. Combine the dry and wet ingredients, then pour into a 4-quart slow cooker. Cover, and cook on medium-high heat for 1–2 hours.

PINEAPPLE CHERRY "DUMP" CAKE

Just dump it all in! Who said vegan baking was hard?

INGREDIENTS
Serves 8

1 (20-ounce) can crushed pineapple, undrained

1 (20-ounce) can cherry pie filling

1 box vegan vanilla or yellow cake mix

½ cup vegan margarine, melted

1. Preheat oven according to directions on cake mix box and lightly grease and flour a large cake pan.

2. Dump the pineapple into the cake pan, then dump the pie filling, then the cake mix on top.

3. Drizzle the cake mix with vegan margarine.

4. Bake according to instructions on cake mix package.

How to Grease and Flour a Cake Pan
Especially with lower-fat cake recipes such as this one, you'll want a well-greased and well-floured pan to prevent the cake from sticking. A nonstick spray works just as well as a tablespoon or so of melted margarine or cooking oil. Coat the pan well, including the sides. Then coat with a light dusting of flour, shaking the pan to cover all the edges.

"SECRET INGREDIENT" CAKE MIX CAKE

This is another one of those unbelievable recipes that only vegans seem to know about. You just have to try it to believe it! As an added bonus, your vegan cake is virtually fat-free!

INGREDIENTS

Serves 8

1 box vegan cake mix

1 (12-ounce) can full-sugar soda (no diet)

1. Grease your cake pan well, as the reduced fat in this cake makes it a bit "stickier."

2. Preheat oven according to package instructions.

3. Mix together cake mix and soda, pour into a cake pan, and bake immediately according to package instructions.

Flavor Combos

Experiment with different flavor combinations just for fun! Try a lemon-lime or orange soda with a yellow cake mix, a cherry soda with chocolate cake mix, and a grape or strawberry soda with a vanilla cake mix.

CHEATER'S PUMPKIN PIE CUPCAKES

Add a handful of raisins or chopped walnuts if you'd like a little texture, or frost and garnish with fall-colored vegan candies.

INGREDIENTS

Yields 1 dozen cupcakes

1 box vegan spice cake or yellow cake mix

1 (16-ounce) can pumpkin purée

¼ cup soymilk

½ teaspoon pumpkin pie spice (if using yellow cake mix only)

1. Preheat oven according to instructions on cake mix package and lightly grease or line a cupcake tin.

2. Combine all ingredients in a large bowl.

3. Fill cupcakes about ⅔ full and bake according to instructions on cake mix.

Chocolate Cheater's Cupcakes

Use a vegan chocolate cake mix and add 1½ tablespoons of cocoa powder. Kick it up a notch with a handful of vegan chocolate chips.

SWEETHEART RASPBERRY LEMON CUPCAKES

Add ½ teaspoon of lemon extract for extra lemony goodness in these sweet and tart cupcakes. Or omit the raspberries and add 3 tablespoons of poppy seeds for lemon poppy seed cupcakes. Sweet and tart— sweetheart! Get it?

INGREDIENTS

Yields 18 cupcakes

½ cup vegan margarine, softened

1 cup sugar

½ teaspoon vanilla

⅔ cup soymilk

3 tablespoons lemon juice

Zest from 2 lemons

1¾ cups flour

1½ teaspoons baking powder

½ teaspoon baking soda

¼ teaspoon salt

¾ cup diced raspberries, fresh or frozen

1. Preheat oven to 350°F and grease or line a cupcake tin.

2. Beat together the margarine and sugar until light and fluffy, then add vanilla, soymilk, lemon juice, and zest.

3. In a separate bowl, sift together the flour, baking powder, baking soda, and salt.

4. Combine flour mixture with wet ingredients just until mixed. Do not overmix. Gently fold in diced raspberries.

5. Fill cupcakes about ⅔ full with batter and bake immediately for 16–18 minutes or until done.

Raspberry Cream Cheese Frosting

Combine a half container vegan cream cheese with ½ cup raspberry jam and 6 tablespoons of softened vegan margarine. Beat until smooth, then add powdered sugar until a creamy frosting forms. You'll need about 2½ cups. Pile it high and garnish your cupcakes with fresh strawberry slices or pink vegan candies.

BASIC VEGAN VANILLA ICING

A simple and basic vegan frosting recipe. Add a few drops of a flavoring extract or food coloring, or just use it as is.

INGREDIENTS

Serves 8

¼ cup soymilk

⅓ cup vegan margarine, softened

2 teaspoons vanilla

3–3½ cups powdered sugar

1. Mix together the soymilk, margarine, and vanilla until smooth.

2. Slowly incorporate powdered sugar until desired consistency is reached. You may need to adjust the amount of sugar.

Frosting Tips

Use an electric or hand mixer to get it super-light and creamy. Frosting will firm as it cools, which also means only frost cakes and cupcakes that are cooled already, otherwise the heat will melt the icing.

CHOCOLATE MOCHA FROSTING

The combination of chocolate and coffee in a frosting adds an exquisite touch to even a simple cake mix cake.

INGREDIENTS

Serves 8

¼ cup strong coffee or espresso, cooled

⅓ cup vegan margarine, softened

2 teaspoons vanilla

⅓ cup cocoa powder

3 cups powdered sugar

1. Mix together the coffee, margarine, and vanilla until smooth, then add cocoa powder.

2. Slowly incorporate powdered sugar until desired consistency is reached. You may need a bit more or less than 3 cups.

VEGAN PEANUT BUTTER FROSTING

Kids will love this creamy frosting, and it's a nice change from the usual flavors, especially when paired with a chocolate cake.

INGREDIENTS

Serves 8

1 cup peanut butter, softened

⅓ cup vegan margarine, softened

2 tablespoons maple syrup

½ teaspoon vanilla

2 tablespoons soymilk

2 cups powdered sugar

1. Whisk together the peanut butter, margarine, maple syrup, vanilla, and soymilk.

2. Slowly incorporate the powdered sugar, using a little bit more or less to get the desired consistency.

CHEWY OATMEAL RAISIN COOKIES

The addition of applesauce keeps these classic nostalgic cookies super-chewy. No egg replacer needed.

INGREDIENTS

Yields 1½ dozen cookies

⅓ cup vegan margarine, softened

½ cup brown sugar

¼ cup sugar

⅓ cup applesauce

1 teaspoon vanilla

2 tablespoons soymilk

¾ cup whole-wheat flour

½ teaspoon baking soda

½ teaspoon cinnamon

½ teaspoon ginger

1¾ cups quick-cooking oats

⅔ cup raisins

1. Preheat oven to 350°F.

2. Beat the margarine and sugars together until smooth and creamy. Add applesauce, vanilla, and soymilk.

3. Sift together the flour, baking soda, cinnamon, and ginger, then add to wet ingredients.

4. Stir in oats, then raisins. Drop by generous spoonfuls onto a cookie sheet.

5. Bake for 10–12 minutes, or until done.

CLASSIC CHOCOLATE CHIP COOKIES

Just like mom used to make, only with a bit of applesauce to cut down on the fat a bit.

INGREDIENTS
Yields about 2 dozen cookies

⅔ cup vegan margarine

⅔ cup sugar

⅔ cup brown sugar

⅓ cup applesauce

1½ teaspoons vanilla

Egg replacer for 2 eggs

2½ cups flour

1 teaspoon baking soda

½ teaspoon baking powder

1 teaspoon salt

⅔ cup quick-cooking oats

1½ cups chocolate chips

1. Preheat oven to 375°F.

2. In a large mixing bowl, cream together the vegan margarine and white sugar, then mix in brown sugar, applesauce, vanilla, and egg replacer.

3. In a separate bowl, combine the flour, baking soda, baking powder, and salt, then combine with the wet ingredients. Mix well.

4. Stir in oats and chocolate chips just until combined.

5. Drop by generous spoonfuls onto a baking sheet, and bake for 10–12 minutes. For a chewy cookie, don't be tempted to overbake them!

Add Some Zing

Want to impress your friends? Shop for vegan white chocolate chips to substitute for regular chocolate, and add about ⅔ cup chopped macadamia nuts. Voilà! White chocolate chip macadamia nut cookies! Just saying it sounds heavenly.

COCOA-NUT-COCONUT NO-BAKE COOKIES

Have the kids help you shape these into little balls, and try not to eat them all along the way!

INGREDIENTS

Yields 2 dozen cookies

¼ cup vegan margarine

½ cup soymilk

2 cups sugar

⅓ cup cocoa

½ cup peanut butter or other nut butter

½ teaspoon vanilla

3 cups quick-cooking oats

½ cup walnuts or cashews, finely chopped

½ cup coconut flakes

1. Line a baking sheet with wax paper.

2. Melt the vegan margarine and soymilk together and add sugar and cocoa. Bring to a quick boil to dissolve sugar, then reduce heat to low and stir in peanut butter, just until melted.

3. Remove from heat and stir in remaining ingredients. Allow to cool slightly.

4. Spoon about 3 tablespoons of mixture at a time onto wax paper and press lightly to form a cookie shape. Chill until firm.

EASY BANANA DATE COOKIES

The daily fast during Ramadan is traditionally broken with a date at sunset, and a version of these simple, refined sugar-free cookies is popular in Islamic communities in northern Africa, though almonds are traditionally added.

INGREDIENTS

Yields 1 dozen cookies

1 cup chopped pitted dates

Water for soaking

1 banana, medium ripe

¼ teaspoon vanilla

1¾ cups coconut flakes

1. Preheat oven to 375°F.

2. Cover dates in water and soak for about 10 minutes until softened. Drain.

3. Process together the dates, banana, and vanilla until almost smooth.

4. Stir in coconut flakes by hand until thick. You may need a little more or less than 1¾ cups.

5. Bake 10–12 minutes, or until done. Cookies will be soft and chewy.

SUGAR-FREE GINGER SPICE COOKIES

A delicious holiday cookie sweetened with maple syrup and molasses instead of refined sugar.
Adjust the seasonings to your taste—add cloves if you like, or omit the allspice and add extra ginger.

INGREDIENTS

Yields 1½ dozen cookies

⅓ cup vegan margarine, softened

½ cup maple syrup

⅓ cup molasses

¼ cup soymilk

2¼ cups flour

1 teaspoon baking powder

½ teaspoon baking soda

½ teaspoon cinnamon

½ teaspoon ginger

¼ teaspoon allspice or nutmeg

½ teaspoon salt

1. In a large mixing bowl, cream together the vegan margarine, maple syrup, molasses, and soymilk. In a separate bowl, sift together the flour, baking powder, baking soda, cinnamon, ginger, allspice, and salt.

2. Mix the flour and spices in with the wet ingredients until combined. Chill for 30 minutes.

3. Preheat oven to 375°F.

4. Roll dough into 1½" balls and place on cookie sheet. Flatten slightly, then bake 10–12 minutes or until done.

CHOCOLATE PEANUT BUTTER EXPLOSION PIE

You can pretend it's healthy because it's made with tofu or toss away all your troubles to the wind and just enjoy it. You'll feel like a kid again.

INGREDIENTS

Serves 8

¾ cup vegan chocolate chips

1 (12-ounce) block silken tofu

½ cup peanut butter, plus ¾ cup

2 tablespoons soymilk, plus ⅔ cup

1 prepared Vegan Cookie Pie Crust (this chapter)

2–2½ cups powdered sugar

1. Over very low heat or in a double boiler, melt the chocolate chips.

2. In a blender, purée tofu, ½ cup peanut butter, and 2 tablespoons of soymilk until combined, then add melted chocolate chips until smooth and creamy.

3. Pour into pie crust and chill for 1 hour, or until firm.

4. Over low heat, melt together ¾ cup peanut butter, ⅔ cup soymilk, and powdered sugar until smooth and creamy. You may need to adjust the amount of sugar.

5. Spread peanut butter mixture over cooled pie and return to refrigerator. Chill until firm.

Make It a Little Less Intense

This really is a rich chocolate and peanut butter flavor explosion, but if you want to tame it down a bit, it's still delicious without the peanut butter topping. Shop for sugar-free vegan chocolate chips at your health foods store or try it with carob chips to make it even "healthier."

PUMPKIN MAPLE PIE

Make a Vegan Cookie Pie Crust (this chapter) with gingerbread cookies to complement the fall spices in this classic American treat.

INGREDIENTS
Serves 8

1 (16-ounce) can pumpkin purée

1 (12-ounce) block silken tofu

½ cup maple syrup

¼ cup sugar

1½ teaspoons cinnamon

½ teaspoon ginger powder

½ teaspoon nutmeg

¼ teaspoon ground cloves (optional)

½ teaspoon salt

1 vegan pie crust

1. Preheat oven to 400°F.

2. Process together the pumpkin, tofu, and maple syrup until smooth and creamy. Add sugar and spices and pour into pie crust.

3. Bake for 1 hour or until done. Allow to cool before slicing and serving, as pie will set and firm as it cools.

For a Sweet Buttery Candied Pecan Topping

Chop ½ cup or so of pecan halves and mix with a couple of tablespoons of maple syrup, a tablespoon or two of melted vegan margarine, and a sprinkle of cloves, nutmeg, or cinnamon. Add to the top of the pie about halfway through the baking time.

VEGAN COOKIE PIE CRUST

Use any kind of store-bought vegan cookie you like for this one: gingersnaps for pumpkin pies, chocolate or peanut butter sandwich cookies for cheesecakes, or wafers for a neutral flavor.

INGREDIENTS
Serves 8

25 small vegan cookies

¼ cup vegan margarine, melted

½ teaspoon vanilla

1. Process cookies in a food processor until finely ground. Or, working in batches, seal cookies in a zip-top bag and crumble using a rolling pin until fine.

2. Add margarine and vanilla a bit at a time until mixture is sticky.

3. Press evenly into pie tin, spreading about ¼" thick. No prebaking is needed.

It's a Garnish Too

Plan on having a few extra tablespoons of this crumbly cookie mix to sprinkle on top of your vegan pie or cheesecake for a sweet topping.

CHOCOLATE RICE PUDDING

For an extra chocolatey flavor, try using chocolate soymilk in place of plain in this recipe.

INGREDIENTS

Serves 4

1 cup white rice

1 quart soymilk

½ cup vegan margarine

1 cup sugar

½ cup vegan chocolate syrup

¼ teaspoon salt

Add all ingredients to a 4-quart slow cooker. Cover, and cook on low heat for 6 hours.

COCONUT RICE PUDDING

The combination of juicy soft mango with tropical coconut milk is simply heavenly, but if mangos are unavailable, pineapples or strawberries would add a delicious touch to this refined, sugar-free dessert.

INGREDIENTS

Serves 4

1½ cups cooked white rice

1½ cups vanilla soymilk

1½ cups coconut milk

3 tablespoons brown rice syrup or maple syrup

2 tablespoons agave nectar

4–5 dates, chopped

Dash cinnamon or nutmeg

2 mangos, chopped

1. Combine rice, soymilk, and coconut milk over low heat. Bring to a very low simmer for 10 minutes, or until mixture starts to thicken.

2. Stir in brown rice syrup or maple syrup, agave nectar, and dates and heat for another 2–3 minutes.

3. Allow to cool slightly before serving to allow pudding to thicken slightly. Garnish with a dash of cinnamon or nutmeg and mangos just before serving.

EASY APPLESAUCE

Homemade applesauce is easy to make and tastes much better than what you can get in the store. It freezes well too, so you can make extra when apples are in season.

INGREDIENTS

Serves 6

10 medium apples, peeled, cored, and sliced

2 tablespoons fresh lemon juice

2 tablespoons water

6" cinnamon stick (optional)

Sugar, to taste (optional)

1. In a 4-quart slow cooker, add the apples, lemon juice, water, and cinnamon stick if desired. Stir to mix.

2. Cover, and cook on low for 5 hours, or until the apples are soft and tender.

3. Purée the apples in a food processor or blender, use an immersion blender, or press through a food mill or large mesh strainer.

4. While applesauce is still warm, add sugar to taste if desired. Store covered in the refrigerator for up to 2 weeks or freeze.

Chunky Applesauce

It's easy to change this recipe into a chunky sauce instead. Once the apples are cooked, mash them with a potato masher instead of blending until smooth.

SUGAR-FREE TOFU CHOCOLATE PUDDING

The genius who first combined chocolate and peanut butter deserves a Nobel Prize. Or at least a MacArthur "Genius Grant." Check your peanut butter brand for added sugar.

INGREDIENTS

Serves 2

1 (12-ounce) block silken tofu

½ teaspoon vanilla

¼ cup peanut butter or other nut butter

¼ cup maple syrup or brown rice syrup

Process all ingredients together until smooth and creamy.

CHOCOLATE MOCHA ICE CREAM

If you have an ice cream maker, you can skip the stirring and freezing and just add the blended ingredients to your machine.

INGREDIENTS

Serves 6

1 cup vegan chocolate chips

1 cup soymilk

1 (12-ounce) block silken tofu

⅓ cup sugar

2 tablespoons instant coffee

2 teaspoons vanilla

¼ teaspoon salt

1. Using a double boiler or over very low heat, melt chocolate chips until smooth and creamy. Allow to cool slightly.

2. Blend together the soymilk, tofu, sugar, instant coffee, vanilla, and salt until very smooth and creamy, at least 2 minutes. Add melted chocolate chips and process until smooth.

3. Transfer mixture to a large, freezerproof baking or casserole dish and freeze.

4. Stir every 30 minutes until a smooth ice cream forms, about 4 hours. If mixture gets too firm, transfer to a blender, process until smooth, then return to freezer.

STRAWBERRY COCONUT ICE CREAM

Rich and creamy, this is the most decadent dairy-free strawberry ice cream you'll ever taste.

INGREDIENTS
Serves 6

2 cups coconut cream

1¾ cups frozen strawberries

¾ cup sugar

2 teaspoons vanilla

¼ teaspoon salt

1. Purée together all ingredients until smooth and creamy.

2. Transfer mixture to a large, freezerproof baking or casserole dish and freeze.

3. Stir every 30 minutes until a smooth ice cream forms, about 4 hours. If mixture gets too firm, transfer to a blender, process until smooth, then return to freezer.

APRICOT GINGER SORBET

Made with real fruit and without dairy, this is a fat-free treat that you can add to smoothies or just enjoy outside on a hot summer day.

INGREDIENTS
Serves 6

⅔ cup water

⅔ cup sugar

2 teaspoons fresh minced ginger

5 cups chopped apricots, fresh or frozen

3 tablespoons lemon juice

1. Bring the water, sugar, and ginger to a boil, then reduce to a slow simmer. Heat for 3–4 more minutes until sugar is dissolved and a syrup forms. Allow to cool.

2. Purée the sugar syrup, apricots, and lemon juice until smooth.

3. Transfer mixture to a large, freezerproof baking or casserole dish and freeze.

4. Stir every 30 minutes until a smooth sorbet forms, about 4 hours. If mixture gets too firm, transfer to a blender, process until smooth, then return to freezer.

STANDARD U.S./METRIC MEASUREMENT CONVERSIONS

VOLUME CONVERSIONS

U.S. Volume Measure	Metric Equivalent
⅛ teaspoon	0.5 milliliter
¼ teaspoon	1 milliliter
½ teaspoon	2 milliliters
1 teaspoon	5 milliliters
½ tablespoon	7 milliliters
1 tablespoon (3 teaspoons)	15 milliliters
2 tablespoons (1 fluid ounce)	30 milliliters
¼ cup (4 tablespoons)	60 milliliters
⅓ cup	90 milliliters
½ cup (4 fluid ounces)	125 milliliters
⅔ cup	160 milliliters
¾ cup (6 fluid ounces)	180 milliliters
1 cup (16 tablespoons)	250 milliliters
1 pint (2 cups)	500 milliliters
1 quart (4 cups)	1 liter (about)

WEIGHT CONVERSIONS

U.S. Weight Measure	Metric Equivalent
½ ounce	15 grams
1 ounce	30 grams
2 ounces	60 grams
3 ounces	85 grams
¼ pound (4 ounces)	115 grams
½ pound (8 ounces)	225 grams
¾ pound (12 ounces)	340 grams
1 pound (16 ounces)	454 grams

OVEN TEMPERATURE CONVERSIONS

Degrees Fahrenheit	Degrees Celsius
200 degrees F	95 degrees C
250 degrees F	120 degrees C
275 degrees F	135 degrees C
300 degrees F	150 degrees C
325 degrees F	160 degrees C
350 degrees F	180 degrees C
375 degrees F	190 degrees C
400 degrees F	205 degrees C
425 degrees F	220 degrees C
450 degrees F	230 degrees C

BAKING PAN SIZES

U.S.	Metric
8 × 1½ inch round baking pan	20 × 4 cm cake tin
9 × 1½ inch round baking pan	23 × 3.5 cm cake tin
11 × 7 × 1½ inch baking pan	28 × 18 × 4 cm baking tin
13 × 9 × 2 inch baking pan	30 × 20 × 5 cm baking tin
2 quart rectangular baking dish	30 × 20 × 3 cm baking tin
15 × 10 × 2 inch baking pan	30 × 25 × 2 cm baking tin (Swiss roll tin)
9 inch pie plate	22 × 4 or 23 × 4 cm pie plate
7 or 8 inch springform pan	18 or 20 cm springform or loose bottom cake tin
9 × 5 × 3 inch loaf pan	23 × 13 × 7 cm or 2 lb narrow loaf or pâté tin
1½ quart casserole	1.5 liter casserole
2 quart casserole	2 liter casserole

INDEX